THE NEW SELL
AND SELL SHORT

WILEY TRADING SERIES

Founded in 1807, John Wiley & Sons is the oldest independent publishing company in the United States. With offices in North America, Europe, Australia and Asia, Wiley is globally committed to developing and marketing print and electronic products and services for our customers' professional and personal knowledge and understanding.

The Wiley Trading series features books by traders who have survived the market's ever changing temperament and have prospered—some by reinventing systems, others by getting back to basics. Whether a novice trader, professional or somewhere in-between, these books will provide the advice and strategies needed to prosper today and well into the future.

For a list of available titles, please visit our Web site at www.WileyFinance.com.

Books by Dr. Alexander Elder

Trading for a Living
Study Guide for Trading for a Living

Rubles to Dollars:
  Making Money on Russia's Exploding Financial Frontier

Come into My Trading Room
Study Guide for Come into My Trading Room

Straying from the Flock: Travels in New Zealand

Entries & Exits: Visits to Sixteen Trading Rooms
Study Guide for Entries & Exits

Sell and Sell Short, First Edition
Sell and Sell Short Study Guide, First Edition

Published by John Wiley & Sons, Inc., Hoboken, New Jersey.

Published simultaneously in Canada.

A previous edition of this book, *Sell and Sell Short* by Dr. Alexander Elder, was published along with a study guide in 2008 by John Wiley & Sons.

All charts unless otherwise noted were created with TradeStation.
Copyright © 2001–2010 TradeStation Securities, Inc. All rights reserved.

For general information on our other products and services or for technical support, please contact our Customer Care Department within the United States at (800) 762-2974, outside the United States at (317) 572-3993 or fax (317) 572-4002.

Wiley also publishes its books in a variety of electronic formats. Some content that appears in print may not be available in electronic books. For more information about Wiley products, visit our web site at www.wiley.com.

ISBN 978-0-470-63239-0 (hardback); ISBN 978-1-118-00555-2 (ebk.);
ISBN 978-1-118-00556-9 (ebk.); ISBN 978-1-118-00557-6 (ebk.)

Printed in the United States of America
V10005320_101718

To Inna Feldman,
the manager of elder.com
whose care, kindness, and integrity
have helped shape our company
for the past twelve years.

CONTENTS

INTRODUCTION

There is a time to grow and a time to decline. A time to plant and a time to reap.

That cute puppy bouncing up and down in your living room will someday become an old, decrepit dog whom you will have to drive to the vet's office to put it out of its misery.

That stock you bought with such great hopes and which you enjoyed watching grow has now rolled over and is cutting into your capital instead of increasing it. It is high time to look for an exit.

Buying is fun. It grows out of hope, great expectations, a chest full of air. Selling is a hard, unsmiling business, like driving that poor old dog to the vet for its final injection. But sell you must.

And once you and I talk about selling—that essential reality at the end of every trade—we will not stop. We will talk about selling short. Amateurs don't know how to short and are afraid of it, but professionals love shorting and profit from declines.

Stocks go down much faster than they rise, and a trader who knows how to short doubles his opportunities. But before you sell short you must learn to sell and sell well.

So let us take off those rose-colored glasses and learn to sell.

WHY SELL?

The markets inhale and exhale. They get a full chest of air and push it out. They must fall just as certainly as they must rise.

To live happily in the markets, you need to get in gear with their rhythm. Any beginner buying stocks knows how to inhale. Knowing when to exhale—when to sell—will set you above the crowd.

We buy when we feel optimistic—or are afraid of missing a good thing. Perhaps you read a story about a new product or heard rumors of a merger. Maybe you ran a database scan or found a promising chart pattern on your screen. You go online or call your broker and place an order to buy. You receive a confirmation—you own the stock. Now the stress begins.

If the stock stays flat and goes nowhere, you feel restless. Did you pick the wrong one again? Other stocks are going up—should you sell yours?

A rising stock creates a different kind of anxiety. Should you take profits, add to your position, or do nothing? Doing nothing is quite hard, especially for men, who are told from childhood "Don't just stand there, do something!" When your stock drops, you feel pain—"I'll sell as soon as it comes back to even."

For many, the most psychologically comfortable position is a slight decline in their stock. It is not sharp enough to be painful, and with the stock near your entry price, there is probably not much reason to sell. No action is required, and you have the perfect excuse to do nothing.

Throw a frog into a pot of hot water and it will jump, but if you heat the frog slowly, you can cook it alive. Traders with no clear selling plans, holding a slowly sinking stock, can suffer a great deal of damage.

Stress is the enemy of good decision making. It is hard to be objective when our skin is on the line. This is why I urge you to write down a plan before you enter a trade. Your plan must list reasons for entering a trade and define three numbers: your entry price, a protective stop, and a profit target.

Make your decision to sell before you buy. This simple rule will allow you to use your intellect instead of some other point of your anatomy and then boil like some poor frog. You are likely to increase your profits, reduce losses, and improve your equity curve by writing down your selling plan before you buy.

Why do so few people do it?

Two reasons. First, most traders have never been taught what you have just read. Beginners and outsiders simply do not have this knowledge. The other reason is that people like to dream. A written plan cuts into their sweet daydreaming business. A vague fantasy of riches feels nice and comfy. Sitting up straight and writing down your specific goals and contingency plans takes away that happy fantasy.

Since you have picked up this book I'd like to think that you have chosen the pleasure of real profits over the sweetness of daydreaming. Welcome to the book, and let us move on to selling and selling short.

ABOUT THE Q&A

It feels exciting to discover an attractive stock and watch it go vertical after you buy. It is just as exciting to see it collapse soon after you short. This joy is only a small part of the game.

You can expect to spend the bulk of your time doing your homework. At times you might scan a long list of stocks and not find anything particularly attractive. At other times you may find a stock that you like, but your money management rules will not allow you to buy. You can put on a trade in moments but spend half an hour documenting it in your diary. The toil of homework takes up the bulk of a serious trader's time. Whoever said "success is 10% inspiration and 90% perspiration" must have come through Wall Street.

I created the questions and answers in this book to help you prepare for the road ahead. My goal was to point out some of the best opportunities, flag some of the worst risks, and get you into the habit of tracking your performance. I often say to my students, "Show me a trader with good records, and I will show you a good trader." I hope this will help you acquire the habit of asking hard questions, testing all ideas on your own data, and keeping good records.

I took great care in crafting the answers in the back of the book. I wanted to go beyond merely saying that A was right and B was wrong—I wanted to explain the reasons behind the answers.

Please do not rush through this book. Trading is a marathon, not a 100-yard dash. Take your time to think and work through a few questions each day. After you have worked through the answers and rated your performance, put it aside for two or three months, then pick it up again and retake the tests to see whether your grades have improved. Trading is like many other serious pursuits—the more you put into it, the more you will get out of it.

Trading is a lonely business, which is why I encourage traders to connect with others and share research and learning. Some of my students have become good friends. Now, by picking up this book and facing its hard questions, you have made the choice to face reality. I wish you success in your trading career.

Dr. Alexander Elder
New York City, 2011

PSYCHOLOGY, RISK MANAGEMENT, & RECORD-KEEPING

To be a successful trader you need an edge—a method of discovering opportunities and placing orders. An edge plus a lot of discipline will put you ahead of the pack.

A beginner has no plan and no edge. He hears different bells on different days and jumps in response to all of them. He may buy today after seeing a piece of news about earnings. He might sell tomorrow after seeing—more likely imagining—a head-and-shoulders top. This is the normal stage of initial ignorance. To move beyond it, to graduate to trading for a living, you need a clear concept for buying and selling. You need to define a trading plan that is fairly clear and bulletproof in order to enjoy a rising equity curve.

My own search for an edge led me to focus on the gap between price and value. Surprisingly few people are aware of it, although when I point it out on a chart they see it immediately.

The concept is quite simple: price and value are not the same. Price can be below value, above it, or equal to it. The distance between price and value may be large or small, increasing or decreasing.

Few technical traders ever think about the difference between price and value. Fundamental analysts are much more attuned to the idea, but they do not own it—technicians can use it as well.

Most buying decisions are based on the perception that price is below value. Traders buy when they think that some future event will increase the value of their trading vehicle.

It makes sense to buy below value and sell above value. To implement this idea, we need to answer three questions: How to define value? How to track its changes? How to measure the distance from price to value?

CHAPTER 1

ON BUYING

Trading requires confidence; but, paradoxically, it also demands humility. Since the markets are huge, there is no way you can master everything. Your knowledge can never be complete.

This is why we need to select an area of research and trading and specialize in it. Let's compare financial markets to medicine. Today's physician cannot be an expert in surgery, psychiatry, and pediatrics. Such universal expertise may have been possible centuries ago, but modern physicians must specialize.

THE THREE GREAT DIVIDES

A serious trader also needs to specialize. He must choose an area of research and trading that appeals to him or her. A trader needs to make several key choices:

- **Technical vs. Fundamental Analysis**

  Fundamental analysts of stocks study the values of listed companies. In the futures markets they explore the supply-demand equations for commodities. Technicians, by contrast, believe that the sum of knowledge about any stock or future is reflected in its price. Technicians study chart patterns and indicators to determine whether bulls or bears are winning the current round of the trading battle. Needless to say, there is some overlap between the two methods. Serious fundamentalists look at charts, while serious technicians like to have some idea about the fundamentals of the market they are trading.

- **Trend vs. Counter-Trend Trading**

  Almost every chart shows a mix of directional moves and choppy trading ranges. Powerful trends fascinate beginners: if you were to buy at a bottom, so clearly visible in the middle of the chart, and hold through the entire rally, you would make a ton of money. Experienced traders know that big trends, so clearly visible in the middle of a chart, become foggy near the right edge. Following a trend is like riding a wild horse that tries to shake you off at every turn. Trend trading is a lot harder than it seems.

  One of the very few scientifically proven facts about the markets is that they oscillate. Markets continuously swing between overvalued and undervalued levels. Counter-trend traders capitalize on this choppiness by trading against the extremes.

  Take a look at the chart in Figure 1.1, and the arguments for and against trend or counter-trend trading will leap at you from the page. You can easily recognize an uptrend from the lower left to the upper right corner. It seems appealing to buy and hold—until you realize that a trend is clear only in retrospect. If you had a long position, you'd be wondering every day, if not every hour, whether this uptrend was at an end. Sitting tight requires a great deal of mental work!

  Swing trading—buying below value and selling above value— has its own pluses and minuses. Trading shorter moves delivers thinner returns, but the trades tend to last just a few days. They require less patience and make you feel much more in control.

  In his brilliant book *Mechanical Trading Systems: Pairing Trader Psychology with Technical Analysis*, Richard Weissman draws a clear distinction between three types of traders: trend-followers, mean-reversal (counter-trend) traders, and day-traders. They have different temperaments, exploit different opportunities, and face different challenges.

  Most of us gravitate towards one of these trading styles without giving our decision much thought. It is much better to figure out who you are, what you like or dislike and trade accordingly.

- **Discretionary vs. Systematic Trading**

  A discretionary trader looks at a chart, reads and interprets its signals, then makes a decision to buy or sell short. He monitors his chart and at some point recognizes an exit signal, then places

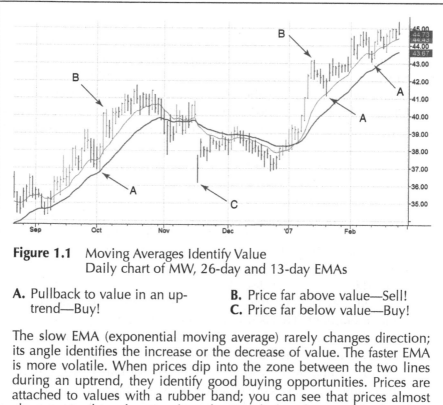

Figure 1.1 Moving Averages Identify Value
Daily chart of MW, 26-day and 13-day EMAs

A. Pullback to value in an uptrend—Buy!

B. Price far above value—Sell!
C. Price far below value—Buy!

The slow EMA (exponential moving average) rarely changes direction; its angle identifies the increase or the decrease of value. The faster EMA is more volatile. When prices dip into the zone between the two lines during an uptrend, they identify good buying opportunities. Prices are attached to values with a rubber band; you can see that prices almost always get only so far away from the EMA before they snap back. When a rubber band extends to the max, it warns you to expect a reversal of the latest move away from value.

an order to exit from his trade. Analyzing charts and making decisions is an exciting and engaging process for many of us.

A systematic trader cannot stand this degree of uncertainty. He does not want to keep making decisions every step of the way. He prefers to study historical data, design a system that would have performed well in the past, fine-tune it, and turn it on. Going forward, he lets his system track the market and generate buy and sell signals.

Systematic traders try to capitalize on repeating market patterns. The good ones know that while patterns repeat, they do not repeat perfectly. The most valuable quality of a good system is its robustness. We call a system robust when it continues to perform reasonably well even after market conditions change.

Both types of trading have a downside. The trouble with discretionary trading is that it seduces beginners into making impulsive decisions. On the other hand, a beginner attracted to systematic trading often falls into the sin of curve-fitting. He spends time polishing his backward-looking telescope until he has a system that would have worked perfectly in the past—if only the past repeated itself perfectly, which it almost never does.

I am attracted to the freedom of discretionary trading. I like to study broad indexes and industry groups and decide whether to trade from the long or short side. I work to establish entry and exit parameters, apply money management rules, determine the size of a trade, and finally place my order. There is a sense of thrill in monitoring the trade and making a decision to exit as planned, jump a little sooner, or hold a little longer.

The decision to be a discretionary or a systematic trader is rarely based on cost/benefit analysis. Most of us decide on the basis of our temperament. This is not different from deciding where to live, what education to pursue, and whether or whom to marry—we usually decide on the basis of emotion.

Paradoxically, at the top end of the performance scale there is a surprising degree of convergence between discretionary and systematic trading. A top-notch systematic trader keeps making what looks to me like discretionary decisions: when to activate System A, when to reduce funding of System B, when to add a new market or drop a market from the list. At the same time, a savvy discretionary trader has a number of firm rules that feel very systematic. For example, I will never enter a position against the weekly Impulse system, and you couldn't pay me to buy above the upper channel line or short below the lower channel line on a daily chart. The systematic and the discretionary approaches can be bridged—just don't try to change your method in the middle of an open trade.

Another key decision is whether to focus on stocks, futures, options or forex. You may want to specialize even further, by choosing a specific stock group or a few specific futures. Making a conscious decision will help you avoid flopping around, the way so many people do.

It is important to realize that in all of these choices there is no right or wrong way. What you select will depend primarily on your temperament, which is perfectly fine. Only greenhorns look down upon those who make different choices.

ONE TRADER'S TOOLBOX

In the first edition of this book, I dedicated an entire section to a description of my trading toolbox—its development and its current state. Some readers liked that, but many complained that they already had this information from my earlier books.[1] As a result, in this edition I decided to limit a discussion of the tools I use to a thumbnail sketch.

Looking at a day's bar or a candle on any chart, we see only five pieces of data: open, high, low, close and volume. A futures chart also includes open interest. This is why I have a rule of "five bullets to a clip"—allowing no more than five indicators on any given chart. You may use six if you desperately need an extra one, but never more than that. For myself, I do well with four: moving averages, envelopes, MACD and the Force Index.

You are not obligated to use the same four indicators. Please feel free to use others—only be sure to understand how they are constructed, what they measure, and what signals they give. Choose a handful of tools, and study them in depth until you become comfortable with them.

What about classical charting, with its head-and-shoulders tops, rectangles, diagonal trendlines, and so on? I believe that much of their alleged meaning lies in the eye of the beholder—traders draw lines on charts to confirm what they want to see.

---

[1]My methods and techniques are described in the following books:

Trading for a Living (1993) has a broad coverage of trading psychology and technical indicators. It introduces the Triple Screen trading system and the Force Index.

Come into My Trading Room (2002) covers psychology and technical analysis but stresses money management and trade planning. It introduces the Impulse system and SafeZone stops.

Entries & Exits (2006) features interviews with 16 traders who share both winning and losing trades. There are my comments on every trade; the album-sized book is printed in color.

If you are going to read only one of these books, I recommend *Come into My Trading Room*, but if you plan to learn more it is better to read them in the order shown above. All of these books also have study guides.

I am suspicious of classical charting because it is so subjective. I trust only the simplest patterns: support and resistance lines as well as breakouts and fingers, also known as kangaroo tails. I prefer computerized indicators because their signals are clear and not subject to multiple interpretations.

Many beginners have a childish faith in the power of technical analysis, often coupled with quite a bit of laziness. Each month I get e-mails from people asking for "the exact settings" of moving averages, MACD, and other indicators. Some say that they want to save time by taking my numbers and skipping research so that they could get right on to trading. Save the time on research! If you do not do your own research, where will you get the confidence to trust your tools during the inevitable drawdown periods?

I believe that successful trading is based on three M's—Mind, Method, and Money. Your Method—indicators and tools—is just one component of this equation. Equally important is the Mind—your trading psychology—and the Money, or risk control. All three are tied together through good record-keeping.

CHAPTER 2

TRADING PSYCHOLOGY AND RISK MANAGEMENT

What are your trading tools? You probably have a computer, some software packages, and a database. You probably visit several trading-related websites and may have a shelf of trading-related books. If you think that this is all, you are overlooking a hugely important trading instrument.

YOUR MIND AS A TRADING TOOL

Your emotions, hopes, and fears have a direct and immediate effect on your trading. What goes on inside your head has a greater influence on your success or failure than any technology.[1] Your decision-making process must be transparent and unbiased to enable you to learn from your experiences and become a better trader.

Trading psychology is discussed in all of my books, but especially in *Trading for a Living*. Let's touch on just a few key points:

- **Solitude is essential**
  When feeling stressed, we tend to huddle and imitate others. A successful trader makes his or her own decisions. You need to isolate yourself while you make and implement your own trading plans. This does not mean becoming a hermit. It is a good idea

---

[1]You can take a test to rate your current trading aptitude at www.spiketrade.com.

to network with other traders, but you should not talk about your trading plans while a trade is still open. Stay alone with your trade, learn all you can, make your own decisions, record your plans, and implement them in silence. You can discuss your trades with the people you trust after closing a trade. You need solitude to focus on open trades.

- **Treat yourself well**
  If your mind is a part of trading, you've got to treat it well. It only seems as though impulsive traders have fun—losers tend to be extremely harsh and shockingly abusive towards themselves. They keep breaking the rules and hitting themselves, breaking and hitting. Beating yourself will not make you a better trader. It is better to celebrate even partial achievements and soberly take stock of your shortcomings. In my own trading, I have a reward system for celebrating successful trades, but do not punish myself for losses.

- **Some traders are destined to fail**
  The markets produce endless temptations, which is why people with a history of poor impulse control are likely to lose in trading. Those who are actively drinking or using substances are highly unlikely to succeed. They may have a few lucky trades, but their long-term forecast is grim. If your drinking, eating, or other behavior is out of control, you are better off not trading until you resolve your addiction problem. Obsessional nit-pickers and greedy people who cannot tolerate losing a dime are also unlikely to do well in trading.

- **It is better not to trade when you are in a foul mood**
  Remember that even a good trader has only a very narrow edge. Anything that reduces that edge shifts the balance of power against you. Feeling calm, relaxed, and in a pleasant mood is extremely important for your success. If you have a severe toothache or if a problem with a spouse distracts you, you would be better off taking a break from the markets. If you feel preoccupied, stand aside until your personal stress clears up.

- **Successful traders love the game more than the profits**
  On Sundays, with my weekend homework completed and plans for the next week drawn up, it is a pleasure to anticipate Monday's opening. A surfer probably has a similar feeling at night, knowing

he'll be going to the beach in the morning. This feeling comes from being prepared.

- **Keeping records: actions are more important than dreams**
  It is easy to talk about discipline on a weekend, when the markets are closed, but let me see you in front of a live screen five minutes after the opening bell. You must write down your trading plans and faithfully implement them. The ability to keep records is an excellent predictor of your future success or failure. If you keep good trading records, you are very likely to succeed. If you fail to keep good records, your chances of successful trading will be slim to none.

RISK CONTROL

If trading is a high-wire act, then risk control means putting on a safety harness. It will save your life in case you slip.

Overtrading means putting on trades whose size is too large for your account. When the stakes become dangerously high, we become stiff with tension, spontaneity goes out the window, and our performance deteriorates. Sensible risk control keeps the size of your trades at a fairly relaxed level.

The two pillars of money management are the 2% and 6% Rules.[2] They will help save your account from the two main causes of trader mortality: the 2% Rule from shark bites and the 6% Rule from piranha bites.

A shark bite is a single disastrous loss that severely damages one's account. A poor beginner who loses one-third of his equity would have to generate a 50% return on his remaining capital simply to break even. The victim of a shark attack loses much more than money: he loses confidence, becomes fearful, and cannot pull the trigger. We can avoid this problem by following the 2% Rule which keeps any loss to a small, livable size.

The 2% Rule prohibits you from risking more than 2% of your account equity on any single trade.

Suppose you have $100,000 in your account—the 2% Rule tells you that your maximum permitted risk on any trade is $2,000. You decide to buy a stock that is selling for $40 and put a stop at $38, risking $2 per share. Dividing your total permitted risk by your risk per share ($2,000 by $2)

---

[2]See *Come into My Trading Room* for details.

tells you that you may trade a maximum of 1,000 shares. You are perfectly welcome to trade a smaller position—but never bigger, which would push your risk above the 2% limit.

The 2% Rule forms the basis of what I call "The Iron Triangle of Risk Control."

1. The distance from your entry price to the stop level defines your maximum dollar risk per share.

2. The 2% Rule defines your maximum risk for the entire position.

3. Dividing your permitted risk by your risk per share gives you the maximum number of shares you may trade.

The 6% Rule requires you to stop trading for the rest of the month once your cumulative loss for that month reaches 6% of your account equity.

Most people tend to push harder when things go badly. We often put on more trades when losing, trying to trade our way out of a hole. In fact, a better response is to step back and take some time off. The 6% Rule forces you to do just that by capping the maximum monthly loss in your account.

A piranha is an aggressive fish found in the rivers of South America. Its main danger comes from the fact that it travels in packs. A careless bull who stumbles into a piranha-infested river might be reduced to a collection of bones. The 6% Rule defines a series of losses after which a bull or a bear must exit the markets and wait on shore.

The 6% Rule forms the basis of the concept I call "Available Risk." Approach every trade with a question—does the 6% Rule allow me to trade? You know how much money, if any, you have lost during the current month. You also know how much money you have exposed to the risk of loss in your open trades. If your previous losses for this month plus your risk on existing trades expose you to a total risk of 6% of your account equity, you may not put on another trade.

Most traders go through emotional swings, feeling elated at the highs and gloomy at the lows, while losing money to sharks and piranhas. If you seriously plan to become a successful trader, the 2% and 6% Rules will convert your good intentions into the reality of safer trading.

CHAPTER 3

ON KEEPING RECORDS

Whenever you put on a trade, you must have two goals. The first, of course, is to make money. The second is to become a better trader.

There is a lot of randomness, and the best-planned trades can go awry. Even a top trader cannot win in every trade—this is a fact of life. On the other hand, becoming a better trader is a realistic and essential goal for every single trade.

You must keep learning from your experience. Whether you win or lose, you must become a better trader after each trade. If you don't, you have simply wasted an opportunity. All that energy and time you put into analysis, all the risks you took with your money—for naught.

The best way to learn is to keep good records. A wannabe trader without records is a dreamer. All numbers relating to your trades must go into a spreadsheet, and a visual record of your trades must go into your diary.

GOOD RECORDS LEAD TO GOOD TRADING

The best way to learn from your experience is to keep good records. They transform your fleeting experiences into solid memories and lessons. Your market analysis and decisions to buy or sell become deposits in your data bank. You can draw on those memories, re-examine them, and use them to grow into a better trader.

The rules of money management will help you survive the inevitable rocky times. The record-keeping methods I am about to share with you will put your learning into a solid uptrend, and your performance will follow. Money management and record-keeping create a rock-solid foundation for your survival and success. The rest—the analysis and techniques—you can pick up from this book, my other books, or those written by other serious authors.

Almost anyone can make an inspired trade, hit the market right, and watch profits roll in. No matter how inspired, a single trade or even a handful of trades will not make you a winner. You need to build a pattern of trades that has a record of success over a long period of time.

Seeing your equity grow quarter after quarter and year after year is the proof of your trading prowess. We tend to become arrogant and careless after a big win or a string of wins. That's precisely when, imagining we can walk on water, we start feeding our equity back into the markets.

Any trader will occasionally hit the market right and score a profit. Even a monkey throwing darts at a stock page will occasionally pick a winner. A single profit does not prove anything. Our most important challenge is to maintain a positive slope of our equity curve. For that you need to keep two sets of records.

TRADER'S SPREADSHEET—BASIC ACCOUNTABILITY

Whenever I talk with traders, I am amazed how few maintain records of their trades in spreadsheets. Many rely on their brokers, but those statements do not provide the necessary level of detail. This is why I recommend using your own spreadsheet. My company, www.elder.com, offers the basic spreadsheet shown on the next page at no charge, as a public service to traders. You can e-mail us at info@elder.com and ask for the template (Figure 3.1).

You do not need to become a spreadsheet expert, but a basic ability to manipulate numbers will give you a much greater degree of control over your trading. If beginners took one tenth of the time they spend looking at indicators and invested that time in learning basic Excel, their payoff would be much greater.

A basic spreadsheet takes just a minute to update after every trade. In my own spreadsheet I have a tab for each of my accounts and a summary tab where I record the value of all accounts on a weekly basis to track my equity curve.

Figure 3.1 shows the headings as well as a few lines from my spreadsheet. The text explains the meaning of every column.

A	B	C	D	E	F	G	H	I	J	K	L	M	N	O	P	Q	R	S	T	U	V	W	X
		2007	Etrade																	Total			
		Symbol	Quant	l/s	Entry	Date	Slippa	Comm	Exit	Date		Slippa	Comm	Fee	P/L	Net		Spike	Webinar	Entry	Exit	Trade	
spike	Shai K	WTW	1,000	s	54.67	02/12/07	$60	$9.99	50.40	2/14/2007		$9.99	$1.68		4,270.00	4,248.34	4,248.34			61%	42%		98% A+

Figure 3.1 A Basic Record-Keeping Spreadsheet

A. Source, group. I always want to know where my picks come from—my own research, the Spike group, webinars, etc. Of course I process all input from others through my own system and accept full responsibility for every trade.

B. Source, individual. If the pick came from a group, such as Spike or a webinar, I want to record the name of the individual whose pick I traded. Some people have an excellent track record, while others, seemingly very smart, lead to losses. I want to track the quality of the tips that come my way.

C. Symbol. One could also add a column for the name of the stock.

D. Quantity. If I exit this position not at once but in two or more trades, I insert a row following this one and split my purchase between two or more rows, depending on the number of exits.

E. Long or short. I use Excel's AutoFormat to color a cell depending on whether it is a long (l) or short (s). Professionals are just as comfortable shorting as they are buying.

F. Entry price.

G. Entry date.

H. Entry order (leave blank if your entry was at the order price). If you did not use a limit order and/or were filled

at a price different from your order level, put the price at which you placed your order here.

I. Entry slippage. Calculates dollars won or lost and colors the cells a shade of red or green depending on the result. Using limit orders occasionally leads to positive slippage.

J. Entry commission. If you insert a line later (see point D), remember to split the commission.

K. Exit price.

L. Exit date.

M. Exit order (similar to column H, above).

N. Exit slippage (similar to column I, above).

O. Exit commission.

P. Fee. Assessed on selling, so if you go short, fill in this cell after receiving a confirmation that you sold short; otherwise fill in after selling your long position.

Q. P/L. Gross profit or loss, before commissions and fees, but after slippage, if any.

R. Net. Net profit or loss after commissions and fees.

S. Net, Spike. So many of my trades come from the Spike group that I have a special column in my spreadsheet for them.

T. Net, webinars. Same idea as column S.

U, V, W, X. These four columns show performance grades on every trade; we will explore them in a later chapter.

TRADING DIARY—YOUR KEY TO LASTING SUCCESS

Make mistakes—but do not repeat them! People who like to explore and learn always make mistakes. Whenever I hire people, I tell them that I expect them to make mistakes—it is a part of their job description! Making mistakes is a sign of learning and exploring. Repeating mistakes, on the other hand, is a sign of carelessness, or some psychological problem.

The best way to learn from your mistakes is by keeping a trading diary. It allows you to convert the joy of successes and the pain of losses into the bankable gold of experience.

A trading diary is a pictorial record of your trades. It documents your entries and exits by using charts with arrows, lines, and comments. I create a diary entry for every purchase or sale. To make sure my diary is always current and up to date I have a rule—no breakfast until my diary for the previous day is completed. This encourages me to update the diary before the market opens and a new trading day begins.

It is important to document every trade. The only exception to this rule is very active day-trading. If you make a dozen trades each day, you may allow yourself to create a diary entry for just every third or fourth trade.

Why a pictorial diary in addition to the spreadsheet?

You probably carry with you photos of people and things you care about. In your wallet, purse, or on your desktop, you have photos of your wife, girlfriend, husband, children, dog, house, or car. Now I also want you to carry the pictures of your trades, so that you get to know them more intimately than before. Creating and maintaining a trading diary is the best way to learn from your experience.

My favorite tool for taking pictures of charts and making notes on them is a program called SnagIt. It makes it easy to capture images from any charting program, draw and write on them, and paste them into your diary. I use it almost daily for updating my diary or sharing trading ideas with friends. Whenever we shoot each other an e-mail, we tend to send charts captured and marked up with SnagIt instead of writing long messages.

My program of choice for keeping a trading diary is Microsoft Outlook. This is a fantastically powerful program, but most people only scratch its surface by using it for e-mail.

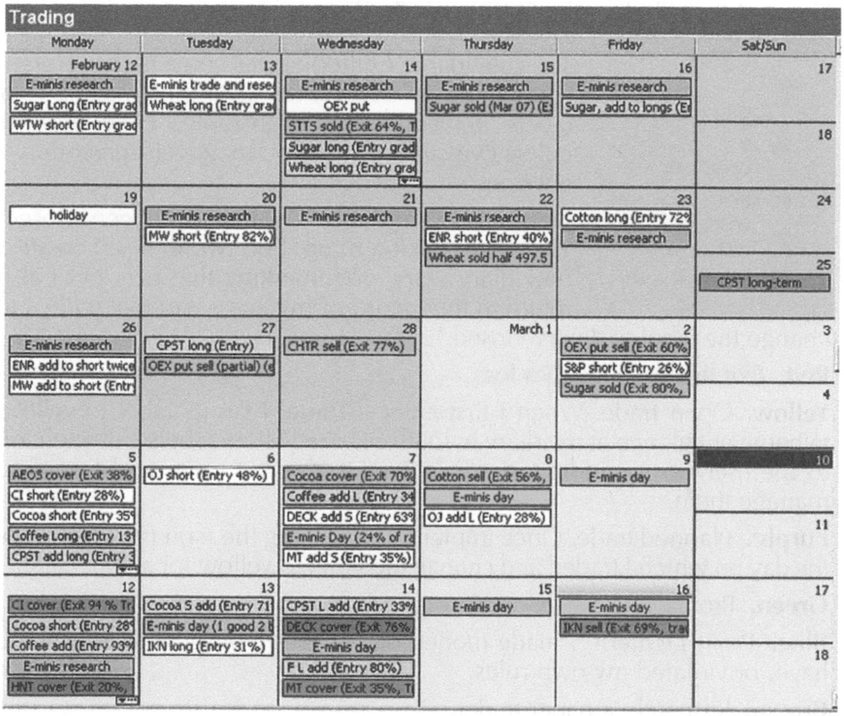

Trading					
Monday	Tuesday	Wednesday	Thursday	Friday	Sat/Sun
February 12 — E-minis research; Sugar Long (Entry gra; WTW short (Entry gra	**13** — E-minis trade and rese; Wheat long (Entry gra	**14** — E-minis research; OEX put; STTS sold (Exit 64%, T; Sugar long (Entry grad; Wheat long (Entry gra	**15** — E-minis research; Sugar sold (Mar 07) (E	**16** — E-minis research; Sugar, add to longs (E	**17** / **18**
19 — holiday	**20** — E-minis research; MW short (Entry 82%)	**21** — E-minis research	**22** — E-minis rsearch; ENR short (Entry 40%); Wheat sold half 497.5	**23** — Cotton long (Entry 72; E-minis research	**24** / **25** — CPST long-term
26 — E-minis research; ENR add to short twice; MW add to short (Entr	**27** — CPST long (Entry); OEX put sell (partial) ((	**28** — CHTR sell (Exit 77%)	**March 1**	**2** — OEX put sell (Exit 60%; S&P short (Entry 26%); Sugar sold (Exit 80%,	**3** / **4**
5 — AEOS cover (Exit 38%); CI short (Entry 28%); Cocoa short (Entry 35; Coffee Long (Entry 13; CPST add long (Entry 3	**6** — OJ short (Entry 48%)	**7** — Cocoa cover (Exit 70%; Coffee add L (Entry 34; DECK add S (Entry 63; E-minis Day (24% of r; MT add S (Entry 35%)	**8** — Cotton sell (Exit 56%; E-minis day; OJ add L (Entry 28%)	**9** — E-minis day	**10** / **11**
12 — CI cover (Exit 94 % Tr; Cocoa short (Entry 28; Coffee add (Entry 93; E-minis research; HNT cover (Exit 20%,	**13** — Cocoa S add (Entry 71; E-minis day (1 good 2 b; IKN long (Entry 31%)	**14** — CPST L add (Entry 33; DECK cover (Exit 76%; E-minis day; F L add (Entry 80%); MT cover (Exit 35%, T	**15** — E-minis day	**16** — E-minis day; IKN sell (Exit 69%, tra	**17** / **18**

Figure 3.2 A Trading Diary in Outlook
See the description of the meanings of colors in Figure 3.3.

Go to the Calendars tab in Outlook, create a new Calendar, and name it Trading. You can view any Calendar in a daily, weekly, or monthly format. I prefer a monthly format, which serves as a table of contents for all of my trades, both open and closed (see Figure 3.2).

Together with two trader friends, Kerry Lovvorn and Jeff Parker, I have created an Outlook add-on especially for keeping a trading diary, which we named AK-47. Initially, the three of us built it for ourselves, but then we offered it to the public, and you can see its description on www.elder.com.

Whenever you click on a calendar to create a new record for a trade, Outlook allows you to label that entry. The labels show up in the monthly view, and if you set a system of rules for coloring labels, each of them will carry a message (see Figure 3.3).

Figure 3.3   Labeling the Entries in a Trading Diary

The calendar in Outlook gives you a list of colors—you can assign a name to each color, making your labels immediately recognizable. Here are the colors I've chosen, but you may well select different ones:

None. Entry into a trade that has been closed. Whenever I exit a trade, I do two things. I create a new diary entry, documenting that exit, but I also return to the record of my entry into that trade and change the label to "entry closed."

Red. Exit that resulted in a loss.

Yellow. Open trade. When I first enter a trade, I set its label to yellow. Whenever I glance at my diary in Outlook, the yellow labels call attention to themselves, reminding me that these trades are open and I need to manage them.

Purple. Planned trade. Once implemented, I drag the icon into the box of the day on which I traded and change the label to yellow for an open trade.

Green. Profit.

Blue. Profit Demerit. I made money on this trade but less than I should have, or violated my own rules.

Brown. Research (a paper trade).

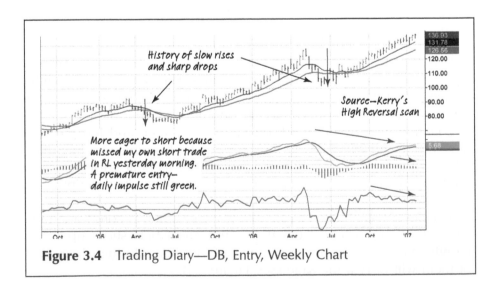

Figure 3.4   Trading Diary—DB, Entry, Weekly Chart

Most of my diary entries include two charts—a weekly and a daily. Depending on the trade, I might also add a monthly or intraday chart. Figures 3.4 and 3.5 show an example of a diary entry.

The weekly DB chart (Figure 3.4) shows the source of a trading idea— an e-mail from a friend who ran several market scans and shared the results with me. Diagonal red arrows mark bearish divergences. Thin vertical arrows show that the stock is prone to sharp drops. There is also a remark chiding myself for being a little too eager to enter. I was very bearish on the stock market and restless after missing an entry into a trade that came from my own scan.

The daily DB chart (Figure 3.5) below shows more bearish divergences and a false upside breakout (a hugely important trading signal). It documents my entry into the trade and grades the quality of my two sell orders on a 100-point scale. Having these charts in front of me today brings the experience of that trade back to life and allows me to learn from it. What did I do right? What did I do wrong? How could I have improved my entry into the trade?

Now, before we move on to the next chapter, would you like to see my exit from that trade, shorting DB? We have already looked at my entry, but what if I told you I forgot how I exited? What if I waved my hands

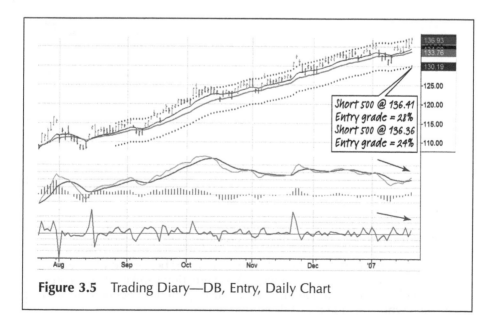

Figure 3.5 Trading Diary—DB, Entry, Daily Chart

in the air and told you that DB went down and I covered? How useful would that be to you?

HOW TO DOCUMENT YOUR TRADING PLAN

I hope that by now I have convinced you that it is essential to keep a trading diary. Will you promise to keep one? If so, I'll open my Outlook again and show you the exit diary. Take a look at Figures 3.6 and 3.7.

I believe that the best format for a trading plan is similar to the diary we have just reviewed. When you scan stocks, you can keep brief notes on the potentially interesting ones in a spreadsheet or on a notepad with three columns: Date, Ticker, and Comment. The idea is to narrow down your search to a few actionable stocks. Once you have a handful of candidates, it is time to work them up and create an action plan for each promising one.

When you find a stock that you think you might want to trade in the days ahead, create a plan for it using the same format as the diary, shown above. Capture a weekly chart using SnagIt, mark its signals with arrows and lines and write on it. Paste the chart with all the markings into a

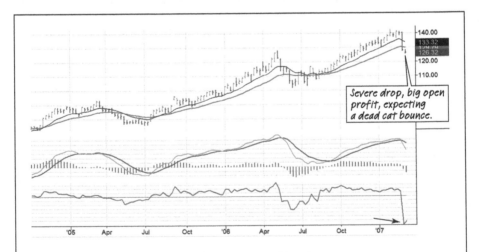

Figure 3.6   Trading Diary—DB, Exit, Weekly Chart

The weekly DB chart shows that the price dropped below the value zone, underneath both moving averages. A severe downspike of the Force Index marks a potential bottom. MACD-Histogram has declined close to the zone where upside reversals tend to occur.

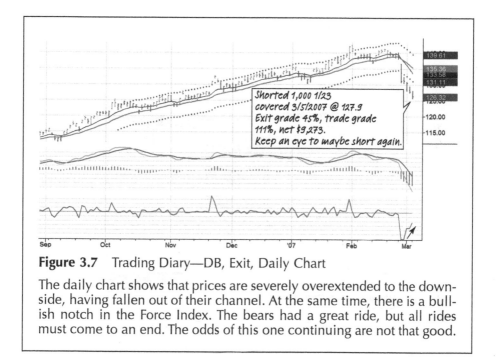

Figure 3.7 Trading Diary—DB, Exit, Daily Chart

The daily chart shows that prices are severely overextended to the down-side, having fallen out of their channel. At the same time, there is a bull-ish notch in the Force Index. The bears had a great ride, but all rides must come to an end. The odds of this one continuing are not that good.

newly created entry in your Outlook Calendar. Now capture a daily chart, mark it up, and paste it into the same Outlook entry, below the weekly chart. Name that Calendar entry after the stock and label it as a planned trade so that you can easily recognize it. Save your newly created entry.

Go to your brokerage house website and place an order or orders for your planned trades. Make sure your broker sends you an alert immediately after your order is filled. Once you know you are in a trade, it is a good idea to place your stop-loss and profit-taking orders using an OCO (one cancels other) order. This way you will not be caught off-guard while away from the screen.

Once you have created a plan for a stock, add its ticker to your monitoring list in the quote window of the program you use for market analysis. The size of the computer screen limits the size of the quote window, which is actually a good thing. I want to monitor only as many stocks as can fit into a single screen, without dividing my attention between dozens of tickers. I like this window (Figure 3.8) to show the key market indexes, such as the S&P 500, as well as separate sections for my long, short, and futures positions. I named the bottom section Monitor, and put the stocks I am considering trading there.

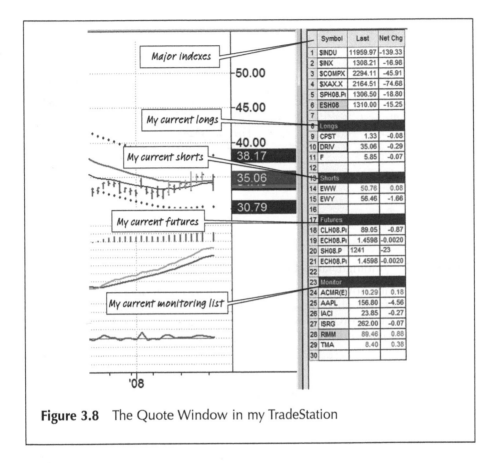

	Symbol	Last	Net Chg
1	$INDU	11959.97	-139.33
2	$INX	1308.21	-16.98
3	$COMPX	2294.11	-45.91
4	$XAX.X	2164.51	-74.68
5	SPH08.P:	1306.50	-18.80
6	ESH08	1310.00	-15.25
7			
8	Longs		
9	CPST	1.33	-0.08
10	DRIV	35.06	-0.29
11	F	5.85	-0.07
12			
13	Shorts		
14	EWW	50.76	0.08
15	EWY	56.46	-1.66
16			
17	Futures		
18	CLH08.P	89.05	-0.87
19	ECH08.P:	1.4598	-0.0020
20	SH08.P	1241	-23
21	ECH08.P:	1.4598	-0.0020
22			
23	Monitor		
24	ACMR(E)	10.29	0.18
25	AAPL	156.80	-4.56
26	IACI	23.85	-0.27
27	ISRG	262.00	-0.07
28	RIMM	89.46	0.88
29	TMA	8.40	0.38
30			

Major indexes
50.00
45.00
My current longs
40.00
My current shorts 38.17
35.06
30.79
My current futures
My current monitoring list
'08

Figure 3.8   The Quote Window in my TradeStation

My quote window always tracks the latest prices and the net changes for the day.

You can see that the exit is graded. Its 45% rating was decent, but the trade grade was very nice. Taking over $9 profit per share on 1,000 shares was a good payday. See the note—"keep an eye on it to maybe short again." The trade does not have to end when you exit a position. There is a lot to review, much to learn, and you can continue to make plans for the future. I hope that this exercise has helped convince you that it is important to keep a trading diary. You need to document your successes and failures and learn from both.

This is the setup I want to see whenever I open my trading program. It shows all the important data at once: the key indexes, my long and short positions in stocks, my futures positions, and my monitoring list.

The chart (truncated in this picture) is on the left, the list on the right. I have set up my TradeStation so that whenever I click a symbol in the quote window on the right, its chart automatically appears in the window on the left.

I also write down key trading messages on my charts, especially the price and size of my entry as well as the target and stop. When the markets become active, it is easy to lose track of things. This is why writing on the chart is very helpful, as illustrated in Figure 3.9.

Once you execute your plan and enter a trade, move its Calendar entry from the day of the plan to the day of the trade. Update the chart and add an intraday chart if you like. Add a few relevant comments—the size of the trade, the entry grade, any comments on the quality of your entry, or the feelings the trade evoked. Change the color of the label from Planned Trade to Open Trade.

Most beginning traders feel out of control, overwhelmed by the sheer volume of the markets. This system for creating plans and monitoring trades will make your work better organized and more likely to be profitable.

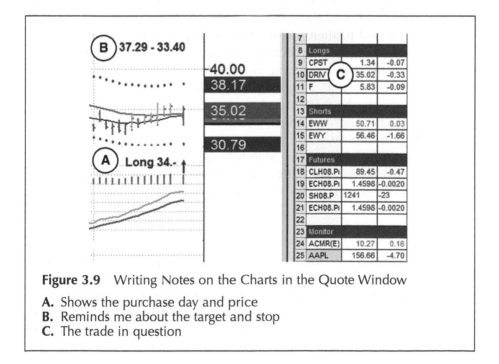

Figure 3.9 Writing Notes on the Charts in the Quote Window

A. Shows the purchase day and price
B. Reminds me about the target and stop
C. The trade in question

If you keep good records, you will be able to recognize any flaws in your method and fix them. Keep doing this long enough, and you may start running out of mistakes! That's when your equity curve will be ready to turn up.

MARGRET'S METHOD—PUT IT ON THE WALL

In addition to the electronic diary, I want to give you a low-tech method for keeping track of planned trades.

You may look at a chart and see a beautiful trade starting to come together—but it is not there yet. You may say to yourself, "If it comes down a bit more and its support holds, I will buy it." What are the chances of you remembering this plan three weeks later, when the stock actually does what you expected?

The best trades come together slowly. You may need to wait for more pieces of the puzzle to emerge before you can pull the trigger and place an order to buy or sell short.

Years ago I adopted a low-tech system my good friend Margret used for keeping track of her trade ideas. On one of my first visits to her tropical penthouse I noticed that her trading room had two bulletin boards with charts pinned to them. Margret explained that whenever she saw a trade starting to come together, she printed out the chart of that stock and marked it up with a red pen, showing what the stock had to do in order for her to buy it. Margret pinned those charts to the bulletin boards. Whenever she walked to her desk she saw the charts with her hand-drawn action signals. There was no way this woman would let a good trade pass her by.

If you decide to implement Margret's method, be sure to take the charts down from the wall after you either enter the trade or cancel the plan. Make sure the visual records on your wall are fresh and up-to-date.

HOW TO GRADE YOUR PERFORMANCE

A person who trades without measuring and grading his performance is like someone who calls himself a competitive runner but does not own a stopwatch. Only a recreational runner can jog around the block without timing himself, to get some exercise and enjoy the scenery. There is no "recreational trading". This is why I suggest grading all trades on three scales: your buy grade, your sell grade, and—most importantly—the overall trade grade.

You can measure the quality of your buying and selling by the location of your trade within that day's range. When you buy, you want to trade as close to the low of the day as possible. When you sell, you want to trade as close to the high of the day as possible.

$$\text{The Buy Grade} = \frac{\text{the high of the day minus buy price}}{\text{the high of the day minus the low of the day}}$$

The result is a percentage: if you buy at the low of the day, your grade is 100%, and if you buy the top tick, your grade is 0. Grades below 20% are poor, above 50% good, and above 80% superb.

$$\text{The Sell Grade} = \frac{\text{the sell price minus the low of the day}}{\text{the high of the day minus the low of the day}}$$

The result is expressed as a percentage: if you sell at the top tick of the day, your grade is 100%, and if you sell at the bottom tick your grade is 0. Here too, you want to score above 80% for an excellent grade, while anything below 20% is poor.

Whenever I trade, my goal is to score above 50% on my entries and exits. This means buying below the midpoint of the day and selling above the midpoint. An entire industry of professional traders makes a living from buying low and selling high. Grading your entries and exits makes you focus on your executions, and that leads to a better performance over time.

If you return to Figure 3.1, you will understand the meaning of columns U and V. They grade the quality of my entries and exits. Psychologically, it is easy to buy high and sell low. Knowing that at the end of the day you will have to grade your entries and exits helps you restrain yourself from chasing intraday rallies or declines.

Whenever you close a trade, you need to measure its quality. While money is important, it does not provide a good measure of an individual trade. The amount you make or lose in a single trade heavily depends on that trade's size as well as the market's current volatility.

The best way to rate your performance in any single trade is to measure the number of points gained or lost against the market's recent volatility. What has been the normal swing of that market in recent months? What percentage of that swing did you catch in your latest trade? Answering these questions will provide a good measure of your performance.

A well-drawn channel on the daily chart provides as an excellent reflection of recent volatility. Our trade grade will show what percentage of that channel we have managed to capture.

For swing trades, I use a channel around the longer moving average on the daily chart. For day-trades, I use a channel on a 5-minute chart, also centered around the longer moving average.

One of the few scientifically proven facts about the financial markets is that they fluctuate above and below value. While prices keep swinging between mania and depression, I rate the quality of each trade by the percentage of the channel it captured.

$$\text{The Trade Grade} = \frac{\text{exit price minus entry price}}{\text{the upper channel line minus the lower channel line}}$$

I measure the channel height on the day I enter a trade—the upper channel line minus the lower line. If you look at Figure 3.1, you will see that column W tracks the percentage of a channel captured in every trade—this is the most important ranking in my records. I call every trade that captures 30% or more of the channel an A trade. Sometimes there are even A+ trades which capture over 30%. Any trade that captures 20% to 30% of a channel gets rated B; 10% to 20%, C; below 10%, a C–; and below zero it becomes a D trade. It is not enough to make profits—it is just as important to earn a good performance grade.

Grading every entry and exit as well as every trade will train you to adopt a demanding and disciplined attitude towards your work. As a private trader, you have no supervisor. To win, you must become your own manager, and that's what trade ratings help you accomplish.

TWO TYPES OF TRADING

There are two key approaches to buying. One is value buying: "buy low, sell high." The other is momentum buying: "buy high, sell even higher."

A value buyer identifies value and tries to buy near or below it. He aims to sell when prices become overvalued. I put two exponential moving averages on every chart and call the space between them the value zone. My software draws a channel parallel to the daily chart's slow moving average that encloses about 95% of all prices for the past three months. The space above the upper channel line identifies an overbought zone, and the space below the lower line an oversold area.

Momentum trading calls for a completely different approach. Momentum traders buy when a stock accelerates and sell when it starts losing momentum.

Are you a value trader or a momentum trader? We make some of the most important decisions in life based on emotion. Some of us are temperamentally drawn to buying low and selling high, suspicious of wild trends. Others scan the markets, looking for runaway trends, then jump aboard and try to hop off before a reversal.

Only you can decide whether to be a value or a momentum trader. Whatever your decision, please keep in mind that having a written plan for buying and selling will put you miles ahead of your competitors. Whatever your method, a person with a plan has a clear advantage over the market crowd.

PSYCHOLOGY, RISK MANAGEMENT, & RECORD-KEEPING

Beginners buy whenever some vague tip floats their way. Experienced traders know that serious buying requires serious research.

Serious buying also requires good money management. There are simple mathematical rules that tell you how much risk you may accept on any given trade as well as on all your open trades combined. Those who violate these rules have a short life expectancy in the markets.

In addition, there are certain psychological techniques that can help make your life in the markets less stressful and more satisfying. Plus, there are highly desirable ways of record-keeping that will help you grow into a mature and successful trader.

That is why, before we get into selling and shorting, you need to answer these questions about psychology and money management, buying decisions, and record-keeping.

Please do not rush as you work through this chapter. Give these questions a great deal of thought and record your answers on pages 30 and 31. Be sure to re-read the appropriate sections in *The New Sell and Sell Short* if you miss any answers.

Please go through all questions in this section and record
your answers prior to turning to the Answers section.

Answer Sheet

Questions	Max. Pts. Available	Trial 1	Trial 2	Trial 3	Trial 4	Trial 5	Trial 6
1	1						
2	1						
3	1						
4	1						
5	1						
6	1						
7	1						
8	1						
9	1						
10	1						
11	1						
12	1						
13	1						
14	1						
15	1						
16	1						
17	1						
18	1						
19	1						
20	1						
21	1						
22	1						
23	1						
24	1						
25	1						

(continues on next page))

Answer Sheet, *continued*

Questions	Max. Pts. Available	Trial 1	Trial 2	Trial 3	Trial 4	Trial 5	Trial 6
26	1						
27	1						
28	1						
29	1						
30	1						
31	1						
32	1						
33	1						
Total points	33						

Question 1—The Stress of Holding a Position

Having bought a stock, most people find themselves in the least stressful position if that stock:

1. Rises slightly
2. Skyrockets
3. Declines slightly
4. Collapses

Question 2—Your Trading Edge

Your trading edge can come from:

1. Fundamental analysis
2. Technical studies
3. Discipline
4. All of the above

Question 3—The Three Great Divides

The three great divides in trading include all of the following, except:

1. Technical vs. fundamental research
2. Trend vs. counter-trend trading
3. Relying on TV news vs. advisory services
4. Discretionary vs. systematic trading

Question 4—Price and Value

Find the incorrect statement about the relationship between price and value:

1. Values change slowly, prices change fast.
2. Studying earnings reports and industry trends allows you to discover value.
3. Moving averages help define the value zone by tracking public consensus.
4. Price equals value at any given moment.

Question 5—Fundamental and Technical Analysis

Which of the following statements about fundamental and technical analysis is incorrect?

1. A fundamentalist calculates the value of the business that issued a stock.
2. Having precise information about the fundamentals tells you exactly which way a stock is going to go.
3. A technician looks for repetitive patterns in price data.
4. A pure technician does not care about earnings or corporate news; he only wants to know the stock ticker and price history.

Question 6—Trend vs. Counter-Trend Trading

The advantages of trend trading over counter-trend trading, include all of the following except:

1. Greater profit potential per trade
2. Lower commission expense
3. More time to make decisions
4. Lower stress level

Question 7—Systematic vs. Discretionary Trading

System trading has all of the following advantages over discretionary trading, except:

1. Knowing in advance what profits or losses to expect over a period of time
2. Less emotional involvement in every trade
3. A greater degree of freedom
4. A method for handling the uncertainty of the markets

Question 8—Technical Toolbox

A technical trader uses a toolbox of indicators in his or her decision-making. Find the correct statement among the following:

1. Selecting the tools that give the signals you want is a sound practice.
2. The more tools, the better the toolbox.
3. "Five bullets to a clip" allows you to use only five indicators.
4. The best indicators are well known, and a trader should use them.

Question 9—Trading Psychology

Find the incorrect statement about trading psychology:

1. If you set your technical system just right, you need not worry about psychology.
2. The mind of a trader continually filters the incoming information.
3. Wishful thinking causes traders to "see" non-existent technical signals.
4. A bullish trader is more likely to overlook sell signals.

Question 10—Trading Discipline

Discipline is essential because the markets present an endless parade of temptations. Please identify the incorrect statement among the following:

1. People with a history of poor impulse control are likely to fail in trading.
2. AA (Alcoholics Anonymous) provides a useful model for dealing with market temptations.
3. If you have a good trading system, discipline is not really an issue.
4. Some traders have personality flaws that make them destined to fail.

Question 11—Dealing with Losses

Traders feel ashamed of their losses. Please review the following statements and find the correct one:

1. In training, punishments are more effective than rewards.
2. If you have taken several right steps and then a wrong one in making a trade, you should punish yourself for it.
3. Successful traders love the game more than the profits.
4. It does not pay to keep records of losing trades.

Question 12—Overtrading

Trading a position that is too large for one's account will lead to all of the following, except:

1. Less spontaneity and greater tension
2. Less calm and adaptability
3. Fear of pulling the trigger
4. A greater focus on the market

Question 13—The 2% Rule

A beginning trader with a $20,000 account decides to implement the 2% Rule of money management. He finds a stock quoted at $12.50 and decides to buy it, with a price target of $15 and a stop-loss order at $11.50. The maximum number of shares this Rule allows him to buy is close to:

1. 900
2. 400
3. 350
4. 200

Question 14—Modifying the 2% Rule

An experienced trader with a $2,000,000 account decides to modify the 2% Rule and cap his risk per trade at 0.25%. He finds a $9 stock which he plans to ride to $12, while putting his stop at $8. The maximum number of shares his Rule allows him to buy is:

1. 2,000
2. 4,500
3. 5,000
4. 12,000

Question 15—The 6% Rule

Find the statement about the 6% Rule that is correct:

1. It will protect your account from a drawdown caused by a bad trade.
2. It will protect your account from a drawdown caused by a series of bad trades.
3. When losses begin to mount, the best response is to trade more actively, to trade your way out of a hole.
4. The 6% Rule needs to be applied after putting on a trade.

Question 16—The Top Two Goals for Every Trade

What are the top two goals for every trade?

1. Make money and test a new system.
2. Face the challenge and feel the joy of victory.
3. Make money and become a better trader.
4. Test your discipline and the ability to implement a plan.

Question 17—Learning from Experience

The best way to learn from experience is:

1. To make lots of trades
2. To keep good records
3. To discuss your trades with friends
4. To review your brokerage statements

Question 18—A Record-Keeping Spreadsheet

Which of the following must be included in a basic record-keeping spreadsheet?

    A. Gross and net P&L

    B. The grade of each trade

    C. Slippage on entry and exit

    D. Source of every trade idea

1. A
2. A and B
3. A, B, and C
4. All of the above

Question 19—Trading Mistakes

Which of the following statements about trading mistakes is incorrect?

1. Intelligent people do not make mistakes.
2. Making mistakes is inevitable when you learn and explore.
3. Repeating mistakes is a sign of impulsivity.
4. Keeping a diary helps you learn from your mistakes.

Question 20—Trader's Diary

Find the correct statement about the trader's diary:

1. There is no need to document your entry if you plan to fill in the diary after you exit.
2. The diaries of losing trades tend to be more educational than those of winning trades.
3. It is essential to create diary entries only for your best trades.
4. An active trader who cannot document all trades can pick and choose what trades to document.

Question 21—Diary Entry

The diary of an entry into a trade must include all of the following, except:

1. The reason for making this trade
2. The buy grade for long or sell grade for short trades
3. Charts of your trading vehicle at the time of the entry
4. The trade grade

Question 22—Trading Plan vs. Diary

Which of the following describes the difference between a Trader's Diary and a Trading Plan?

1. Contains charts in two timeframes.
2. The charts are marked up to identify buy or sell signals.
3. The document is named after the stock ticker.
4. Buy or sell grades are recorded.

Question 23—The Monitoring Screen

The window for monitoring stocks in your trading software should include all of the following, except:

1. Key market indexes
2. Your open positions
3. The stocks you consider trading
4. The stocks you have exited

Question 24—Comments on the Screen

Keeping your comments about open positions on the screen is useful for all of the following reasons, except:

1. It reminds you how long you have been in a trade.
2. It helps you see whether you are winning or losing in an open position.
3. It helps you keep track of your profit target and stop-loss order.
4. It helps you measure your performance.

Question 25—Pinning a Chart to a Wall

"Margret's method"—pinning a chart to a wall and marking the trading signals, for which you will be waiting—has all of the following advantages, except:

1. It forces you to clearly express what price or indicator action you expect.
2. It keeps you from forgetting a plan.
3. Removing the charts from the wall if your plans change helps keep your mind fresh.
4. Keeping charts on a wall ensures that you will act when the time is right.

Question 26—Sources of Trading Ideas

Which of the following can serve as sources of trading ideas?

   A. Maintaining a short list of stocks whose signals you follow.

   B. An electronic scan of a stock market database.

   C. Tips from friends and advisory services.

   D. Mass media news.

1. A
2. A and B
3. A, B, and C
4. All of the above

Question 27—Grading Buys and Sells

Find the incorrect statement about grading buys or sells:

1. The closer you buy to the low of the bar, the better your grade.
2. The closer you sell to the low of the bar, the better your grade.
3. Selling above the midpoint of the bar earns a positive grade.
4. Buying in the lowest quarter of the bar earns an excellent grade.

Question 28—Grading Completed Trades

Find the correct statement about grading completed trades:

1. Money is a good measure of the quality of each trade.
2. A long-term trend trader can use channels to measure the quality of trades.
3. A trade capturing over 30% of a channel earns an "A."
4. A trade capturing less than 20% of a channel earns a "D."

Question 29—Buying

Find the incorrect statement about buying:

1. The principle of value buying is "buy low, sell high."
2. The principle of momentum buying is "buy high, sell even higher."
3. The upper channel line identifies the level of depression and the lower channel line the level of mania in the markets.
4. Momentum trading works well in runaway trends.

Question 30—Value

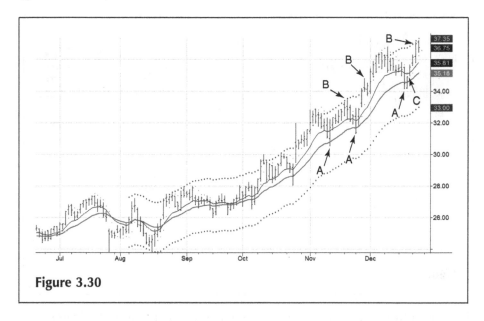

Figure 3.30

Please match the following descriptions with the letters on the chart:
1. Value zone
2. Below value—consider buying
3. Overvalued—consider selling

Question 31—A Trade Diary

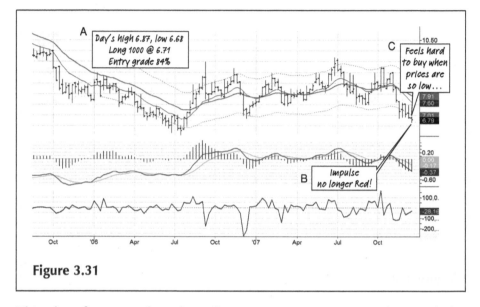

Figure 3.31

This chart from a trader's diary illustrates an entry into a trade. Match the following with the letters on the chart:

1. A technical comment on a chart pattern that led to a trade
2. A performance rating
3. A psychological comment

Question 32—Grading a Trade

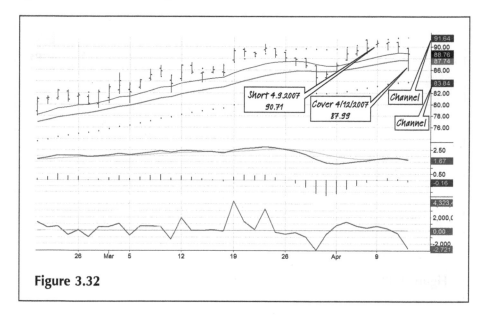

Figure 3.32

This chart shows one of the trades in which I piggybacked a Spike pick.*
The weekly chart is not shown here, but you can see bearish divergences of MACD Lines and the Force Index on the dailies. The question,
however, is about grading this trade: short at 90.71, cover at 87.99, upper
channel line at 91.56, lower channel line at 83.67. What is the trade
grade?

1. Trade Grade A: Over 30% of the channel
2. Trade Grade B: 20–30% of the channel
3. Trade Grade C: 10–20% of the channel
4. Trade Grade D: Below 10% of the channel

*See www.spiketrade.com

Question 33—Value Buying vs. Momentum Buying

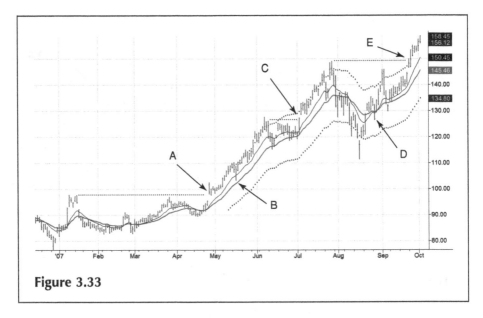

Figure 3.33

Take a look at the letters on this chart and identify value buying or momentum buying zones.

1. Value buying zones
2. Momentum buying zones

ANSWERS TO QUESTIONS

PART ONE:

PSYCHOLOGY, RISK MANAGEMENT, & RECORD-KEEPING

Question 1—The Stress of Holding a Position

Answer 3 Declines slightly

Sitting back and doing nothing feels easy; thinking and making decisions is hard. While a collapse in your stock feels painful, the rise is also stressful because it forces you to think about your exit strategy, targets, stops, and so on. Most people are surprisingly comfortable sitting with a slightly losing position and hoping for better.

Question 2—Your Trading Edge

Answer 4 All of the above

An edge is a method of discovering opportunities and placing orders that gives a trader an advantage over the majority of competitors. A trader with either a technical or a fundamental edge still needs discipline to implement trading signals.

Question 3—The Three Great Divides

Answer 3 Selection "Relying on TV news vs. an advisory service" is incorrect.

A serious trader needs to specialize by choosing those areas of research and trading that appeal to him. Choosing between technical or fundamental analysis, trend or counter-trend trading, and discretionary or systematic trading are all serious choices. Your selections depend to a great degree on your temperament and personality. A successful trader is an independent person. Hooking yourself up to the feeding line of either TV news or an advisory service is really no choice at all, since there is so little difference between them.

Question 4—Price and Value

Answer 4 Selection "Price equals value at any given moment" is incorrect.

Prices are easily seen while you need to look for values. Prices can change quickly in response to the mood of the masses, while values change slowly. Each price is a momentary consensus of value, but that consensus keeps changing, overshooting value on the way up or down. A simple tool, such as a pair of moving averages, helps you get a general idea of where the value is and which way it is moving—and allows you to trade accordingly.

Question 5—Fundamental and Technical Analysis

Answer 2 Selection "Having precise information about the fundamentals tells you exactly which way a stock is going to go" is incorrect.

Having precise information about the fundamentals does *not* forecast exactly which way a stock is going to go. The problem with fundamental analysis is that values change slowly but prices fluctuate fast. In the short run, prices can even move against the fundamentals. Whether you are primarily a fundamentalist or a technician, you want to know how the other side lives and thinks. Having both a fundamental and a technical view of a stock provides a deeper understanding of its trends and reversals.

Question 6—Trend vs. Counter-Trend Trading

Answer 4 Selection "Lower stress level" is incorrect.

Trend trades last longer than counter-trend moves, giving you more time to make trade-related decisions. They promise greater profits by covering longer distances. Commissions are lower in trend-following trades than in active swing trading. Still, it would be incorrect to expect a lower stress level. Riding a trend is like riding a bucking horse that tries to shake you off. Holding on to a trend-following trade requires a great deal of patience and self-assurance—a lot of mental work.

Question 7—System vs. Discretionary Trading

Answer 3 Selection "A greater degree of freedom" is incorrect.

System traders who have done a lot of backtesting can have a fairly high level of confidence knowing what profits or losses to expect down the road. If they have the discipline to follow all the signals of their system, they will lower their stress level, insulating themselves to a degree from uncertainty in the markets. What they give up is the freedom to make decisions as market conditions change, creating new threats or opportunities.

Question 8—Technical Toolbox

Answer 3 "Five bullets to a clip" allows you to use only five indicators.

A typical beginners' mistake is to overstuff their toolbox; they also tend to use different tools at different times to confirm their preconceptions. It is much better to limit yourself to a small number of well-tested tools. Which tools are used, however, may very well vary among different traders.

Question 9—Trading Psychology

Answer 1 Selection "If you set your technical system just right, you need not worry about psychology" is incorrect.

The sheer volume of information available to us is so immense that no human can process everything. Our eyes, ears, and brains filter out much of incoming data. We become consciously aware of only a small part of market information. Our wishes, hopes, and fears filter out much of the rest. Trading systems have their advantages, but it would be a humanly impossible task to switch off our personal psychology, in the markets or anywhere else.

Question 10—Trading Discipline

Answer 3 Selection "If you have a good trading system, discipline is not really an issue" is incorrect.

The seemingly easy riches that glitter on every screen seduce many traders to plunge into the market without considering its very real dangers. You need discipline to set up and follow your decision-making tree. You must decide when to step in and when to stay out. People who cannot resist temptation are likely to do poorly in trading, no matter how smart they are.

Question 11—Dealing with Losses

Answer 3 Successful traders love the game more than the profits.

Rewarding people tends to improve their performance much more than punishments. It pays to be kind to yourself while learning how to trade. Give yourself sufficient time to learn; celebrate even partial successes. Keep good notes of all your trades—you will probably learn more from losses than from wins. Trade a small size, so that you can focus on the game and not on the money. You can always increase your trading size later, after you become more knowledgeable and secure.

Question 12—Overtrading

Answer 4 Selection "A greater focus on the market" is incorrect.

When stakes become dangerously high, people become stiff with tension and are afraid to pull the trigger. The spontaneity and ease of adjustment deteriorate, and performance goes down accordingly. A trader whose position is too large for his account is not focusing on the market. He is focusing on the money. The feeling of tension clouds his mind, preventing him from reading the market's signals. One of the key goals of money management is to put your mind at ease by setting realistic position limits and providing a safety net for your account.

Question 13—The 2% Rule

Answer 3 350

A trader who decides to risk no more than 2% of his account in any given trade may risk the maximum of $400 in a $20,000 account. Of course, he is free to risk less. Buying a stock at $12.50 and putting a stop at $11.50 means risking $1 per share. In a perfect world, this rule would have allowed him to buy 400 shares, but in reality this trader will have to pay a commission when he buys and again when he sells; he can also expect to be hit with slippage. This is why 350 shares is the correct answer. He may buy even fewer shares but he may not buy a greater number.

Question 14—Modifying the 2% Rule

Answer 2 4,500

As a rule, the larger the account, the lower the percentage a trader will risk on any single trade. The maximum for him is the same as for everyone else—2%; still, he may go up to that absolute limit only when he sees an exceptional opportunity. At other times he is likely to limit his risk to well below 1%. For a trader with a $2,000,000 account, a quarter percent comes to $5,000—quite a bit to bet on a single trade. Risking $1 per share means a theoretical maximum size of 5,000 shares. In practice, the size has to be reduced, to pay commissions and to cover possible slippage.

Question 15—The 6% Rule

Answer 2 It will protect your account from a drawdown caused by a series of bad trades.

The 2% Rule is designed to limit risk on any single trade, but the 6% Rule will protect you from the damage caused by a series of bad trades. The 6% Rule will force you to step back when losses begin to mount; this is the opposite of what most traders do, as they dig themselves a deeper hole by frantic trading. The time to apply the 6% Rule is before you enter a trade, not after. It helps you to see whether you can afford the risk of an additional trade.

Question 16—The Top Two Goals for Every Trade

Answer 3 Make money and become a better trader.

The main reason to trade is to make money, but there is a fair bit of randomness in the markets, and not every trade can be profitable. On the other hand, becoming a better trader is a very reachable goal for every trade. Whether you win or lose, you must become a better trader at the conclusion of each trade. You must keep learning both from your winning and losing trades. Testing your discipline and the ability to implement a plan are key components of learning to become a better trader.

Question 17—Learning from Experience

Answer 2 To keep good records

A human mind has a limited capacity to remember. Keeping good records allows you to transform fleeting experiences into solid memories. Using your notes as your "extracranial memory" allows you to re-examine your experiences and grow into a better trader. A trader who uses money management rules to protect his equity and who keeps good records to learn from his experience is on the road to success.

Question 18—A Record-Keeping Spreadsheet

Answer 4 All of above

The purpose of keeping a trader's spreadsheet is to record hard facts about your trading. In addition to such basic data as entry and exit prices, you need to calculate slippage, track the quality of your sources, and grade your performance for every entry and exit for each trade as well.

Question 19—Trading Mistakes

Answer 1 Selection "Intelligent people do not make mistakes" is incorrect.

Mistakes are part and parcel of learning and exploring—which is why intelligent people often make them. There is nothing wrong with making a mistake—the problem is repeating the same mistake. Keeping a diary helps you avoid this problem.

Question 20—Trader's Diary

Answer 2 The diaries of losing trades tend to be more valuable than those of winning ones.

Losses force traders to stretch their minds and learn new things. It is important to study all aspects of a trade and document your entry while the details are still fresh in your mind. An active trader who can record only some trades needs a disciplined system, such as recording every second, fifth, or even tenth trade, regardless of whether that trade was a winner or a loser.

Question 21—Diary Entry

Answer 4 Selection "The trade grade" is incorrect.

You want to record your reason for entering a trade to help you discover which signals produce better results. It pays to analyze any market in more than one timeframe: one longer-term, another shorter-term, for a deeper understanding of what is happening. If you follow this rule, you will need to save entry charts in more than one timeframe. While you must rate your entry at the end of the day, you won't know your overall trade grade until you close it out.

Question 22—Trading Plan vs. Diary

Answer 4 Buy or sell grades are recorded.

A trading plan uses the same format as the diary. It shows charts in multiple timeframes, marked up with trade signals. They are named in the same way, even though their labels are different. The one difference is that a trading plan cannot include buy or sell grades—you will know them only after you put on a trade.

Question 23—The Monitoring Screen

Answer 4 Selection "The stocks you have exited" is incorrect.

It is essential to monitor your open positions, whether long or short. It is also important to keep an eye on key market indexes, such as the Dow or the Nasdaq. Needless to say, you want to keep a short list of stocks you are thinking of trading on the front burner. The stocks you have exited would only clutter your screen. If you do not plan to re-enter them any time soon, move them to a separate window or tab.

Question 24—Comments on the Screen

Answer 4 Selection "It helps you measure your performance" is incorrect.

If your trading software allows you to write on the screen, take advantage of this feature. Marking your entry date and price will help you see at a glance where you stand in that trade. Marking up your target and stop levels will allow you to be more alert both to trouble and to profit-taking opportunities. What an on-screen note cannot do is measure your performance. That is something to be accomplished in your Trader's Spreadsheet and transferred into your Diary.

Question 25—Pinning a Chart to a Wall

Answer 4 Selection "Keeping charts on a wall ensures that you will act when the time is right" is incorrect.

Printing out a chart and marking up the signals that will prompt you to act is an effective way of monitoring your trading ideas. Seeing those charts whenever you approach your desk provides a powerful reminder of your plans. The bulletin board needs to be periodically purged, to prevent it from turning into an archive of old ideas. Still, no system, no matter how logical, will force you to act—only you can supply the motivation.

Question 26—Sources of Trading Ideas

Answer 4 All of the above.

You can pick up your ideas everywhere. A great Russian poet Anna Akhmatova wrote, "If only you knew from what muck poems grow, knowing no shame." The key point is that all of those ideas are the raw material for your trading system. You may toss 20 ideas into the grist-mill of your system, and in the end put on a single trade—that would be a reasonable percentage.

Question 27—Grading Buys and Sells

Answer 2 Selection "The closer you sell to the low of the bar, the better your grade" is incorrect.

You want to buy as near the low of the bar and sell as near the high of the bar as possible. Buying in the top quarter or selling in the bottom quarter of the daily bar is a loser's game; buying below or selling above midpoint is very good, while buying in the bottom quarter or selling in the upper quarter of the daily bar gives you an excellent grade.

Question 28—Grading Completed Trades

Answer 3 A trade capturing over 30% of a channel earns an "A."

Money, reflected in the equity curve of your account, provides a good measure of your overall trading skill, but it is a poor measure of any individual trade. Channels provide a good yardstick for swing trades, but a long-term trader needs a different measure, such as the percentage by which he multiplied his capital. The quality of short-term swing trades is best measured by comparing gains to the height of the channel on the daily chart. Capturing at least 30% of that channel earns you an A, 20% a B, 10% a C, while a loss gets a D.

Question 29—Buying

Answer 3 Selection "The upper channel line identifies the level of depression and the lower channel line the level of mania in the markets" is incorrect.

In quiet markets, it makes sense to try to buy at or below value and use channels to sell above value. Momentum trading, such as buying upside breakouts, works better in runaway trends. When prices rise above the upper channel line, they identify a flash of unsustainable optimism, a zone of market mania. When they fall below the lower channel line, they identify the zone of fear and pessimism.

Question 30—Value

Answer 1. C
     2. A
     3. B

If each price is a snapshot, then a moving average is a composite photograph, a reflection of value in the market. If you buy near the moving average, you'll be buying value. If you buy below the EMA, you'll buy undervalued assets. One of the very few scientifically proven facts about the markets is that prices oscillate above and below value. When you sell above the upper channel line, you sell overvalued assets.

Question 31—A Trade Diary

Answers 1. B
2. A
3. C

A visual diary of a trade must include several components. It is essential to mark technical trade signals or comment on the strategy that led to this trade. A Diary must include a quality rating for every entry, exit, and the entire trade. Beginners need to record their feelings during each trade, but more experienced traders tend to become unemotional about their trades and may skip such comments.

Question 32—Grading a Trade

Answer 1 Trade Grade A: Over 30% of the channel.

Shorting at $90.71 and covering at $87.99 gained $2.72, before commissions. The channel was $7.89 tall at the time of the trade. The trade covered 34% of the channel, earning an A grade. It pays to concentrate on points and percentages, and not count money while in a trade.

Question 33—Value Buying vs. Momentum Buying

Answers 1. B and D
2. A, C, and E

The principle of value buying is "buy low, sell high." The principle of momentum buying is "buy high, sell even higher." Value buying means going long when prices pull back to or below value. Buying on a break-out above an important earlier peak is a prime example of momentum buying. Notice several additional buying opportunities besides those marked with letters on this chart.

GRADING YOUR ANSWERS

If a question requires only one answer, you earn a point by answering it correctly. If a question requires several answers (for example, "Which two of the following four statements are correct?"), rate your answer proportionately. If you answer both correctly, give yourself a point, but if only one, then half a point.

28-33: Excellent. You have a good grasp of buying, managing money, and keeping records. Now is the time to turn your attention to selling.

21-27: Fairly good. Successful trading demands top performance. Look up the answers to the questions you've missed, review them, and retake the test in a few days before moving on to the next section.

Below 21: Alarm! Scoring below the top third may be acceptable in some professional fields, but it is deadly in trading. Professional traders are waiting for you in the markets, ready to take your money. Before you do battle with them, you must bring yourself up to speed. Please study the first section of *Sell and Sell Short* and then retake the test. If your grade remains low on the second pass, look up the books recommended in that section and study those as well.

PART TWO

HOW TO SELL

Y ou need to write down a selling plan *before* you place your buy order. Putting a plan on paper has a powerful psychological effect on most people. It reduces stress, which leads to an increase in profitability. We make our best decisions when we feel relaxed. Writing down your exit plan reduces tension by separating your two jobs: analysis and trading.

Give your "analyst" the luxury of peace and quiet, as he thinks and writes down his plan while the markets are closed. Give your "trader" the luxury of simplicity—a map with which to run, focusing only on implementing decisions. Keep these two jobs separate. Let the analyst think. Let the trader execute. Let them work as a team instead of pushing and stepping on each other's shoelaces.

Warren Buffett, perhaps the most successful investor in the world, says that when you buy a stock you become a partner of a manic-depressive fellow he calls Mr. Market. This character runs up to you every day, offering to buy you out or sell you his share. You should ignore Mr. Market most of the time because he is crazy.

Occasionally Mr. Market becomes so terribly depressed that he offers to sell you his share for a pittance—and that's when you should buy. At other times he becomes so manic that he offers you an insanely high price for your share—and that's when you should sell. Unfortunately, Mr. Market's mood is so contagious that it sweeps most people off their feet. They buy when he is manic and sell when he is depressed—which is precisely the wrong thing to do. Writing down your exit plan before you enter a trade helps you protect yourself from undue influence.

You can view this part of the book as a sellers' menu. You can choose just one dish, or you can choose several techniques and combine them. Also, you will see that different menu choices are more appropriate under different market conditions.

You need to be very clear about your timeframe for selling. Are you putting on a position trade whose duration will be measured in months? Does your analysis point to a swing trade that will last a few days? Or perhaps you are in front of a live screen, angling for a day-trade?

If this is a day-trade, you've got to have your finger on the trigger as you sit in front of the screen. One of the worst mistakes made by chronic losers is converting a day-trade gone bad into a long-term position. On the other hand, watching a live screen is counterproductive when you are in a position trade. A swing trader who watches a live screen almost always gets shaken out of his position; he sees a minor signal and gets out too early, missing the big trend he planned to catch.

THE THREE TYPES OF SELLING

Whenever you prepare to buy a stock, ask yourself whether you plan to hold it for the rest of your life and leave it to your heirs. Since your answer is most likely "no," the next question must be: what will prompt you to sell this stock?

- How high does your stock need to fly for you to say "Enough!" and take profits? Do you have a specific price in mind, or a price range where you will consider selling? Is there an indicator pattern that will tell you the uptrend is becoming tired and it is time to take profits? The best time to answer these questions is before you enter a trade!

- What if your decision to buy was wrong, and the stock begins to slide? How low does it have to fall for you to pull the trigger and shoot? The worst time to make such a decision is when you own the falling stock. As it keeps sliding lower and lower, it will repeatedly flash signs of being oversold. Again and again, it will seem that the decline is at its end and about to reverse. If you are not prepared to take a quick and small loss, you can keep hoping and deluding yourself for a long time. Many traders suffer serious damage and sell in disgust only when they can no longer take the pain. The best time to decide at what price level to be rid of a stock is before you buy it!

- Finally, you might decide to sell a stock if it does not move as you expected or if it traces a suspicious chart or indicator pattern. What does this stock have to do to challenge your bullish outlook? I call this "selling in response to engine noise." As you become more experienced, your ears will become more attuned to such noises.

In summary, we can divide selling options into three main categories:

1. Sell at a target above the market.
2. Be prepared to sell below the market, using a protective stop.
3. Sell before the stock hits either a target or a stop—because market conditions have changed and you no longer want to hold it.

We will review these choices one at a time. Remember, trading is a huge field, and no one can master every method. It pays to be aware of many methods, but select the one that appeals to you, and train yourself to become good at using it.

CHAPTER 4

SELLING AT A TARGET

Once you select a buy candidate, you need to ask several questions:

1. What do you think is the profit target—how high is this stock likely to rise?

2. How low does it need to fall to convince you that your decision to buy was wrong and the loss should be cut?

3. What is this stock's reward-to-risk ratio, what is the relationship between its potential reward and risk?

Professional traders always ask these three questions. Gamblers do not bother with a single one.

Let us begin by tackling the first question: What is the stock's profit target?

A good way to set a target for a swing trade is to use either a moving average or a channel. To estimate a profit target for a long-term trade it pays to examine long-term support and resistance.

Putting on a trade is like jumping into a fast-moving river. You can walk up and down the shore, looking for a spot to jump in. Some people spend a lifetime on the shore, paper-trading their way through life.

You are safe on the shore: your skin is dry and your cash is earning interest in a money market account. One of the very few things in trading you can totally control is the moment you decide to jump in. Do not allow restlessness or anxiety to push you in before you find a good spot.

While you are looking for a place to jump in, there is another important area to scout. You must look downstream, where white water marks the boulders. You need to scan the distant shore for what may be a good place to get out of the water before you hit dangerous rapids. You must set up a profit target for your trade.

When I first began to trade, I had the misguided notion that I was going to get into a trade and get out when "the time was right." I thought that setting a profit target would reduce my potential profit. An amateur who gets into a trade with no clear idea of a profit target is pretty certain to become confused and lose his bearings.

Kerry Lovvorn hit the nail on the head when he said during his interview for *Entries & Exits*: "People want to make money but do not know what they want from the markets. If I am making a trade, what am I expecting of it? You take a job—you know what your wages and benefits are going to be, what you're going to be paid for that job. Having a profit target works better for me, although sometimes it leads to selling too soon."

In this chapter I will show you several trades from my diary, including an entry, an exit, and a follow-up. Since this is a chapter about selling, I will focus on the exits from long trades, saying just enough about the entries to provide a general idea of the reasons for a trade.

Before we begin, let me comment on the follow-up charts in this book. Some of them may look impressive, with my exit nailing the top, but often you'll see that more money was left on the table than taken from it.

Beginners who look at charts are often mesmerized by powerful trends. Experienced traders know that big trends are clear only in retrospect. All trades are perfectly visible in the rearview mirror, but the future is vague, changeable, and unclear. Putting on a trade is like riding a wild bronco. As you shoot out of the gate at a rodeo, you know that if you can stay on horseback for 50 seconds you'll be considered a very good rider and earn a prize. The time to ride a long distance will come later and on a different horse. We will discuss selling long-term positions later in this chapter.

As you look at these trades, most of which come from my personal trading diary, please pay attention to several features. Notice that I grade every trade in three ways—the quality of my entry and exit and, most importantly, the overall quality of the trade. I always write down my source of the idea for the trade. It can be my own homework, a Spike pick, or something from a webinar. I have cells in my record-keeping spreadsheet that trace a total P&L for every source of ideas, for obvious reasons. I want to know who to listen to in the future and who to ignore.

As we begin setting profit targets, let me list the tools available to us. My favorites are:

1. Moving averages
2. Envelopes or channels
3. Support and resistance zones
4. Other methods

SELLING AT A MOVING AVERAGE

Robert Rhea, a prominent market technician during the first half of the twentieth century, described the three stages of a bull market. During the first stage, prices recover from the oversold excesses of the preceding bear market—they rise from deeply undervalued levels back to value. During the second stage, rising prices reflect improving fundamentals. Finally, during the third and final stage, prices rally on enthusiasm, optimism, and greed—people buy "because prices have always gone up." Rhea, who had done a great deal to popularize the Dow Theory, was writing about bull markets that lasted several years. I found that I could apply his concept to shorter timeframes.

We have already discussed how moving averages reflect a longer-term consensus of value. When prices crash below a moving average and drag it down, a bear move is in progress. When prices stop declining and the moving average flattens out, we need to become alert to the possibility that the bear may be dead.

The markets run on a two-party system. When the bear party loses power, we anticipate that the next election will go to the bulls. The first target for a bullish move is a rally back to value, up to the moving average.

This approach to buying below value and setting the profit target in the value zone works especially well with the weekly charts. The Triple Screen trading system calls for making strategic decisions on the weekly charts and implementing them on the dailies, where you make tactical choices on the timing of buying and selling.

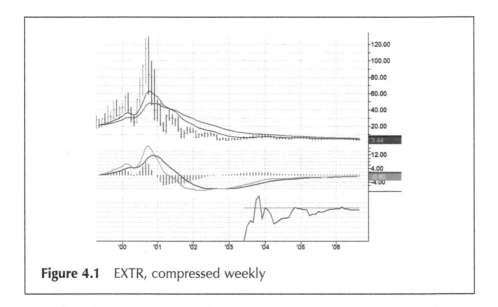

Figure 4.1 EXTR, compressed weekly

I received an e-mail from a trader friend about a stock he has been trading. Kerry pointed out that the stock had recently broken below its multiyear low and had stabilized. Whenever I look at a stock I haven't seen in a while, I pull up its weekly chart (Figure 4.1) and compress it

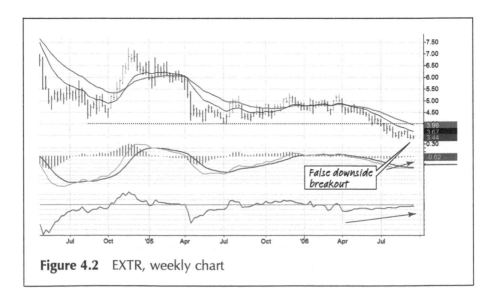

Figure 4.2 EXTR, weekly chart

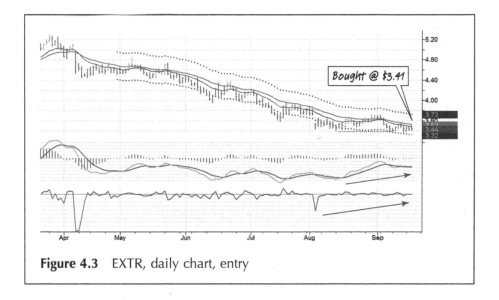

Figure 4.3   EXTR, daily chart, entry

so that the entire history fits into a single screen. I want to see at a glance whether the stock is cheap or expensive, relative to its own history. EXTR, with a high above $120 and a low near $3, was trading below $3.50, giving an absolutely clear answer to this question.

Next, I open up the stock's weekly chart and review its history over the last two or three years (see Figure 4.2). This format allows me to identify long-term price and indicator patterns. Here you can see that the stock's price has recently broken below its long-term support at $4.05. The decline had stalled and the trend had changed from down to sideways. Both the MACD-Histogram and the Force Index were trending higher—a bullish sign. I decided that a rally was likely to carry prices into the value zone on the weekly chart. That zone was between $3.67 and $3.96, between the two moving averages.

At the right edge of the daily chart (see Figure 4.3), EXTR shows a false downside breakout—one of the most bullish signs in technical analysis. It is confirmed by a bullish divergence of MACD Lines. In addition, the bullish divergence of the Force Index is sending an important message—the attempted downside break had no power. My decision— go long EXTR, with a stop at 3.31 and a target of 3.81, above the upper channel line. The distance from the latest closing price to the target was 37 cents, down to the stop 13 cents. The reward-to-risk ratio was nearly 3:1—not the greatest ratio but certainly very acceptable.

EXTR			Upchannel	Downchannel	Day's High	Day's Low	Grade
Entry	$3.45	20-Sep-06	3.74	3.31	$3.50	$3.41	56%
Exit							
P/L						Trade	

It was a nice entry on a quiet day—buying in the lower half of the daily bar, for a 56% entry grade. The day after I bought EXTR, it weakened, and the following day touched a new low. It must have triggered some stops, punishing those who like to place their stops immediately below the latest low. It is important to make an allowance for the normal noise of the markets and place your stop a little farther away, in an area where you do not expect the prices to go.

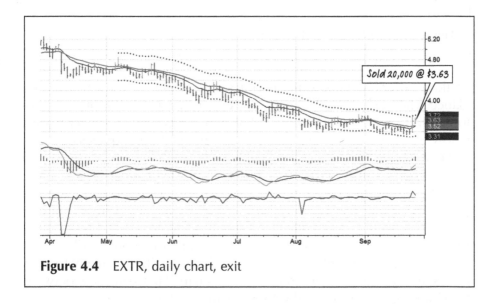

Figure 4.4   EXTR, daily chart, exit

EXTR	20-Sep-06	Date	Upchannel	Downchannel	Day's High	Day's Low	Grade
Entry	$3.45	20-Sep-06	3.74	3.31	$3.50	$3.41	56%
Exit	$3.63	27-Sep-06			$3.66	$3.56	70%
P/L	$0.18					Trade	42%

The following week EXTR exploded to the upside, almost reaching its upper channel in a single day. It closed near the high, but the following day had a narrow range and could not rise any higher. I saw this as a sign of resistance and sold at 3.63 (see Figure 4.4).

I chose not to hold out for more than the market seemed willing to give. I treat a selling target as a working estimate. If the market appears very strong, I will try to ride the price move beyond the initial target. If it appears weak, I will get out earlier.

This was a very nice exit, selling near the high of the day, for a 70% exit grade. Even more rewarding was the trade grade. Taking 18 cents out of a 43-cent channel produced a 42% trade grade—an A+ trade. I bought below value and sold near the overvalued level.

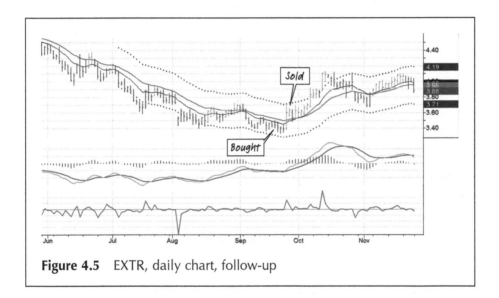

Figure 4.5   EXTR, daily chart, follow-up

One of the essential values of keeping a Trading Diary is that it encourages you to return to every closed-out trade a month or two later (see Figure 4.5). It makes you re-evaluate your performance with the benefit of hindsight. If you keep learning from your experiences, you will become a better trader tomorrow than you are today!

In retrospect, I could have held much longer—but at the time of the exit there was no clear way of knowing that those rallies would come. There are two sure-fire ways to nail every bottom and top. One is to paper-trade on old charts; the other is to lie about your trades. For the real traders risking real money, fast dimes are better than slow dollars.

You have to develop a style of trading that feels comfortable to you and follow it without regrets. Regret is a corrosive force in trading. If you kick yourself for leaving some money on the table today, you will reach out too far tomorrow—and fail.

And now let us review another trade.

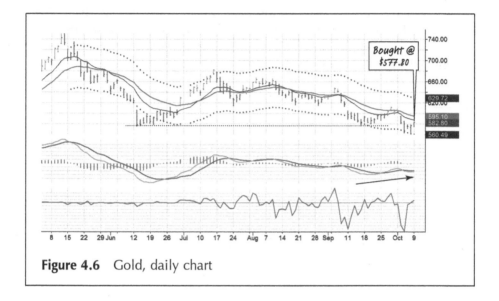

Figure 4.6   Gold, daily chart

One of the advantages of the futures markets is that there are so few of them. Unlike thousands of stocks, you can easily review a couple dozen key futures markets as part of your weekend homework. This is how I became aware of the following pattern in the gold market.

At the right edge of the daily chart (Figure 4.6), gold has broken below the support line but closed above it. I learned from David Weis, a frequent guest instructor in our Traders' Camps, that a false downside breakout is one of the most bullish signals in technical analysis. The Impulse system on both the weekly (not shown) and the daily chart has turned blue, saying that the worst of the downtrend was over, permitting buying.

Notice a severe downspike of the Force Index several days ago. Such downspikes identify the areas of panic and a washout of weak longs, clearing the air for an advance. A bullish divergence of both MACD Lines and MACD-Histogram between September and October bottoms delivered a powerful buy signal. I bought December gold on 10/10/2006 at $577.80, with the target near the weekly value zone, above $630 and a stop just below the recent lows.

		Upchannel	Downchannel	Day's High	Day's Low	Grade
Entry	$577.80	628	559	$580.80	$573.00	38%
Exit						
P/L					Trade	

The entry day's high was $580.80, low $573, making my entry rating 38%—just about a passing grade. My target: a move across the EMAs, towards the upper channel line.

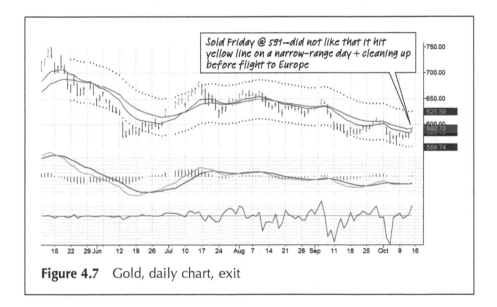

Figure 4.7   Gold, daily chart, exit

I sold three days later, on Friday 10/13 (see Figure 4.7). On the technical side, I did not like a very narrow range on the day gold hit its slower moving average on the daily chart. The value zone serves as natural resistance for both upmoves and downmoves. The narrow range showed a lack of progress in an area where resistance could be expected. On the psychological side, I had an incentive to sell that had nothing to do with the market. I had a ticket to fly to Europe the following week and wanted to reduce my market positions to a minimum. I did not want to hold anything that might require time, attention, and babysitting. I guess you could say I was looking for a reason to get out.

		Upchannel	Downchannel	Day's High	Day's Low	Grade
Entry	$577.80	628	559	$580.80	$573.00	38%
Exit	$591.00			$594.20	$587.60	52%
Trade						19%

My exit grade was 52%, meaning that I sold just above the midpoint for the day. My trade grade was a B–, as I took $13.20 out of a $69 channel. Quite a decent grade, but it certainly left room for improvement.

Now, without a Diary, one would close out this trade and move on. The Diary allows us to look back—how good was this trade in retrospect? Let us revisit gold two months later (see Figure 4.8).

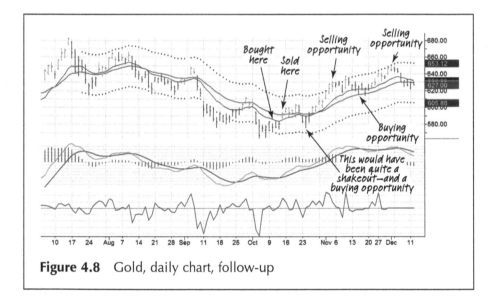

Figure 4.8   Gold, daily chart, follow-up

When we look back with the benefit of hindsight, we must be careful not to be swept off our feet by the powerful trends that are clearly visible only in retrospect. Four days after my exit, gold reached a top and collapsed right back to my entry level. It made two more very tradeable swings from the value zone between the EMAs to the overvalued zone near the upper channel line on the daily charts. I had bought below value and sold above it—a very reasonable sale, considering the fact that gold was just coming out of its bear market and one had to be very cautious betting on the bulls. When in doubt, get out!

SELLING AT ENVELOPES OR CHANNELS

We have seen how moving averages on the weekly and daily charts serve as profit targets for the rallies that jump off the bear market lows. Later, after a bullish trend has been established, you will rarely see such targets. As prices keep chugging higher, moving averages start lagging behind them. This is why moving averages do not make good targets during steady uptrends.

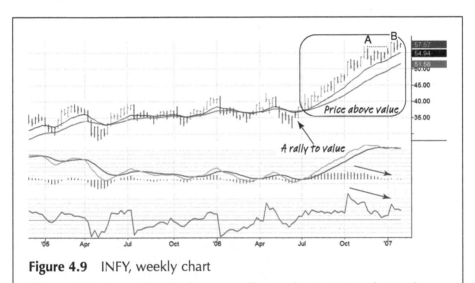

Figure 4.9   INFY, weekly chart

This weekly chart of INFY shows a rally to value in 2006; that's when a weekly moving average would have worked as a target. It was followed by a powerful upmove during which prices stayed above value for months. Clearly, a moving average would not have provided a target under these conditions. We need to find another tool for targeting exits during uptrends.

Before we continue our search for suitable targets, let us take a look at an important pattern on this weekly chart (see Figure 4.9). It shows one of the most powerful signals in technical analysis—a bearish divergence between prices and weekly MACD-Histogram. Following peak A, MACD-H declined below zero—I call this "breaking the back of the bull." The stock rallied to a new bull market high at point B, but the indicator traced a much lower, almost non-existent peak. That

was a loud warning to the bulls. This signal was confirmed by a multitude of other bearish signs—a breakout of prices to a new high with no
follow-through; a bearish divergence of the Force Index; and completely
flat MACD Lines.

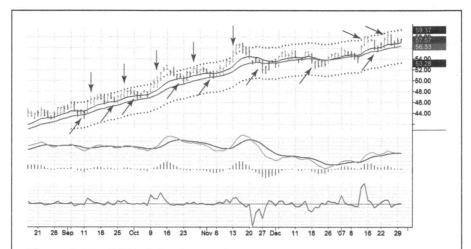

Figure 4.10 INFY, daily chart

While the weekly chart of INFY shows prices running above their moving average for months, the daily chart of the same stock during the
same time shows a very different pattern. Prices keep running higher
within their price channel, as if on invisible rails. Such orderly patterns
are fairly typical in steady uptrends. A stock keeps moving up, fluctuating
between value (its moving average) and the overvalued level at its upper
channel line.

When a stock is rallying in this manner, the space between the two
EMAs, the value zone, is a good place to buy. The upper channel line
shows where that stock becomes overbought and marks a good zone for
profit-taking.

We can see the shorter-term action on the daily chart, shown in
Figure 4.10. Trading a stock in such an uptrend—repeatedly buying at
value and selling at the upper channel line—may feel like going to a
cash machine, although I'm reluctant to use the phrase because nothing
in the markets is as simple as going to an ATM. Still, you can see a steady
repetitive pattern, as the stock oscillates between its value zone, which
also keeps rising, and the overvalued zone, which also keeps rising.

This pattern gives traders a set of good profit targets—selling at the upper channel line.

If moving averages help define value, then channels or envelopes drawn parallel to those averages help define overbought and oversold zones. Ideally, we want to buy below value, below the moving averages, and sell at an overvalued level, near the upper channel line. We will grade our performance by the percentage of the channel we can capture in our trade, keeping in mind that anything above 30% will be considered an A trade.

During one of my monthly webinars, a trader named Jeff Parker suggested looking at CEGE (see Figure 4.11). I run these webinars once a month, and each consists of two sessions a week apart. A couple of dozen traders gather in a virtual classroom to review the markets and specific stocks. Many participants bring up their picks for me to review. If I like a pick very much, I announce that I will probably trade it the next day. That was the case with CEGE.

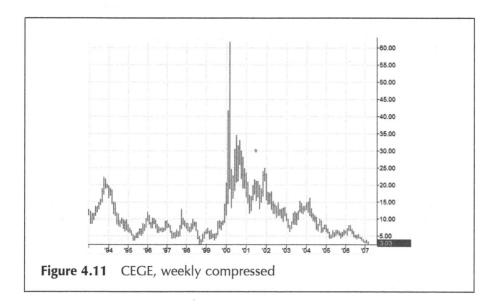

Figure 4.11   CEGE, weekly compressed

Compressing the weekly chart of CEGE into a single screen, you can see that the stock had rallied above $60 in the happy days of the 1990s bull market. It then crashed and burned, tried to rally a few times, but sank below $3 near the right edge of the chart. By then

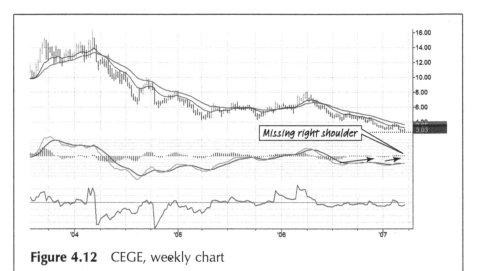

Figure 4.12   CEGE, weekly chart

The weekly chart shows a powerful combination—a false downside breakout accompanied by a bullish divergence of MACD-Histogram. The Impulse system has turned blue at the right edge, permitting buying. The latest bullish divergence was of a "missing right shoulder" type, meaning the indicator could not even decline below zero. It showed that the bears were running out of breath.

it had slid more than 95% off its bull market peak. I call stocks that have fallen more than 90% "fallen angels" and often look for buy candidates among them. My entry into CEGE is shown in Figures 4.12, and 4.13.

When our webinar resumed the following week, we revisited CEGE. Jeff, whose pick it was, spoke about it being very overbought. Prices had shot up towards the upper channel line, without quite reaching it, and stalled for two days. MACD-Histogram reached an overbought level. Since I had a number of long positions at the time, I decided to prune my holdings by selling CEGE shortly after it opened the following day (Figure 4.14).

My exit grade was only 6%, as the stock rallied sharply after I sold it. It was a poor grade, but one cannot score highly on every sale—the important thing is to work to keep the average grade above 50%. My trade grade, however, was an A—I took 36% out of this stock's channel.

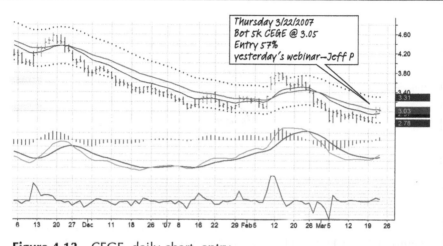

Figure 4.13 CEGE, daily chart, entry

The daily chart showed that the first rally from the oversold lows had already taken place. Prices were in the value zone on the daily chart. The upper channel line on the daily chart presented an attractive target for the next leg of the rally. At the same time, there was a good possibility that prices could overshoot this target, in view of a very bullish pattern of the weekly chart.

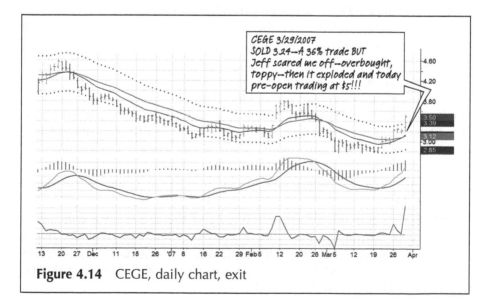

Figure 4.14 CEGE, daily chart, exit

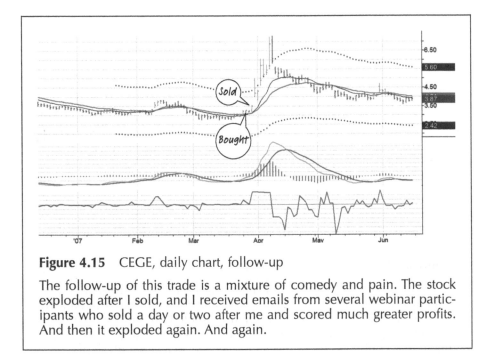

Figure 4.15 CEGE, daily chart, follow-up

The follow-up of this trade is a mixture of comedy and pain. The stock exploded after I sold, and I received emails from several webinar participants who sold a day or two after me and scored much greater profits. And then it exploded again. And again.

A few days after I exited, Jeff called, kicking himself for having sold too soon (see Figure 4.15). I tried to humor him—look, by having sold early we freed ourselves from the stress of having to decide what to do with the super-profits of a runaway trend! Seriously, though, this trade provided several important lessons.

First of all, it is important to have confidence in your profit targets and not sell too soon. Second, it does not pay to kick yourself over a missed opportunity. This will only lead to reckless trading down the road. I told Jeff that he had to congratulate himself for having picked such a great stock. If you keep buying good stocks, some of them will bring you windfall profits.

In Figure 4.15, notice how much wider the channels are on the follow-up chart. I use a program called Autoenvelope which automatically draws channels that contain approximately 95% of the recent price data. When prices jump, an Autoenvelope becomes wider. This is a reminder that in trading we never shoot at a stationary target—the target always moves, making the game harder. Here I took profits near the channel wall—but a few days later the "wall" moved!

CEGE returned to narrow daily ranges after its brief price explosion. It began to sink back towards the base where Jeff and I had bought, working its way towards becoming an attractive buy once again.

Holding Out for More

When it comes to the good things in life, the majority of people want more—a bigger house, a shinier car, perhaps even a newer and better spouse. I remember being stopped dead in my tracks at a party where I talked to a couple; the husband had just received an important promotion and the wife spoke of wanting to "upgrade our friendships." The entire advertising industry pushes us to reach for more. Many people spend their lifetime in a mindless race, like caged animals chasing their tails. This endless race tends to become very dehumanizing.

When people engaged in the rat race come to the market, they also tend to reach for more, more, more. Even a profitable trade brings them no joy; it burns them to see that they neither bought the bottom, nor sold the top, but left some money on the table. Their bitterness drives them to either buy too early or sell too late. People who keep reaching for more usually underperform those of us who follow tested methods.

Those who reach out for more than the market is willing to give often end up with much less.

The power word in life, as well as in trading, is "enough." You have to decide what will make you happy and set your goals accordingly. The pursuit of your own goals will make you feel in control. To always crave more is to be a slave to greed and advertising. To decide what is enough is to be free.

Do not get me wrong—I am not suggesting you take a vow of poverty. I like flying business class, living in a nice place, and driving a powerful car as much as any other guy. What I am saying is this: find the level at which you will be satisfied—and be happy when you get there. This is much better than always feeling off-balance, short, chasing after an ill-defined "more."

And what to do if "more" somehow falls into your lap? What if one month you hit the market just right, and earn super-profits in your account? The experience of super-profits unhinges most people. Craving even more, they climb farther out on a limb and take wild risks until their super-profits turn into super-losses. To stay cool and calm, you need a personal plan for managing profits—we will return to this in the chapter on personal dividend.

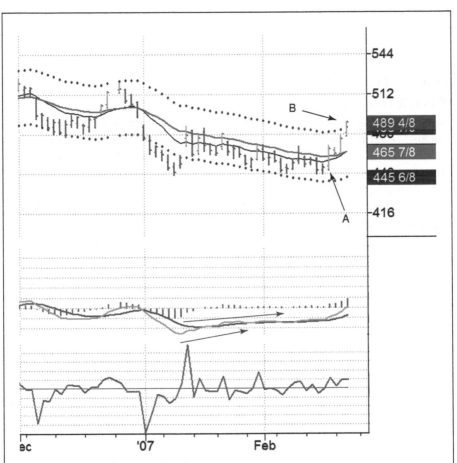

Figure 4.16 Wheat, daily chart

A. Bullish patterns on weekly and daily charts—go long.
B. Took profits on 1/3 of the position, held the rest.

This chart of wheat shows a purchase near the lows, following multiple bullish divergences. Prices accelerated and punched above the upper channel line. I was so bullish on wheat at the time (based on the weekly charts—not shown) that I took only partial profits. I violated my rule and did not sell above the upper channel line.

For a trader who always craves more, the idea of taking profits near the upper channel line can feel very stressful. Some trades do not reach their target while others overshoot it.

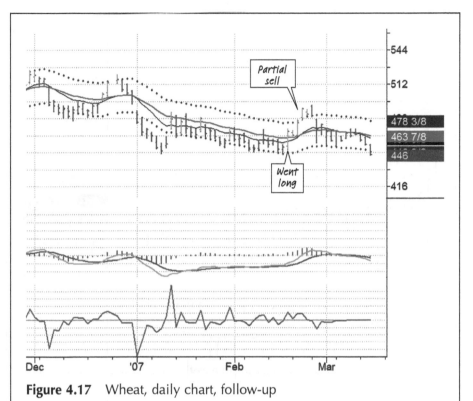

Figure 4.17   Wheat, daily chart, follow-up

Wheat continued to reward greed for two more days after my partial exit. Prices kept hovering above the upper channel line but then collapsed. I had to scramble as my open profits melted away. The entire profit for this wheat trade would have been much greater had I gratefully accepted what the market was giving me, instead of reaching for more.

You cannot become fixated on the channel as an iron-clad profit target. If the market starts acting weak, there is nothing wrong with accepting less than your initial target. Neither trade shown above quite reached the upper channel line. EXTR missed it by a bit, gold by a wide margin—but both ended up very profitable. Paradoxically, being willing to accept less often gives you more. See a trading example in Figures 4.16 and 4.17.

Powerful moves that overshoot their targets and keep on going cause stress for greedy traders. A trader looks at a market from which he exited

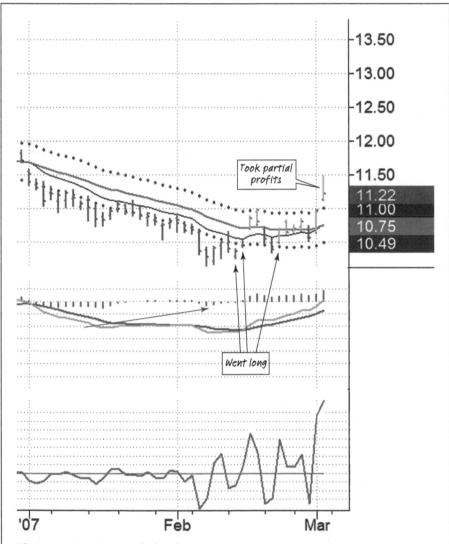

Figure 4.18 Sugar, daily chart

Sugar prices jumped soon after the rollover. The chart above shows that the entire day's bar popped above the upper channel line. In the face of such great strength I took only partial profits on my longs, but held the remaining two-thirds of my position. I was so impressed with sugar's strength—which confirmed my bullish forecast—that I ignored the fact that the bar above the upper channel closed near its low—a suspicious sign of weakness.

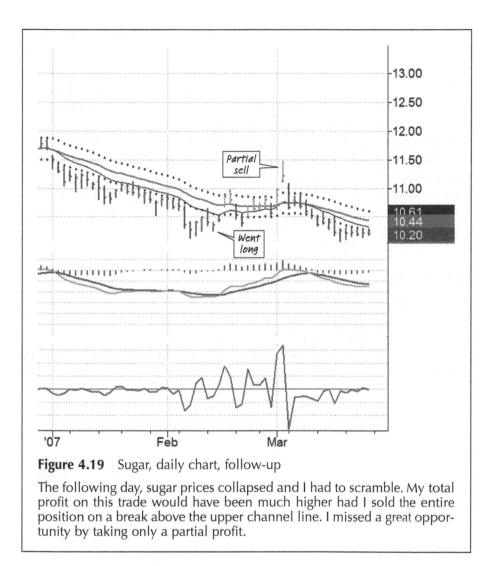

Figure 4.19 Sugar, daily chart, follow-up

The following day, sugar prices collapsed and I had to scramble. My total profit on this trade would have been much higher had I sold the entire position on a break above the upper channel line. I missed a great opportunity by taking only a partial profit.

with a nice profit and kicks himself if that market continues to move in the same direction—only now without him.

Let us review another trading example (see Figures 4.18 and 4.19). In January 2007 I became very bullish on sugar, on the basis of weekly charts (not shown). I began building a long position in the March 2007 contract, eventually taking profits and rolling over into May.

I am sure that we could find examples of prices rising above the upper channel line and continuing "to walk the line," rising with the channel. Of course it happens, but that is not the point. My point is that "enough" is better than "more." It leaves you feeling calm and in control—and feeling this way leads to greater profitability in the long run.

This brief discussion raises one other important point, which we already discussed in Chapter 2, page 10, "Treat yourself well." Not all my trades are successful—some lose money while others, such as the ones shown above, earn less than what was available. When I recognize a mistake, I do not beat myself over the head. I create a diary entry, analyze what happened, and learn as much as I can from my failings. I accept my imperfections, and as long as I learn something from a trade, that is a good and productive experience.

A Rally Stumbles

What if you set a profit target for your trade at the envelope but later come to believe that the rally has even greater potential? How much longer can you hold? Experience has taught me it is better not to overstay trades. Still, occasionally situations occur in which a rally rockets higher, and it feels tempting to hold on for a bit more than initially planned.

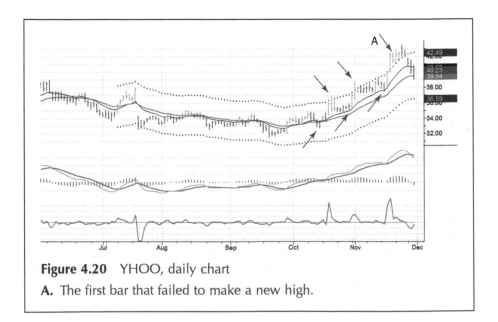

Figure 4.20 YHOO, daily chart

A. The first bar that failed to make a new high.

Once prices blow through your initial target, where will you take profits? There is an option that appeals to me. I wait for the first day when the price fails to reach a new high for this move and sell either near the day's close or soon after the opening the following day.

Here, as with everything else in trading, it is important not to try to reach for extremes. The top tick of a rally is the most expensive one in the market—fortunes have been lost hunting for it. The logic behind the "no-new-high" sell rule is straightforward. When a super-powerful move cannot reach a new high, it tells you that the bulls are starting to run out of breath and reach even higher, but I have long ago given up on trying to catch the absolute top. Remember, the top tick is the most expensive one.

Figure 4.20 shows a YHOO rally that began in October. At first, it moved like so many other trades—below value, followed by a rally to the upper channel line, then a drop back to value, followed by another rally to the upper channel line. Following the second rally, prices barely declined, showing that the bulls were very firm and not giving way to the bears.

After prices touched their value zone in November, they staged an explosive move to the upper channel line. They reached it within a day and rocketed higher the following day. On the third day of this rally, the bulls appeared to either have lost confidence or taken a rest. The range on the third day was narrow and the volume thin, reflected by falling Force Index. Even more important, the bulls failed to lift prices to a new high for this rally. That was the signal to sell.

Prices did rally a little higher on subsequent days, but the bulk of the upmove was over. Three days after the "no-new-high" day, prices began to sink back towards value. Selling early beats selling late. Only someone with a crystal ball can call the top of every move, but those who live by a crystal ball must get used to swallowing a lot of ground glass. It is important to trade without regrets. Remember—the power word is "enough."

SELLING AT RESISTANCE LEVELS

Moving averages provide targets for rallies from deeply oversold levels. Channels or envelopes provide targets for short-term traders. These tools help catch short-term swings—but such moves seem puny to long-term position traders. We used to call such people investors, before the world accelerated and everyone became a trader. Long-term traders, whose time horizon is measured in months or even years, need bigger targets.

A deer hunter needs a bigger gun than someone who goes out shooting rabbits.

Support and resistance zones provide targets for long-term trades. We can identify support and resistance by looking for price levels where a great deal of trading has taken place, clearly more than the areas immediately above or below.

To have confidence in any technical tool we must understand how it works and what it measures. If we are going to rely on support and resistance, we need to understand the reality behind them.

Each price tick reflects an agreement between a buyer and a seller, but it also represents the opinion of the crowd that surrounds these two people. Had the crowd disagreed with either the buyer or the seller, someone would have stepped in, and that trade would have happened at a different price level.

The more transactions occur at a certain price level, the more people believe that level represents value. A congestion zone on a chart tells you that many market participants consider that level a fair value and are prepared to buy or sell there.

If you look at any chart, you'll notice that prices almost never move in a straight line. Instead, prices stay within a range, swirling like water behind an earthen dam. Once the dam breaks, prices surge until they find another basin. They will now spend a long time filling that basin, until another dam breaks and prices surge again.

If each tick represents a transaction between a buyer and a seller, then a trading range represents a general consensus of value between masses of buyers and sellers. When prices lap at the edges of a range, amateurs become excited. They expect breakouts and buy at new highs or sell at new lows. Professionals, on the other hand, know that most breakouts are false and are followed by retracements. They tend to trade in the opposite direction, selling at the upper edges of congestion zones and buying at the lower edges. Once in a blue moon the amateurs win, but in the long run it pays to trade with the pros.

This back-and-forth action draws trading ranges on many charts. A range is a horizontal pattern with fairly clear upper and lower boundaries that identify support and resistance. A price range represents a huge financial and emotional commitment by crowds of buyers and sellers. If you glance at the average daily volume inside the range, multiply it by the number of days in that range and then by the average price of the stock during that time, you will immediately realize that a trading range for a single stock can quickly run into billions of dollars.

Have you ever noticed that people tend to become a little emotional about money?

Do you think that a crowd with a billion dollars' worth of commitments might want to act when those commitments are threatened?

Support and resistance are built on two powerful emotions—pain and regret. People who have bought in the range only to see prices drop feel pain. They are waiting for prices to return so they can "get out even." Their selling, driven by pain, is likely to put a lid on any advance. People who sold short in the range are also waiting for a pull-back. They regret that they did not short even more. Their regret will lead them to sell short when prices return to the level where they shorted, resisting the advance. Pain and regret put a damper on a rally into a trading range or a decline into that range.

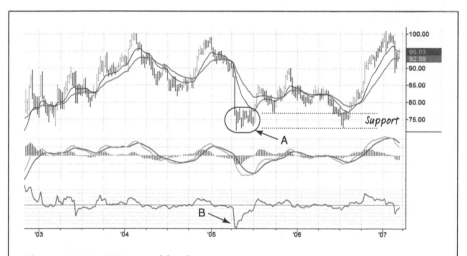

Figure 4.21 IBM, weekly chart

A. Half a billion shares traded at approximately $75—about 37 billion dollars within this range.

B. Notice how downspikes of the Force Index help identify important market bottoms. Can you find two more downspikes on this chart?

Let us review examples of support and resistance on the charts of some popular markets: IBM and the euro.

In 2005 IBM (see Figure 4.21) fell into the $73–$78 zone, spent about three months there, and then erupted into a rally. Half a billion shares traded in that zone, with an approximate total value of $37 billion. You can feel how much emotion was attached to that huge pool of money! When IBM fell back into that zone a year later, there were enough buyers who regretted that they had missed the boat earlier. They soaked up the supply and pushed IBM back up, up, and away.

How can we set profit targets for massive rallies? Looking into IBM's history on the same chart you can see that in recent years whenever the stock got into the $95–$100 zone, heavy selling drove it down. Think of those poor folks who bought near $100 in 2004. After sweating and suffering through the bear trend they were waiting for IBM to rise back to their purchase price, so that they could "get out even."

Of course, "even" is never really even. Think of the lost interest, the depreciation of money, and the loss of opportunity. Think of the mental burden of sitting on a losing position, unable to concentrate on better opportunities. These losers are waiting, ready to dump millions of shares when the stock finally returns to their purchase price. If you were one of the smart traders who bought near $75, would you expect the rally to stall near the $100 level? That zone of overhead resistance would have been a very sweet level for placing your profit target.

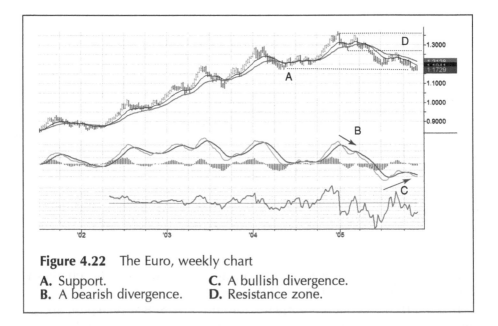

Figure 4.22 The Euro, weekly chart
A. Support. **C.** A bullish divergence.
B. A bearish divergence. **D.** Resistance zone.

The euro (Figure 4.22) erupted from the gate soon after its creation in 2001, rising from 85 cents to $1.36 within three years. A severe bearish divergence in 2005, marked by a red arrow on the chart, capped the uptrend and sent prices lower. The euro found support near the 2004 lows, then dipped below that level, shaking out weak holders.

Keep in mind that support and resistance are not made of plate glass. They are more like wire fences, and bulls and bears can lean on them. As a matter of fact, some of the best buy signals occur after the bears manage to push prices slightly below support. This sets off stops and takes out the weak holders before the bulls resume control and lift prices again.

At the right edge of Figure 4.22, we see a bullish divergence. The last bar has turned blue. This change of the Impulse system tells us that the bears are slipping, and buying is now permitted.

If we go long here, what will be the target for the upmove? We can expect resistance in the congestion zone, between 1.3 and 1.35, the area of the 2005 top.

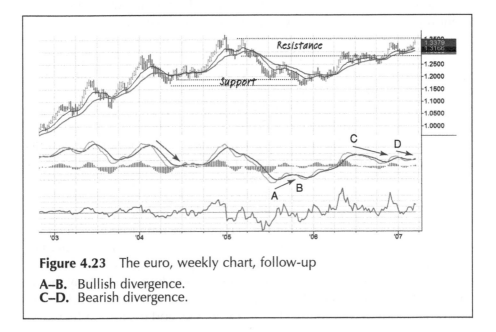

Figure 4.23 The euro, weekly chart, follow-up

A–B. Bullish divergence.
C–D. Bearish divergence.

Currencies are notoriously hard to trade since they move nearly 24 hours a day. You may be peacefully asleep while your competitors halfway across the globe are picking your pockets. If you are a swing trader, looking to catch price moves that last a few days to a few weeks, you are better off staying away from currencies. Leave them to day-traders and to long-term position traders. These people can benefit from the currencies' well-established tendency to run in long trends.

To follow up on the chart of the euro, in Figure 4.23 we see a combination of signals—a bullish divergence of MACD, a false downside breakout, and the Impulse system turning blue on the weekly chart. They confirmed each other in area B, giving an especially strong message to buy. The entry into this long trade in the euro worked out extremely well. The buy signal allowed us to set a reasonable long-term profit target—at the resistance in the trading range of the 2005 top.

After the euro hit resistance at point C, it stalled and went flat for several months. At the same time, the new MACD-H peak C, the highest in over a year, showed that bulls were at record strength. This meant that the price level associated with this indicator peak was likely to be exceeded.

That's exactly what happened near the end of 2006 and again in early 2007, but on those occasions, MACD-Histogram was giving different messages. Its bearish divergences signaled that the upmoves were nearing their ends.

Looking at support and resistance helps you set reasonable targets for long-term moves. The great value of long-term targets is that they help you fix your eyes on a remote but reachable goal. This helps you hang on to a long-term move and not get thrown off by the short-term action of prices or indicators or both.

Another benefit of having a long-term target is that it reminds you to sell in a predetermined zone. Many traders become more bullish near the tops, along with the rest of the market crowd. A target tells you when your goal has been reached. You have set it, and now it tells you to take profits, go home, take a nice vacation, and look for the next trade.

Psychologically, it is much harder to trade long-term trends than short-term swings. In short-term trading you are active, watching the market every day, ready to adjust your stops and profit targets, add to your position, take partial profits, or exit the trade altogether. Many of us find this feeling of control very satisfying. The emotions tend to be different in long-term trading. There are weeks and even months when

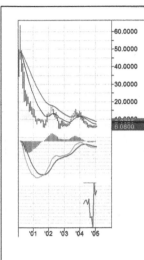

Figure 4.24   STTSY monthly

My attention was drawn to STTS, since renamed STTSY, during a monthly webinar in November 2004. One of our most active participants at the time was Jackie Patterson, a Californian who had left her job to become a full-time trader. She was a good stock-picker, but no stock she brought up had gotten me as excited as STTSY.

This computer-chip testing company traded above $60 in the happy days of the 1990s bull market but fell below $6 during the bear market. It was one of those "fallen angels" we have already discussed. The idea, of course, is to buy after a stock stops declining. It is OK to buy cheap but not OK to buy on the way down.

The weekly chart appeared extremely attractive. It showed that after the stock crashed from above $60 to below $6, it bounced above $17. Another fall, below $5, was followed by a bounce to nearly $16. This puppy's behavior made it clear that even after it lost over 90% of its value it had no desire to die. A stock that has survived a bear market becomes a prime buying candidate for the next bull market.

you do nothing. You recognize short-term tops and bottoms but restrain yourself from doing anything, as you wait for your long-term target to be hit. That's why having a price target is so important—it increases your psychological holding power.

To conclude our discussion of profit targets at support and resistance, let me share another trade from my diary (see Figure 4.24). It will illustrate techniques, as well as some psychological points. It will show why it is harder to hold a long-term position than a short-term trade. And it will allow us to discuss several important issues relating to the management of a trade, beyond simply setting a profit target.

Zooming into the right edge of the weekly chart (Figure 4.25), the picture became even more attractive. The stock established three lows during the past six months at $5.50, $5.40, and $5.37. This pattern told me that the support was solid. Even when the stock was pushed to a slightly lower low, it refused to accelerate to the downside, but instead recoiled and came back up. Those quick stabs seemed to indicate that some powerful interests were trying to push the stock a little lower in order to frighten holders into selling so they could buy up their shares.

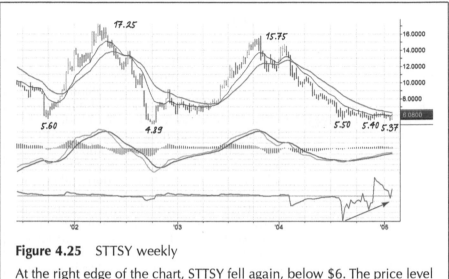

Figure 4.25 STTSY weekly

At the right edge of the chart, STTSY fell again, below $6. The price level below $6 emerged as a very strong support zone. In looking at the chart, it became evident that the zone near $16 provided very strong resistance. Whenever STTSY rose to that level, it seemed to hit a ceiling and come tumbling back down to the floor.

The bears were so weak that MACD-Histogram stayed above zero during the latest decline. The Force Index, in the bottom pane of the chart, showed three stabs to the downside—each more shallow than the next, confirming that the bears were becoming weaker.

When the Impulse system went blue at the right edge of the chart, it removed the last prohibition against buying. I bought 10,000 shares at $5.99. My plan was to hold until STTSY reached $16, which I figured might take a couple of years. I was looking to clear a $100,000 profit on this trade.

As the stock began to move in my favor, I added another 5,000 shares at $6.13, but a few weeks later offloaded that lot at $6.75, clearing 62 cents and booking a quick profit on that side bet. My plan was to hold for the long haul, but this turned out to be much more stressful than trading in and out.

STTSY briskly rallied to $8.16, then sold off back to my buying point. I was convinced that my initial plan was correct and continued to

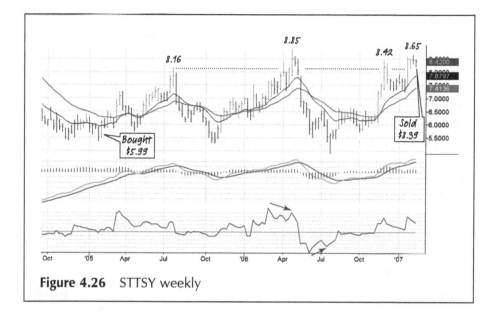

Figure 4.26 STTSY weekly

hold. STTSY rallied again, this time to $8.85. I saw multiple signals of a top, including a bearish divergence of the weekly Force Index, marked by a red arrow on the chart (Figure 4.26). Focusing on my target of $16, I clenched my teeth and held. The decline quickly wiped out nearly $30,000 of paper profit, and the position briefly went negative, as STTSY dipped below my entry point. I held on to my original plan, focusing on the bullish details, such as a "kangaroo tail"—a one-bar stab towards the lows. It was accompanied by a bullish divergence of the Force Index, marked with a green arrow on the chart. STTSY rallied again, this time up to $8.42, but holding long-term was becoming less and less fun.

During this trade I made a multitude of swing trades in other stocks. Trading short-term was a lot more fun and profitable. I also held a handful of other long-term positions, similar to STTSY, as my plan was to teach myself to hold for the long haul. Still, my position in STTSY was starting to feel like a headache. I'd had enough of those rallies into the $8–$9 zone, followed by declines back down to the purchase point, with no profit to show for my work or patience.

In February 2007, two years after I bought STTSY, the stock rallied to $8.65, slightly better than its previous high of $8.42. There the rally stalled and the weekly ranges became narrow. Such signs often precede price declines. I felt the weight of STTSY on my shoulders and gave an order to sell, getting out of my 10,000 shares at $8.29. Instead of hitting my $100,000 target, I cleared less than $24,000 on this trade—$27,000, taking into account a side bet on STTSY early in the game. I was happy to be out of STTSY, liberated from having to look at the stock as it gyrated up and down. Still, I had gotten into such a habit of watching it that I kept an eye on it (see Figure 4.27). What I saw turned out to be highly amusing, to say the least.

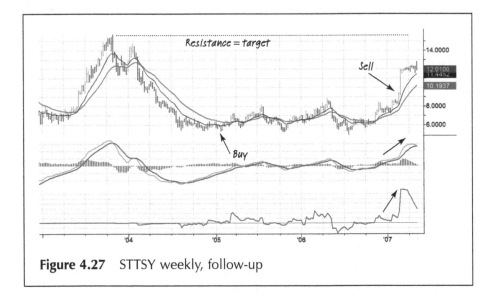

Figure 4.27   STTSY weekly, follow-up

Just a few days after I felt relief from selling STTSY, the stock stood on its hind legs and roared. Two weeks later it traded at nearly $12. Most indicators confirmed the great strength of the bulls by reaching new record highs. They signaled that whatever brief weakness may intervene, the bulls were very strong and that $12 was likely not the final peak in STTSY. The stock appeared ready to go higher, and the initial target of $16 looked very realistic.

Did I buy it back? Of course not! My two-year entanglement with STTSY was over. The relatively small profit I took out of its spectacular move would be the only money I'd make out of it—much less than what was available. So why show this trade here? Is there anything we can learn from it? Yes, quite a lot. Here are the lessons, in no particular order:

1. First of all, my entry into this trade was excellent. I had correctly identified an important bottom and acted in good time. Second, my profit target for the trade appears to have been on track, even though I could not hold long enough to get full benefit from my analysis.

2. This trade confirmed to me that I am temperamentally better suited for shorter-term trading. Since I am determined to learn to hold long-term, I must adapt by adding some elements of short-term trading to my long-term positions. I decided that in future long-term trades I will establish a core position that I will hold from start to finish—its smaller size will produce less stress. At the same time, I will put on larger short-term trades in the direction of my long-term trade. Looking back on Figure 4.26, there would have been every reason to buy extra on the way up, sell when tops were formed at the upper dashed line, and buy again whenever the stock fell back to its original buy zone near the lower dashed line.

3. This trade reminds us that it is important to treat yourself well. Your mind is a trading instrument, and beating yourself up for mistakes, such as getting out too early, would be like slapping your computer—it does not improve performance. My goal is to learn from my mistakes, not to punish myself for them.

4. Last but not least, I want you to see that even experts make mistakes. I still make them. The idea is to weed out gross mistakes, such as not using a diary or violating money management rules. Once you've done that, you can concentrate on the lesser ones.

Whenever you put on a trade, you have two goals: to make money and to become a better trader. You may or may not reach the first goal, but you must reach the second. If you do not learn from your trades, you are wasting your time and money. During this trade, I kept good notes, both in a spreadsheet and in a visual format in my diary, allowing me to extract lessons from the experience. The money profit was relatively small, but the trading lessons were multiple and rich.

As I write this book, I have several long-term trades going. There is a major U.S. industrial concern whose stock, I believe, wants to rise from $7 into the $20+ range. I am even more excited about a little Nasdaq number that trades for a bit over a dollar. It traded near $100 in the 1990s—this fallen angel lost over 99% of its value. I acquired the bulk of my position below $1 and expect to hold it until the stock reaches $20 a couple of years from now. With both stocks, I have a core position that I do not touch and a bigger short-term position that I keep putting on and taking off, actively trading in the direction of the trend. The lessons of STTSY are continuing to help me.

CHAPTER 5

SELLING ON A STOP

If you compare buying a stock to getting married, using a stop is like signing a prenuptial agreement. If your happy relationship hits the rocks, the prenup will not take away the pain, but it will reduce the hassle, the uncertainty, and the expense of the separation. What if you are a happy bull but discover that your beloved stock has been sneaking out and getting between the sheets with a bear? Any breakup is going to hurt, but the best time to decide who gets what is when you still tenderly hold each other's hands.

A stop provides an essential reality check for any trade. Yes, you love this stock. Yes, you have great expectations. But what if it doesn't work? Have all your previous stock ideas worked out well? Or has there been one or two that did not? More than one or two? Many? Is there any doubt then that you need a stop? You need to examine the chart and decide where you want to get out if that trade starts going against you.

Even a profitable trade deserves to have a protective stop. Stops help you sell when the stocks turn against you. Some traders also like to ride runaway trends using trailing stops that follow rapidly moving prices.

Once you put on a trade, a pernicious "ownership effect" sets in, making it much harder to decide when to sell. The best time to make that decision is before you enter a trade.

Think of that old-fashioned jacket that hangs in your closet. You cannot bring yourself to throw it away—because it is yours, you are used to having it, you've always had it. At least that useless jacket does not cost you anything beyond taking up space in your closet (and in your mind, I might add—holding a useless possession creates a tiny dead spot—and after a while many little dead spots merge into bigger dead zones). At least you won't have to pay rent for the jacket that hangs there. On the other hand, having a dead trade in your account can become very expensive, even downright ruinous.

A single bad trade can punch a hole in your account. A group of bad trades can destroy it.

Another side effect of not using stops and holding on to bad trades is that they interfere with making good trades. Just as a toothache interferes with your planning a losing trade grabs more of your attention than it deserves. It prevents you from seeking out new and better trades. Whenever a trade that's gone against you has your nerves tied in a knot, it makes it harder for you to get into a new trade. Holding on to a losing trade costs you money, pain, and missed opportunities.

A trading system without stops is not a system—it is a joke. Trading such a system is like racing a car without seatbelts. You may win several races, but the very first accident could kill you.

Stops are your link to reality. You may have beautiful ideas of profits, but deciding where to put a stop forces you to look at the possible downside. It makes you ask the essential question: Is the potential profit worth the risk?

Every trade deserves a protective stop. Follow this simple rule: you may not put on a trade unless you know exactly where you will place your stop. You must make that decision before you enter a trade. In addition to the stop, you need a profit target to evaluate that trade's reward-to-risk ratio. A trade without a target is like a gambling chip.

About 20 years ago one of my friends hit a rough patch and went to work as a broker. I moved one of my accounts to him, and whenever I called to place an order, he would not let me get off the phone until I also gave him a stop. My friend has since grown into a successful money manager, but I remember him as the most disciplined broker I ever had.

And what about moving stops? Markets change, prices change, and your outlook on a stock may change. You may become more bullish, more bearish, or less certain. As your perception of risk and reward changes, you may want to move your stop. How can you do it? In a market where everything is permitted—most of all losing money—what rules will you set for moving stops?

The absolutely essential rule of moving stops is that you may move them only one way—in the direction of the trade. When you go long and place a stop below the market, you may move it up but never down. When you go short and place a stop above the market, you may move it down but never up.

Using stops is a one-way street. You may tighten them but never loosen them.

You buy a stock because you expect it to go up. Had you expected that stock to go down, you would not have bought it. If it starts going down, it tells you that your decision was poor. Moving your stop farther away to accommodate your mistake would only compound the error. Don't do it.

Let us summarize what we have discussed so far:

- You need stops; a trade without a stop is a gamble.
- You need to know where you'll put your stop before you enter a trade (if the reward-to-risk ratio is poor, do not enter that trade).
- Whenever you change a stop, you may move it only in the direction of the trade.
- Everybody needs hard stops; only expert discretionary traders are allowed to use soft stops, discussed below.

If you have any doubts about these points, please go back and reread this chapter. If you agree, let us move forward and discuss how to place stops.

An important footnote about stops—it is perfectly fine to re-enter a market after it hits your stop. Beginners often make a single stab at a stock and leave it alone after it kicks them out. Professionals, on the other hand, see nothing wrong with trying to buy or sell short a stock again and again, like trying to grab a slippery fish, until they finally get a hold of its gills.

THE IRON TRIANGLE

The main purpose of using stops is to protect yourself from adverse moves by limiting your loss on a trade to a predetermined amount. The secondary purpose is to protect paper profits. With loss control the key purpose of stops, it is no wonder that setting stops is tightly linked with money management.

The process of risk control works in three steps:

1. Set a stop on the basis of chart analysis and then calculate the dollar risk per share by measuring the distance from the planned entry price to the stop level.

2. Use your money management rules to calculate the maximum amount you may risk on a trade and decide how much you will risk.

3. Divide the number of dollars in line 2 by the number of dollars in line 1 to find out how many shares you may trade.

I call this the Iron Triangle of risk control. One side is your risk per share, another your total permitted risk per trade. The third side, derived from the first two, gives you the maximum trade size.

Size, as the joke goes, does not matter. What matters is risk.

As a trader, you do not really trade IBM or EBAY or soybeans—you trade money and deal in risk. This is why you must set your position size on the basis of risk.

Compare buying 1,000 shares of a $20 stock and placing your stop at $17 to buying 2,000 shares of a $40 stock and placing your stop at $39. Even though the size and the cost of the second position is greater, the amount of risk is lower.

Let us review the three steps outlined above, followed by a few trading examples:

1. **Calculate dollar risk per share.**
   Suppose you decide to buy a stock that is trading at $18. Now suppose that your chart analysis indicates that if this stock falls below $17 it will cancel the bullish scenario. You decide to place a protective stop at $16.89. Your risk per share then will be $1.11. It could become even higher in the case of slippage, but $1.11 is a reasonable estimate.

2. **Calculate dollar risk per trade.**
   Suppose you have $50,000 in your trading account and follow the 2% money management rule explained above. This means that your maximum risk per trade is $1,000. That is actually quite a lot of risk for a modest account. Many would decide to risk less than 1%.

3. **Divide your risk per trade by risk per share.**

This is how you find the maximum number of shares you may trade. If your maximum permitted risk per trade is $1,000 and the risk per share in the planned trade is $1.11, your maximum number of shares is below 900. Remember, the $1,000 maximum allowed risk per trade must cover commissions and slippage. Also, there is no law that says you must go up to the maximum permitted risk on every trade. You are not allowed to risk more, but you are perfectly welcome to risk less.

What if you have big expectations for that $18 stock? You may want to give it some extra room and place a stop as far away as $15.89, but then your risk per share would be $2.11. Since the maximum permitted risk for the trade would remain the same, your maximum purchase would drop to 470 shares.

On the other hand, if you sit in front of the screen, watching that stock like a hawk, you may put a stop at $17.54, and risk only 46 cents per share. Your maximum permitted risk will remain $1,000, but now you will be able to trade a 2,170-share block.

Decisions about stops are tightly linked to decisions regarding profit targets. You must weigh the amount of risk you are willing to take against the potential reward you are trying to reap. As a rule of thumb, I am attracted to trades with reward-to-risk ratio of 3:1 or better. I would be very reluctant to enter a trade whose reward-to-risk ratio is 2:1 or lower.

Using stops is an essential practice. Before we discuss the wide variety of stops available to you, let us clarify two extremely important distinctions. We must choose whether to use market or limit orders for our stops. We also need to look into the choice between soft and hard stops.

MARKET OR LIMIT ORDERS

All orders can be divided into two broad groups—market and limit orders. A market order is filled at what brokers call the best price—but what is in fact any price and often the worst price. An alternative to a market order is a limit order. It demands an execution at a specific price—or no execution at all. A limit order helps you avoid slippage.

A market order guarantees you an execution but not the price. A limit order guarantees you the price but not the execution. You must choose because you cannot have both in the same trade. You have to decide what is more important to you—an execution or an avoidance of slippage? You may answer this question differently at different times.

Suppose you've bought 1,000 shares of a $19 stock, and your research indicates that if it declines to $17.80, the uptrend will be over. You call your broker or log onto his website and place a stop order to sell 1,000 shares at $17.80, good until cancelled. Normally, a stop order is placed below the market as an MIT order—"market if touched." If you put your stop at $17.80, it will become a market order to sell 1,000 shares the moment that stock trades at $17.80. Your position is now protected.

A market order is a slippery thing. In a quiet market, you may get filled at $17.80. Occasionally, you may get very lucky, and if prices bounce after touching $17.80, you may get filled at $17.81 or $17.82. What is much more likely to happen, however, is that during a sharp downdraft the stock will not linger at $17.80. You put your MIT stop at $17.80, but when you get your fill, it is at $17.75. This slippage on 1,000 shares has just cost you $50—probably several times larger than your commission.

Prices move smoothly only in quiet markets but they can jump across several price levels when the action heats up. Putting an MIT order at $17.80 does not guarantee you'll be filled there. In a fast decline you may suffer slippage. If a sudden piece of very bad news hits your stock, it may gap all the way down to $16, or even lower.

A stop is not a perfect tool for protecting your profits or reducing losses—but it is the best tool we have.

Stung by slippage, some traders switch to limit orders. I almost always use limit orders for entering trades and taking profits at target levels. A limit order says, in effect, "my way or the highway." I will only do business at a level that suits me, and will not accept slippage on an entry or on profit-taking. If I miss entering a trade as a result of a limit order, I do not complain—there will be many other trades in the future. If you try to enter a trade using a limit price and do not get filled, you lose nothing.

The situation with protective stops is completely different. If you miss an exit from a trade, you can get caught in a waterfall decline. A trader can lose a lot while fiddling with limit orders, trying to save a few pennies. When the trouble hits, run without haggling. That is why

I use limit orders for entries and profit-taking but switch to MIT orders when using stops.

HARD AND SOFT STOPS

A hard stop is an order you place in the market. A soft stop is the number you keep in your mind, prepared to act as soon as the market reaches that level.

I am a little reluctant to discuss soft stops here. It is a topic for professional and semi-professional traders, and I am concerned that some beginners may misunderstand and misuse it. For most beginners, a soft stop is like no stop at all.

This reminds me of a TV commercial—a company advertised a soft drink by showing people on motorbikes zooming up and down steep slopes. Splattered across the bottom of the screen in big white letters was a warning: "All tricks performed by trained professionals. Kids: do not attempt to duplicate at home!" And that's exactly what I'd like to say about soft stops.

If the topic is so dangerous, why not leave it out of the book altogether?

Because I want this book to be useful for the people who are rising to a higher level of expertise and may find hard stops too rigid. I want to put control into your hands, trusting you to make reasonable decisions.

Just remember that hard stops are for everybody, but soft stops are only for the pros or serious semi-pros.

Whatever method you use for setting stops, in the end you will come up with a number—the level for your stop for the next trading day. Will you make that number a hard or a soft stop?

A hard stop goes into the market as a specific order—you actually give it to your broker. The big plus of a hard stop is that it allows you to take your eyes off the market. It is perfect for those who cannot be in front of the screen during trading hours or do not like making decisions in real-time. Beginners must use hard stops because they have neither the expertise nor the discipline to make decisions in real-time.

Professional systematic traders use hard stops, but professional discretionary traders may use either hard or soft stops. A pro can do his research, come up with a number for a stop, and enter it into his record-keeping system—but he may not necessarily give that order to his broker. He may watch that level, prepared to exit if prices get near it, but give himself a bit of latitude.

Using soft stops requires iron discipline and full-time attention to the screen. You have no business using soft stops if you are not in front of the screen, ready to execute a trade when the market hits your level. You also need absolute discipline. A beginner who freezes in fear and keeps hoping for a lucky break when the market turns against him should not be using soft stops.

Soft stops can provide a terrific benefit by allowing more flexibility than hard stops. As the market starts heading down towards your stop you may decide that the stock looks heavy and get out earlier; you may cut losses sooner and save more money. On the other hand, you may decide that a decline on low volume could be a fakeout move and hold the stock a little longer, giving it a chance to recover. An experienced professional can benefit from the flexibility of a soft stop, but too much freedom is deadly for beginners.

A trader has no right to use soft stops until he or she has traded profitably for at least one year. Even then you may adopt soft stops only slowly and continue to use hard stops when you are away from the screen.

Since the decision-making process for establishing stop levels is the same for hard and soft stops, I will not be making any further distinction between them in this chapter. We will discuss how, where, and when to place your stops. You will need to decide whether those will be hard or soft, depending on your level of expertise.

A BAD PLACE

The worst misconception about stops is that one should place them on long positions immediately below the latest low. This idea has been around for a long time and became very popular because it is simple and does not require much thought. Even I took this bait early in my trading career and passed it on to others—until reality hit me on the head.

The trouble with such stops is that markets very often trace out double bottoms, with the second bottom slightly lower than the first. I could fill a book with charts showing this pattern. The level immediately below the latest low is where amateurs cut and run, while professionals tend to buy.

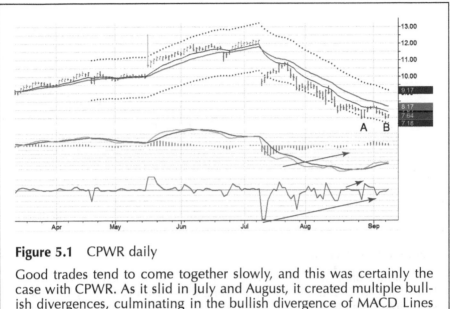

Figure 5.1   CPWR daily

Good trades tend to come together slowly, and this was certainly the case with CPWR. As it slid in July and August, it created multiple bullish divergences, culminating in the bullish divergence of MACD Lines in August. It reached the low of 7.46 at point A in August. Any trader who bought and put his stop "a penny below the latest low" got tossed out in September, when the stock briefly fell to 7.44 at point B. The question at the right edge is this: where will you put your stop if you buy here?

Whenever prices approach a bottom area, I become alert to the possibility that they could penetrate to a lower low. If prices fall to a new low, while the indicators fall to a more shallow low, creating a bullish divergence, I wait for prices to rally slightly. When they rise above the level of the first bottom, they flash a buy signal. I consider this false downside breakout one of the strongest and most reliable trading signals—a double bottom with a bullish divergence, with the second bottom slightly deeper than the first (see Figures 5.1 and 5.2).

It boggles the mind to think of the thousands of people who, year after year, put their stops slightly below the latest bottom. Why do people put their stops at precisely the level where they are most likely to be hit? Why do they sell at the level where the professionals are likely to be buying?

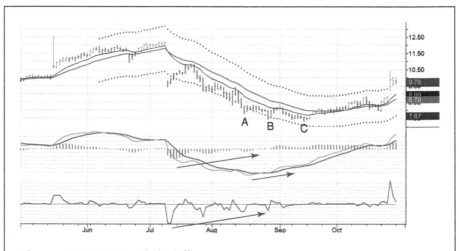

Figure 5.2   CPWR, daily follow-up

The market often meanders while it gathers steam for a dash. CPWR briefly fell to 7.32 at point C, punishing those who casually place their stops immediately below the latest low. That is where beginners cut and run, while professionals tend to go shopping in those areas.

Was that fishing expedition a crime? Probably not—just a pack of savvy pros trading against the unprepared and fearful amateurs.

Crowds crave simplicity. Putting a stop a penny below the latest low is so simple, anyone can do it. And the bulk of trading literature reinforces this pattern.

Professional traders keep exploiting the crowd's tendency to place stops a penny below the latest low. They know where those stops are. There is no law that prohibits professionals from looking at charts. The pros expect to find clusters of stops just beyond the edges of congestion zones.

As a stock sinks towards the level of an important low, its trading volume tends to dry up. All eyes are on that stock, but there is not a lot of activity, as people wait to see whether the support will hold. A small sell order, thrown at the market while buy orders are thin, can push the stock down, below its previous low. That's the area where many serious pros love to operate.

As the falling stock sets off the stops of public customers, the pros snap up shares at a discount. If there are so many shares for sale that

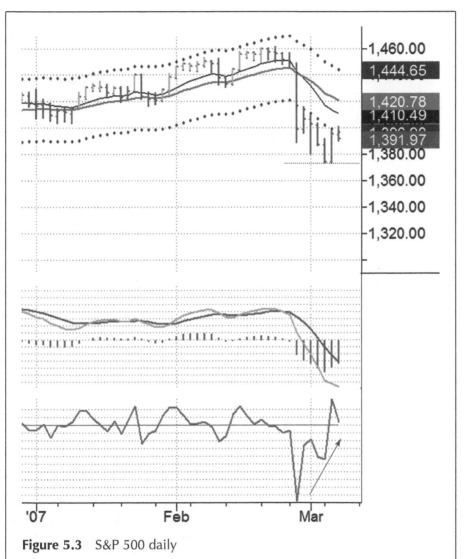

Figure 5.3   S&P 500 daily

In a sharp mini-crash in February 2007 the Standard & Poor's 500 index fell out of its channel but then appeared to have found a bottom, with the Impulse system turning blue.

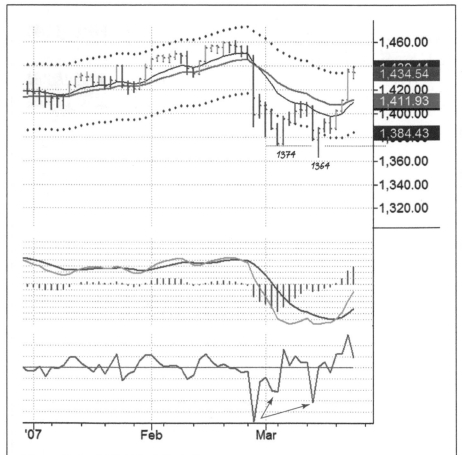

Figure 5.4 S&P 500 daily follow-up

Prices bounced strongly enough to hit the upper channel. Unfortunately for many beginners, prices stabbed below the first low before flying off. Their expectation of a rally was correct, but tight stop placement would have led to a loss instead of a profit.

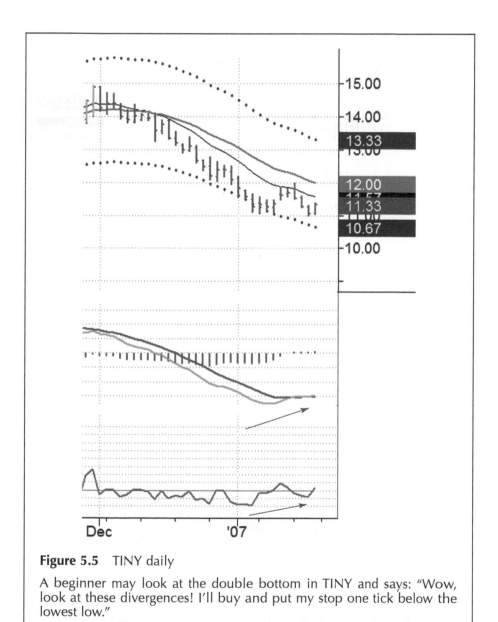

Figure 5.5 TINY daily

A beginner may look at the double bottom in TINY and says: "Wow, look at these divergences! I'll buy and put my stop one tick below the lowest low."

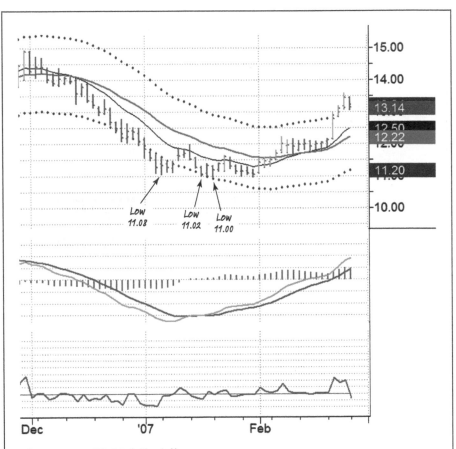

Figure 5.6   TINY daily follow-up

TINY was a stock in a promising industry, with exciting technical patterns.
It did build a base in early January and rallied about 25%. Trouble is, it
flew up only after it kicked out early buyers who put their stops a penny
below the latest low. That low was 11.02, and the primitive stops were
taken out when the stock briefly fell to 11.

the stock accelerates down, they quickly cut their losses and let it
slide, but this rarely happens. Normally, the number of shares sold by
the people with stops is not that great. As their sales get absorbed and
the decline stalls, the pros jump in, joining the feeding frenzy, buying
below the lows. The stock rises back into the range, leaving behind a

brief downspike—a trace of the pros' fishing expedition. They have just scared a bunch of anonymous amateurs into selling them goods at a discount. Has this ever happened to you?

Where should we put our stops? Please review Figures 5.3 through 5.6 to see a few examples.

Putting a stop a penny below the latest low tends to be a losing proposition. What are the alternatives? Let us review several possible solutions.

REDUCING SLIPPAGE—TIGHTER BY A PENNY

Looking at most charts, you can make a fairly good guess about where careless traders would place their stops. When crowd members use stops, they tend to place them at very obvious levels. They slap them immediately below support when long or immediately above resistance when short. In the financial markets, it pays to do things differently from the majority. Let us discuss several alternatives to those obvious levels.

If you make your stops tighter, you'll reduce your dollar risk per share, but you'll also increase the risk of a whipsaw. If you place your stops farther away, you will reduce your risk of a whipsaw, but your losses per share will become heavier when your stops get hit. Both approaches have their pluses and minuses, but you must choose one for any given trade. Like so many choices in the markets, your decision will depend on your attitude.

My approach to using stops has formed gradually, largely as the result of painful experiences. When I first began to trade I did not use stops. After several beatings from the market I learned that I needed stops for protection. I began using them, but placed them in an amateurish way—a tick below the latest low on long positions or a tick above the latest high when going short. Needless to say, I kept getting stopped out by whipsaws.

To add insult to injury, I noticed that when I placed my stops the usual way, one tick[1] below the latest low, it exposed me to a great deal of

---

[1] I was surprised by how many people wrote to me after reading my previous books and asked what a tick is. Let me explain it for those who do not know how to Google their questions—a tick is the smallest price change allowed in a given trading vehicle. As I write this, a tick for most U.S. stocks is a penny. A tick in corn is 1/8 of a penny. A tick in sugar is 1/100 of a penny. Your broker should have a brochure with the information about the tick size for any market you care to trade.

slippage. A stock would decline to the level where my stop had been set, but when I received my confirmation, the fill would be several ticks lower. There were so many stops at my level that when the stock hit it, it just went flying. With all those sell orders, including my own, flooding the market, the buyers were momentarily overwhelmed.

What could I do about it? The pain of losing provided plenty of motivation. I decided to tighten my stops and began placing them not one tick below the latest low, but at the actual low level. Looking at many charts, I saw that there had been very few instances when a stock declined exactly to its previous low and held there, without going a tick lower. Normally, it either held well above that low or went well below it. This meant that placing a stop one tick below the low did not add to my safety margin. I began placing my stops at the actual low, instead of going one tick lower.

This method largely eliminated slippage on my stops. Time after time, a stock would come down to its previous low and just boil there. There would be a great deal of activity but not much movement. Then the stock would fall a tick below its old low and hit an air pocket—whoosh!—falling several ticks within moments.

I realized that the level of the previous low was where the pros re-jigged their positions. There was very little slippage there. Once the stock fell a tick below its previous low, it was in public stops territory, and the slippage became hot and heavy. With that discovery, I began placing my stops at the exact level of the previous low—and my slippage drastically diminished. I used that method for many years—until I switched to an even tighter method of placing stops.

NIC'S STOP—TIGHTER BY A DAY

In a Traders' Camp in 2003, I met a trader by the name of Nic Grove. His story, is in some way typical of how people come to trading. As a young man growing up in Australia, Nic was involved in his family's real estate business, then went out on his own as a commercial landscaper. By the time he turned 50, he grew tired of the routine and sold his business. He flew to Paris, rented a small apartment, and started learning French. Looking for something to do and generate income, Nic stumbled into trading. He happened to read my book, came to a Camp, and gradually we became good friends.

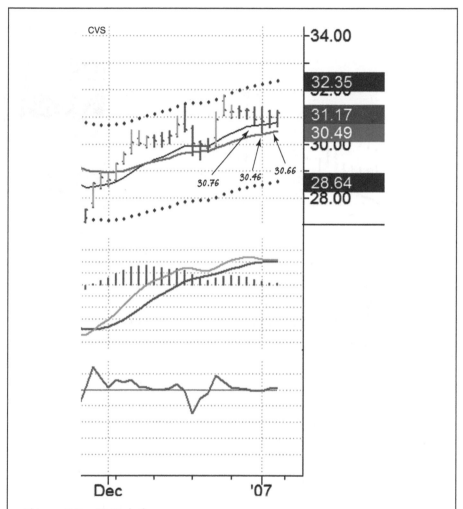

Figure 5.7 CVS daily

CVS is in an uptrend on the weekly chart (not shown). This daily chart shows that it has declined into its value zone between the two EMAs. The lowest low of the decline was $30.46, bracketed by two higher lows, $30.76 and $30.66. If we go long CVS, Nic's stop would belong slightly below the lower of those two bracketing lows. Since the lowest of them was $30.66, I would put a stop at $30.64 or even $30.59—on the other side of a round number.

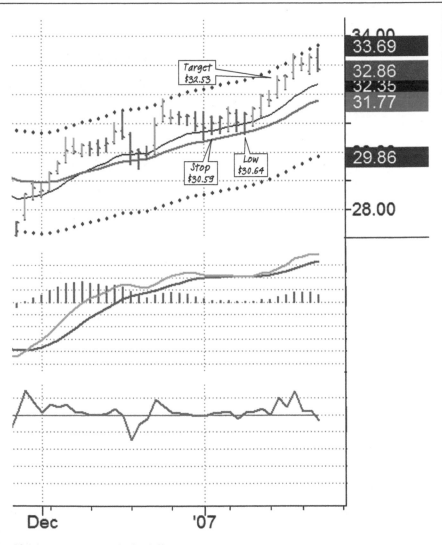

Figure 5.8 CVS daily follow-up

CVS hung around its value zone for a few more days before it took off and hit the target at the upper channel line. The stop below the second lowest low was never endangered.

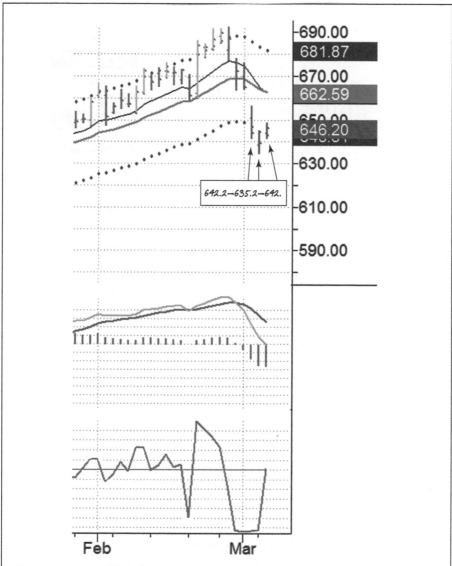

Figure 5.9 Gold daily

Gold, while in a bull market on the weekly chart (not shown), got hit by a piece of bad news and was driven down. It fell below its lower channel line, a deeply oversold area. The lowest point of the decline was $635.20, bracketed by two lows: $642.20 and $642. I would place a stop slightly below the lower of the two, avoiding the round numbers—$641.90 or $641.40.

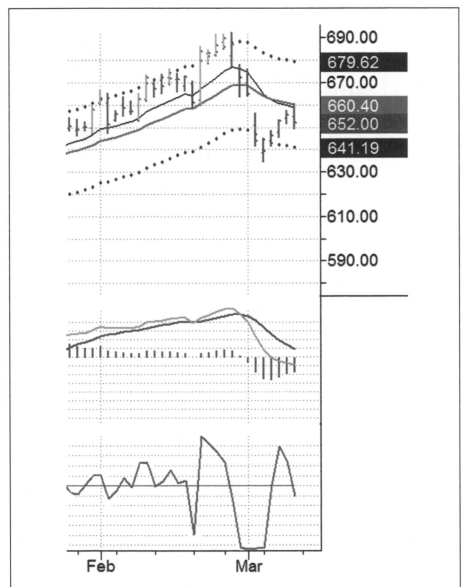

Figure 5.10 Gold daily follow-up

Gold rallied to $659.80, into its value zone between the two EMAs and appears to have stalled. The stop was not hit, but now would be a good time to take profits—since gold is at value and does not seem to be going up.

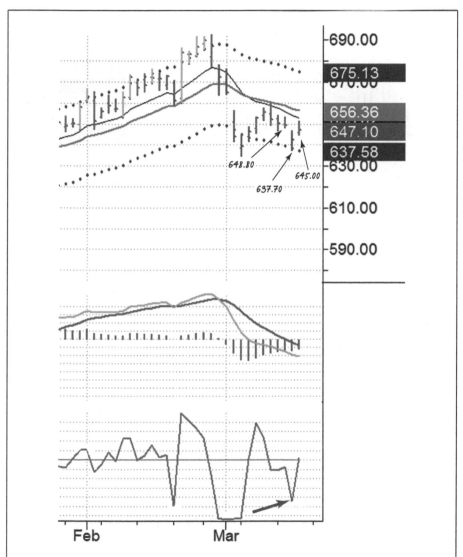

Figure 5.11   Gold—2nd follow-up

Gold punched its lower channel line for the second time. The second decline was less powerful than the first, leading to a bullish divergence of the Force Index. At the right edge, gold looks like an attractive buy again. The lowest low of this decline was $637.70, bracketed by the lows of $648.80 and $645.00. I would put "Nic's stop" slightly below the lower of the bracketing lows, at $644.40.

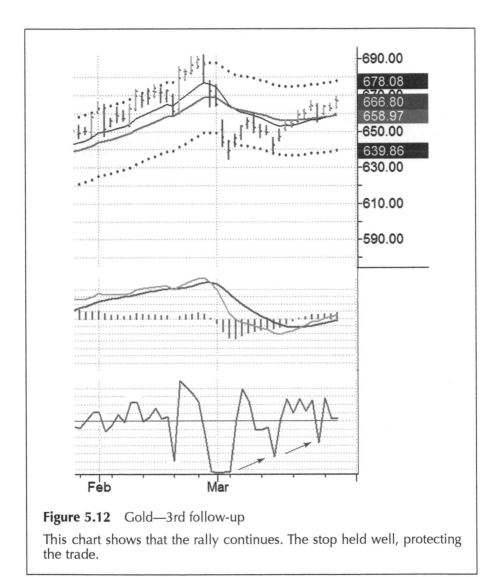

Figure 5.12   Gold—3rd follow-up

This chart shows that the rally continues. The stop held well, protecting the trade.

During a bull market Nic and I were sharing research and buying stocks that had been temporarily driven down to their EMAs. We wanted to hold them for a rally back to their upper channel line, using a fairly tight stop. Nic suggested looking for the low where most people would place their stops and then examine the bars that bracketed that low on each side. He would then place his stop a little below the lower of those two bars. This concept is easier to illustrate than to describe—please see Figures 5.7 through 5.12.

This very tight method of placing stops is especially suited for short-term swing trading. Trying to catch a bottom can be dangerous. A very tight stop like this one does not allow any time for dreaming. It tells the market to put up or shut up.

WHEN TO USE WIDER STOPS

The planned duration of your trade will influence how far from the entry to place your stop. As a rule, a shorter time horizon calls for tighter stops, while a longer timeframe requires wider stops.

All timeframes have advantages and disadvantages. One of the key benefits of longer-term trades is that they give you the time to think and make decisions. At the other end, if you are day-trading and stop to think, you're dead. Longer-term trading gives you more time to think and make decisions, but the cost of this luxury is the greater distance from your entry price to a stop. A stock can meander much more in three months than in three hours. As traders we shoot at a moving target; given more time, the targets will move a great deal more.

A beginning trader is better off staying away from day-trading. This extremely fast game tends to destroy amateurs. Nor would I recommend long-term trend-trading for those who are just starting out. The best way to learn is by making many small trades, keeping a diary, and practicing entries and exits. Long-term trades do not provide enough activity to gain that experience.

Swing trading is a good place to learn trading. Once you have a year under your belt during which your equity curve shows an uptrend with shallow drawdowns, you'll know that you are becoming good. Then you can decide whether to continue to focus on swing trading or to expand your horizons. If, at that point, you decide to learn long-term trading, you will need to use wider stops. You need them to avoid whipsaws. The only logical place for a stop is the level where you do not expect prices to go.

Think about it—if you go long and place a stop below the market, you want to have it at a level where you do not expect prices to decline. You want your stop at a level that could be reached only if the trend reverses.

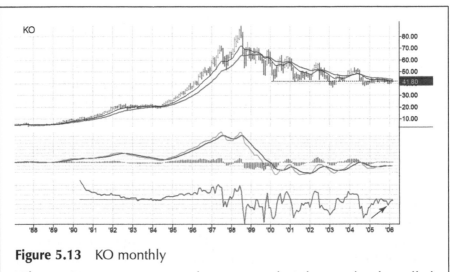

Figure 5.13 KO monthly

When trying to put on a very long-term trade (what used to be called an investment), it pays to begin by analyzing a monthly chart. This chart of KO (Coca-Cola) shows 20 years' worth of history. You can see a bull market that took the stock from under $4 (split-adjusted) to nearly $90 in 1998, followed by a bear market slide to below $40. The area below $40 emerged as strong support, which has stopped four declines since 2001. At the right edge of the chart, the monthly Impulse system has turned from red to blue, permitting buying.

If you identify an uptrend and go long, your stop belongs at a level that is safe from the normal chop of prices. A major uptrend is swingier than a little price move, and your stops have to be wider.

The principle of Triple Screen is to make a strategic decision on a long-term chart (Figure 5.13) and a tactical plan on a short-term chart (Figure 5.14). With the monthly chart permitting buying, we turn to the weekly chart to decide where to enter.

Suppose you're trading a $100,000 account and following the 2% Rule. If you place your stop at the level we discussed, your maximum trade size could be nearly 600 shares.

A stop on a long-term position must be wide, but not so wide as to kill the trade size. Remember that professional traders will often take several stabs at a trade.

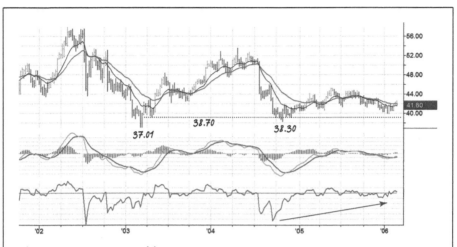

Figure 5.14 KO weekly

The trend of the shorter timeframe changes ahead of the longer time frame. The upside reversal is already under way on the weekly chart. A bullish divergence of the Force Index helps identify a bottom, and prices have already risen above their EMAs. This chart supports our buying decision. Prices are close enough to value to buy here. To set a price target, I prefer to turn to the longer-term chart. A level of about $60, approximately half-way back up to the top, would seem like a reasonable estimate. But what about a stop?

The latest low was $38.30 and the lowest low next to it ("Nic's Stop") $38.75. If you put your stop at that level, you will risk a bit more than $3 per share.

Now let's take a look at what happened to KO going forward (see Figure 5.15).

Wider stops are a feature of long-term trades. The key point to keep in mind is that as the width of your stops increases, the size of your trade must decrease, making sure you stay within the iron triangle of good money management.

MOVING STOPS

The "iron triangle" links protective stop with position size. It makes you enter each trade with a clear stop in mind, but as time goes on,

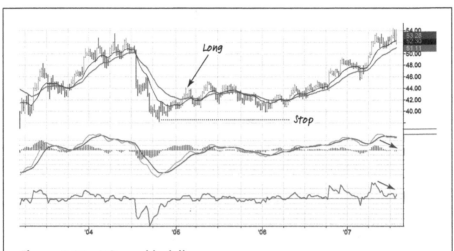

Figure 5.15   KO weekly follow-up

Talk about patience! Had you bought KO at the level we discussed, you would have had to wait nearly a year before the uptrend got going. Prices did sink below the entry level but never violated their stop. At the right edge of the chart, prices have just broken out above their 2004 high. Several indicators are tracing bearish divergences. Shall we hold to our initial target of near $60 or take profits here? This is the sort of dilemma that long-term traders have to deal with.

you'll face a choice. On the one hand, you may leave both the stop and the profit target in place. On the other hand, you may want to move your stop to protect a share of your paper profits. Of course, you may only move your stops in one direction—up for longs and down for shorts. You may tighten your grip on a trade but never loosen it.

Some traders use trailing stops, moving them in the direction of the trade. Others may start out with a traditional stop but then, as prices approach their target, decide that the market wants to go farther. A trader who thinks that the trend is likely to move beyond his initial target may cancel his profit-taking order and switch to a trailing stop. This would allow the trade to run as far as it can before it sets back and hits the stop. Making this switch requires the same calculations as at the beginning of the trade—balancing the potential reward against the very real risk. When you switch from a target to a trailing stop, you must be willing to give up a part of your profit.

There are pros and cons to trailing stops, like with everything else in trading. On the plus side, a trailing stop can deliver extra profits if the trade moves beyond your target. On the minus side, you risk giving back some profit if the trend reverses.

There is a variety of techniques available for placing trailing stops:

- You can use a multibar low as a trailing stop; for example, you can keep moving your stop to the lowest low of the last three bars (but never against your trade).

- You can trail prices with a very short moving average and use its level for a trailing stop.

- You can use a Chandelier stop—every time the market makes a new high, move the stop within a certain distance from the top—either a specific price range or a number based on an ATR (average true range). Any time your stock makes a new high, you place your stop within that distance from the top, like hanging a chandelier from the ceiling (this method is described in *Come into My Trading Room*).

- You can use a Parabolic stop (described below).

- You can use a SafeZone stop (described below).

- You can use a Volatility-Drop stop (described below, for the first time in trading literature).

- You can use a Time Stop and get out of your trade if it does not move within a certain time. For example, if you enter a day-trade and the stock does not move within 10 or 15 minutes, it is clearly not doing what you expected, and it is best to scratch that trade. If you put on a swing trade that you expect to last several days, but then a week goes by and the stock is still flat, it is clearly not confirming your analysis and the safest action would be to get out.

If you become interested in trailing stops, test them like any other method. Write down your rules, then test them on the charts. If the system works on paper, begin implementing it with real money, while keeping good records. Test the method on small size trades, so that neither profit nor loss would matter to you. Then you can concentrate

A Parabolic Stop

The Parabolic system, presented in 1976 by J. Welles Wilder, Jr., was one of the first attempts to include the concept of time in setting stops. The system moves the stops closer to the market each day. In addition, it accelerates whenever a stock or a commodity reaches a new extreme in the direction of the trade.

$$Stop_{tomorrow} = Stop_{today} + AF \times (EP_{trade} - Stop_{today})$$

Where $Stop_{today}$	= the current stop
$Stop_{tomorrow}$	= the stop for the next trading day
EP_{trade}	= the extreme point reached in the market in the current trade. If long, this is the highest since the purchase day. If short, this is the lowest low since the shorting day
AF	= the Acceleration Factor

On the first day in a trade, Acceleration Factor equals 0.02. This means you must move your stop by 2% of the distance between the extreme point and the original stop. AF increases by 0.02 each day the rally reaches a new high or a decline reaches a new low, up to the maximum of 0.20.

Losers go broke by hanging onto losing positions and hoping for a reversal. The Parabolic system protects traders from indecision.

The Parabolic system is extremely useful during runaway trends. When prices soar or crash without a pullback, it is hard to place stops using normal chart patterns or indicators. Parabolic is a great tool for placing stops under those conditions.

The Parabolic system works well in trending markets but leads to whipsaws in trendless markets. It can generate spectacular profits during price trends but chop up an account in a trading range. Do not use it as an automatic trading method.

Adapted from *Trading for a Living* by Dr. Alexander Elder,
John Wiley & Sons, Inc., 1993

on mastering the new approach and leave money-making for later, after you have developed confidence in your new method.

A SAFEZONE STOP

SafeZone stops are based on the concept of signal and noise in the financial markets. If the price trend is the signal, then the counter-trend

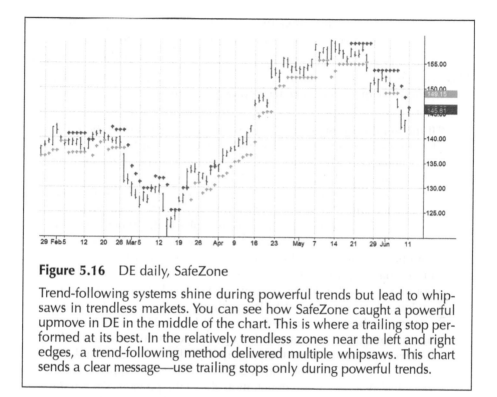

Figure 5.16 DE daily, SafeZone

Trend-following systems shine during powerful trends but lead to whip-saws in trendless markets. You can see how SafeZone caught a powerful upmove in DE in the middle of the chart. This is where a trailing stop performed at its best. In the relatively trendless zones near the left and right edges, a trend-following method delivered multiple whipsaws. This chart sends a clear message—use trailing stops only during powerful trends.

moves are the noise. Engineers build filters to suppress noise and allow the signals to come through. If we can identify and measure market noise, we can place our stops outside of the noise level. This allows us to stay in the trade for as long as the signal identifies a trend. This concept was described in detail in *Come into My Trading Room* and has since been implemented in several trading programs.[2]

We can define a trend in a variety of ways, including something as simple and straightforward as the slope of a 22-day EMA. When the trend is up, we define noise as that part of each day's range that protrudes below the previous day's low, going against the trend. When the trend is down, we define noise as that part of each day's range that protrudes above the previous day's high. A trader needs to select the length of

---

[2]Elder.com includes SafeZone in its Elder-disks for several popular programs, such as TradeStation, MetaStock, eSignal, TC2007, and StockFinder.

the lookback period for measuring all the "noisy" penetrations. That lookback period must be short enough to make it relevant for current trading—approximately a month of the latest data on the daily charts (Figure 5.16).

To quote from *Come into My Trading Room*:

> If the trend is up, mark all downside penetrations during the lookback period, add their depths, and divide the sum by the number of penetrations. This gives you the Average Downside Penetration for the selected lookback period. It reflects the average level of noise in the current uptrend. Placing your stop any closer would be self-defeating. We want to place our stops farther away from the market than the average level of noise. Multiply the Average Downside Penetration by a coefficient, starting with a 2, but experiment with higher numbers. Subtract the result from yesterday's low, and place your stop there. If today's low is lower than yesterday's, do not move your stop lower since we are only allowed to raise stops on long positions, but not to lower them.
>
> Reverse these rules in downtrends. When a 22-day EMA identifies a downtrend, count all the upside penetrations during the lookback period and find the Average Upside Penetration. Multiply it by a coefficient, starting with a 2. When you go short, place a stop twice the Average Upside Penetration above the previous day's high. Lower your stop whenever the market makes a lower high but never raise it.

Like any other method, SafeZone is not a mechanical gadget to replace independent thought. You have to establish the lookback period and choose the coefficient by which to multiply the normal noise to obtain the SafeZone stop. Usually, a coefficient between 2 and 3 provides a margin of safety, but you must research it on your own market data.

VOLATILITY-DROP TRAILING STOPS

One trader who likes to use trailing stops is Kerry Lovvorn, whose method is designed to keep him in a trade for as long as prices are running in his favor but get out soon after they start pulling away from their recent extremes.

I do not use a trailing stop until my target is hit. At that time the trade has fulfilled its duty, but the market may be moving in a way that seems to have potential for an additional reward. When the market hits my target, I have a choice. I can take profits, be happy, and go on to the next trade. But then maybe my target was too conservative, and there is greater profit potential left in the move. I do not want to give all my accumulated profit from this trade back but am willing to risk a portion to find out whether the move has more life left in it. My decision depends on how much profit I am willing to give back to find out. The challenge of a trailing stop is the same as that of any other stop—where to set it. If you set it too tight, you may as well go ahead and exit the trade.

Once the market gets going, it can go much farther than we can ever imagine. We can set a trailing stop and let the market decide how far it wants to go and when to take us out.

Using trailing stops is my way of saying—hey, if the market is willing to give me more, this is how much I am willing to give up to find out. I think of it in terms of the price I have to pay to play the game. This is similar to the calculations I make when putting on a fresh trade—weighing reward against risk. The question is the same: How much am I willing to pay? Once I decide to switch to a trailing stop, my decision has been made, and I let the market decide how far to go next.

I call my trailing stop a Volatility-Drop. If the market is willing to go crazy and have this huge momentum move, I am willing to stay with it. Suppose I use Autoenvelope to set my price target when I enter the trade. The normal width of the envelope is 2.7 standard deviations. If I want to switch to a trailing stop once that target is reached, I will place it one standard deviation tighter—at 1.7 standard deviations. As long as the move continues along the border of a normal envelope, I'll stay with it, but as soon as the price closes inside of the tighter channel, I'll be out. A programmer could take it and make it automatic—either intraday, or end-of-day.

How do you decide whether to take profits at the initial target or switch to a trailing stop?

If my target is hit and I see bearish signals, I won't use a trailing stop. If I see a negative price action—like a wide bar closing near the low on heavy volume, I will take my profit at a target and be gone. But when the market is moving well, with higher highs and

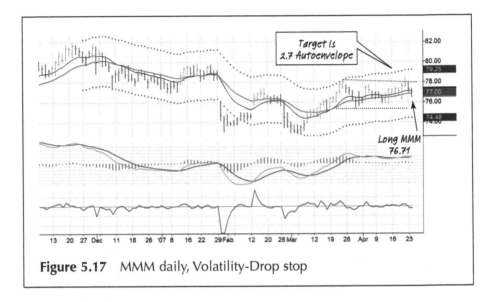

Figure 5.17 MMM daily, Volatility-Drop stop

higher lows, I will follow. It's like a beautiful girl—you are going to follow her along. I make the decision when my target gets hit— I need to see a positive enough action to switch to a trailing stop.

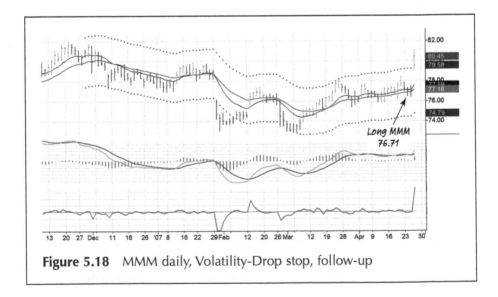

Figure 5.18 MMM daily, Volatility-Drop stop, follow-up

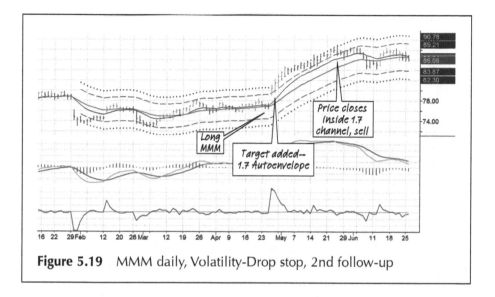

Figure 5.19 MMM daily, Volatility-Drop stop, 2nd follow-up

How often do you switch from a target to a trailing stop?

I do it in about two-thirds of my trades. It doesn't always work in
my favor. Sometimes I set a trailing stop, and five minutes later I get
stopped out. About half the time a trailing stop gives me a little
more profit than the original stop. The big payoff comes from
those rare cases of oversize profits in runaway moves.

Like any market tool, trailing stops are not for everybody, but
they help me in my decision making. They are good for the people
who find themselves struggling to decide whether to get out of the
trade or stay in it. Using a trailing stop shifts the decision away
from you and hands it over to the market. That's what drove me
to use trailing stops.

This chart (Figure 5.17) illustrates an entry into a trade. The
weekly (not shown) was neutral. The daily showed a narrow trading range. I call this pattern "a squeeze play" and try to catch a
breakout from it. The recent tall peak of MACD-Histogram led me
to expect an upside breakout, and I took a long position inside the
squeeze.

Two days later MMM had erupted from its squeeze and flew
above my target, which was at the upper channel line, at 80.63
(Figure 5.18). The action was extremely strong, with the entire bar

above the channel. I immediately decided to switch to a trailing stop and drew a second Autoenvelope on the chart, at only 1.7 standard deviations. My plan was to sell after MMM closed inside that narrower channel (see Figure 5.19).

MMM continued to "walk the line" for several more weeks until it finally contracted and closed inside the narrower channel. I exited on May 24 at 87.29, a big improvement over the initial 80.63 target. Notice how different Autoenvelope looks in retrospect—by the time we get to the exit, the entry appears quite different. This is because Autoenvelope is based on the last 100 bars action, and as the market becomes more volatile, Autoenvelope becomes wider.

Kerry's Volatility-Drop tactic provides a useful trading tool and delivers an important message. Trailing stops are suitable only during certain periods. When the markets are quiet and orderly, a trader is better off with his original profit target and stop. When the markets embark on powerful moves, a trader may switch to a trailing stop.

CHAPTER 6

SELLING "ENGINE NOISE"

Imagine driving your car on a routine trip. Gradually, you become aware of a hard rattling noise, which becomes louder whenever you step on the gas. Will you continue to drive? Will you keep your foot on the accelerator, hoping that maybe the noise is nothing serious and will go away? Or would you pull over and get out of the car to investigate?

Hard noise and gradual loss of power could be the signs of engine trouble. Maybe you're lucky and it's no big deal, just a branch caught in the undercarriage or some other nonsense that is easy to remove or fix. On the other hand, something could be seriously wrong with the car. Continuing to drive while ignoring the signs of danger could lead to serious damage down the road.

You might enter a trade as casually as running an errand. Maybe the trip will be uneventful, but if you hear hard noise or see steam coming from under the hood, do not press on. Take your foot off the gas pedal, pull over, and step out of the car to investigate what's happening.

There is no reason to hold every trade to its planned target. You have to listen to the market. Perhaps it wants to give you more than you expected, but maybe it wants to give you less. As a trader, you need to keep an eye on what is happening and get out when you suspect engine trouble.

System traders and discretionary traders differ in many ways. For a system trader, a stop is set in stone. He has placed it, along with an order for taking profits at the levels his system gave him; he does not need to look at the screen intraday. A discretionary trader plays a different game.

He also has a target and a stop, but he is allowed to exit the market sooner or hold a little longer if his analysis suggests a different course of action.

This permission to change course in the middle of a trade has different meanings for different people. My friends among system traders find it stressful. Discretionary traders, on the other hand, consider this ability to change plans liberating. Yes, I have my plan, yes, I have my stop, but I also have the luxury of choice: I can tighten my stop if I do not like how the market is acting, or take profits early. Or, if I like how the market is acting, I can continue to hold past my profit target and try to take more money from the trade than originally planned.

Let us review several situations in which a discretionary trader may change his or her exit tactic in the middle of a trade. I have named these exits "engine noise" because when you first got into a trade you planned to drive somewhere else, but the noise coming from the engine prompted you to pull over. Please keep in mind that selling in response to "engine noise" requires a high level of experience. If you are a beginner, you may want to skip this chapter and return to it later, after you've become a more proficient trader.

WEAKENING MOMENTUM

If your stock starts to act sloppy, there is nothing wrong with taking a profit and standing aside, ready to repurchase. The time to become suspicious of an open position is when its progress starts slowing down—when the stock starts moving sideways rather than up. There are many measures of market momentum, extensively described in trading books. The following example uses MACD-Histogram, a popular indicator, to gauge momentum (see Figure 6.1).

Buy and sell signals are clearly visible on old charts, but the closer we get to the right edge, the foggier they become. Trends and reversals are hard to recognize in real time. There are almost always conflicting signals at the right edge of a chart, but that is where we must make our decisions. This is why a shorter-term trading approach makes sense—buying near value and selling in the overvalued zone.

If our plan is to buy value and sell above value, what would make us change this approach? When a savvy short-term trader sees a divergence between MACD-Histogram and price, he or she is ready to sell without waiting for the upper channel to be hit. Maybe prices will

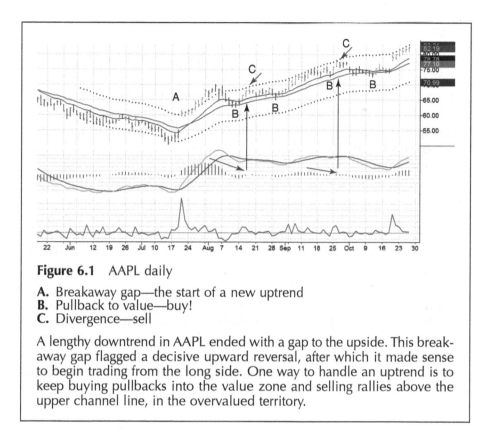

Figure 6.1 AAPL daily

A. Breakaway gap—the start of a new uptrend
B. Pullback to value—buy!
C. Divergence—sell

A lengthy downtrend in AAPL ended with a gap to the upside. This break-away gap flagged a decisive upward reversal, after which it made sense to begin trading from the long side. One way to handle an uptrend is to keep buying pullbacks into the value zone and selling rallies above the upper channel line, in the overvalued territory.

reach it or maybe they won't, but meanwhile, it makes sense to grab a profit and re-evaluate the situation from the sidelines. This chart shows how both bearish divergences were followed by pullbacks into the value zone. Those pullbacks created good opportunities to re-establish long positions.

If you do not like how your long position is acting, you have two choices. If you're in a short-term trade, you can just shoot it, accept a lower profit than planned, and move on. If you are in a long-term trade, you probably do not want to sell your entire position. You may want to take partial profits and maintain your core position, with an eye towards repurchasing the shares you've sold at a lower price. This technique allows you to take more than one dollar's profit out of a one dollar move. Let me open my diary to illustrate both approaches.

AN "ENGINE NOISE" EXIT FROM A SHORT-TERM TRADE

One of my favorite sources of leads for short-term trades is the Spike group. Its members generate dozens of short-term picks every weekend, and I almost always select one of them to trade in the week ahead. This particular week, I liked IKN; Jim Rauschkolb who suggested it had sent in the Spike submission form shown in Figure 6.2. This long trade involved risking 25 cents per share to make 57 cents (see Figures 6.3 and 6.4).

My exit grade was 69%, a high rating, thanks to selling in the upper third of the day's range. The overall trade grade was a middling 18%, reflecting the percentage of the channel I had caught on the daily chart. Since a 20% rating equals a "B", 18% rated a B–. That Spike pick won a Bronze for the week, meaning it was the third best pick of that week, in a very difficult market environment. My discretionary exit has nailed down a profit.

There is nothing terribly exciting about this trade, which is precisely why I show it here. There is very little excitement about day-to-day trading, with thrilling trades few and far between. A reasonable trading idea comes in, an entry gets fumbled a bit, the trade does not go as well as expected, but the exit is clean, and in the end a bit of profit drops to the bottom line, nudging up the equity curve. This is what much of trading for a living is about.

My Pick:	**IKN**	Long ▼	Select your trade direction
Price Entry:	**$14.19**	Limit ▼	Select your entry order type
Protective Stop:	**$13.84**		
Price Target:	**$14.76**		

Discussion:

Trade date: March 12, 2007
Average daily volume:579,455
Earnings Date: None in near future
Risk to Reward ratio: 1 to 1.63

Market Group: MG761- Business/Management Services. Impulse blue closed above Fast EMA.

Weekly Chart: Impulse is blue. Pulling back to value.

Daily Chart: Impulse turned green, FI(2) shows a bullish divergence. RSI(21) hit bottom last week and is starting higher. Price movement higher Friday with volume.

Figure 6.2   IKN plan

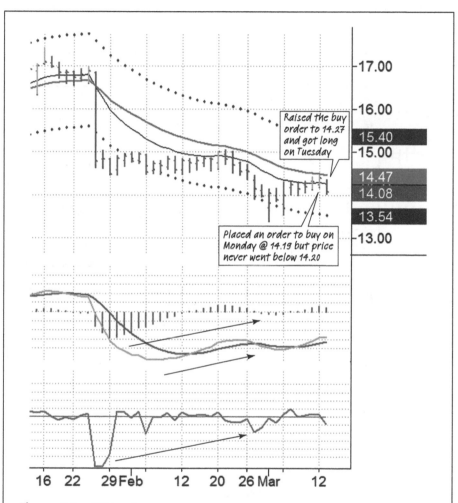

Figure 6.3 IKN entry

I placed my order to buy IKN on Monday at 14.19, exactly where the Spiker who chose it had recommended buying. IKN was strong that day and its low for the day was $14.20. My buy order was not filled, but after the close I felt even more bullish. After studying support and resistance on intraday charts, I raised my buy order for the next day to $14.27. The market quickly reminded me that it does not pay to move your entries. IKN declined and, after filling my buy order, closed at 14.08, near the day's low. My entry grade was only 31%, as I bought in the upper third of that day's bar.

IKN	long	Date	Upchannel	Downchannel	Day's High	Day's Low	Grade
Entry	$14.27	14-Mar-07	15.4	13.54	$14.37	$14.05	31%
Exit							
P/L						Trade	

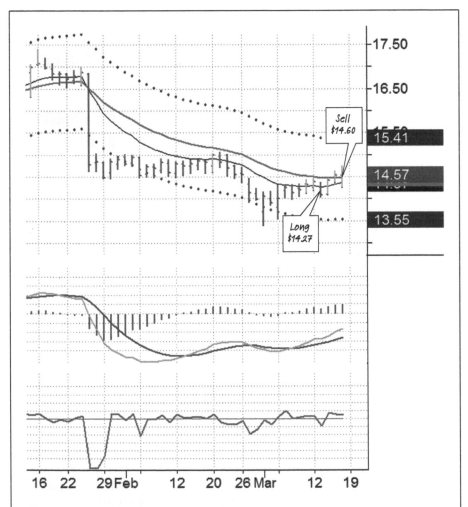

Figure 6.4   IKN exit

On Friday, March 16, IKN took out the previous day's low, then turned up
and rallied above its longer-term moving average (the yellow line). With
the weekend approaching, I decided not to wait and took profits while
prices were above value. I sold my IKN at $14.60.

IKN	long	Date	Upchannel	Downchannel	Day's High	Day's Low	Grade
Entry	$14.27	14-Mar-07	15.40	13.54	$14.37	$14.05	31%
Exit	$14.60	16-Mar-07			$14.75	$14.27	69%
P/L						Trade	18%

A DISCRETIONARY EXIT FROM A LONG-TERM TRADE

In January 2007 I received an e-mail from a friend who told me about his great bullishness on Ford Motor Company. The firm had just indicated it was likely to announce its biggest quarterly loss in the company's history,

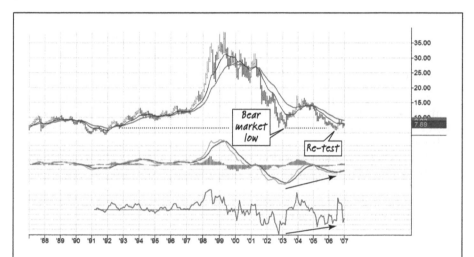

Figure 6.5 F monthly

A quick look at a 20-year long monthly chart of Ford revealed a bull market top near $40, followed by a vicious bear market, which took the stock down to $6 in 2003. Ford bounced, then slowly slid to a slightly lower low in 2006. I love this pattern of a slightly lower low, accompanied by massive bullish divergences. With the company prospects very appealing, according to my fundamentalist friend, and a monthly chart very constructive, it was time to look at a weekly chart.[*]

---

[*]There was also a psychological confirmation. That winter I used the same limo driver, a nice young man who was interested in stocks but did not know who I was. On the last ride, feeling generous, I told him I was buying Ford. He was so shocked—because of all the bad fundamental news—that he turned sharply back towards me—and I was afraid he'd skid the limo off the icy turnpike. A contrarian loves buying stocks that the crowd hates.

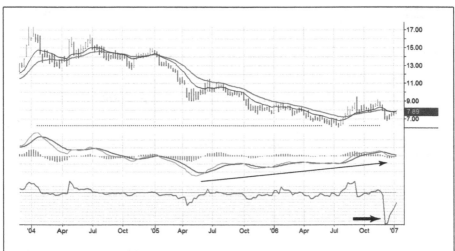

Figure 6.6 F weekly

The weekly chart confirmed multiple bullish divergences at the 2006 bottom and added another strong buy signal—a deep spike of the weekly Force Index, marked by an arrow on the chart. Such a downspike reflects a huge volume of sales, as a mass of traders gives up on a stock and dumps its shares on the market. This downspike of the Force Index revealed that the holders had reached what some call a "puke point," tossing out their former possessions. After weak hands are eliminated, only strong holders remain and a stock is ready to advance (this signal works well at bottoms but its reverse is not useful for calling tops).

but my friend Gerard de Bruin outlined his reasons why the new CEO would turn the company around. He was a retired money manager whose approach to finding stocks was based on the fundamentals. I respected his judgment and took a look at the stock (see Figures 6.5 and 6.6).

I've already described my approach to trading tips. A tip is merely a trigger for doing one's own research. I like it when a tip comes from a fundamental analyst. Since my own work is primarily technical, it provides a multidimensional view of a stock.

I developed a plan to accumulate a fairly large position in F and hold it for several years, with a tentative target near $20, about halfway back to the top. Since this plan took a very long-term view, I had no intention of chasing any rallies, including the one at the end of January. I was going to wait and accumulate my position during short-term declines.

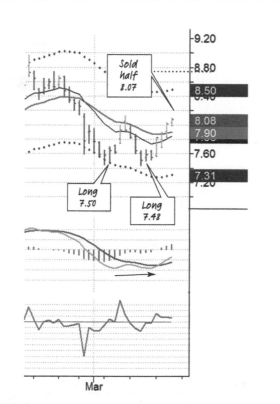

Figure 6.7 F daily

I acquired the first position—about one-fifth of what I meant to accumulate—at $7.50 and the second at $7.48. Both were purchased near the lower channel line on the daily chart, when the Force Index dipped below zero. The two bottoms were separated by a brisk rally. Another rally erupted from the second bottom, but I saw a bearish divergence of the Force Index and a slightly overbought position of MACD-Histogram, which made me concerned that the rally was running into resistance. I implemented my plan by selling the more expensive of the two positions at $8.07, planning to repurchase double its size when prices fell back towards the $7.50 support. The chart above shows these three steps in my Ford campaign—buying at $7.50 and $7.48, then selling half at $8.07.

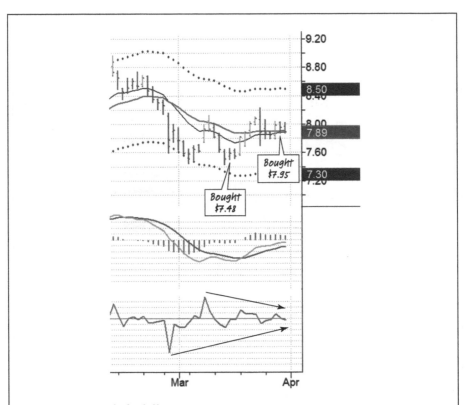

Figure 6.8 F daily follow-up

The day after I sold, F spiked up a little, and then cracked but refused to sink. Its rise had been capped, but there had been no follow-through to the downside. My overall stance on Ford was bullish. A stock that refuses to go down probably wants to go up. I thought that the risk of missing a rally was greater than the risk of being caught in a decline, and placed a new buy order.

  I bought the same number of shares at $7.95 as I sold at $8.07. As I write this, F is well above $9, and I continue to use declines to build up my long position, while using rallies to take partial profits.

My plan continues in effect to this day, as I keep buying on declines, selling part of my position on rallies, and repurchasing on subsequent declines. I keep on selling more expensive, recently acquired shares, while maintaining the core position of older, cheaper ones for the long haul. Figure 6.7 illustrates the first three steps in this game, while Figure 6.8 illustrates the fourth.

This long-term position was established on a combination of two inputs: a fundamental tip and strong technical signals. The buying and selling campaign depends on keeping an ear out for engine noise and selling at the slightest signs of sputtering. When the engine sounds good, I repurchase sold shares at a lower level. All the while, I maintain the core position for the long haul.

SELLING BEFORE EARNINGS REPORTS

Most fundamental information is reflected in stock prices. I say to fundamental money managers that I feel as though they are working for me. Whenever they buy or sell on the basis of their research, their actions create stock patterns that a technical analyst can recognize. When it comes to fundamental analysis, at the very minimum, you need to know to what industry group a stock belongs. Stocks, like people, move better in groups. It is a good idea to go long stocks in strong groups and sell short stocks in weak ones.

One of the problems with fundamental information is that it flows into the markets in bursts rather than in a steady stream. A chunk of fundamental information can hit a stock and make it leap. This is especially likely to happen when a company releases its earnings reports.

Earnings are important because in the long run they drive stock prices. When you buy a stock, you are in effect paying for future earnings and dividends. This is why many analysts, fund managers, and traders closely watch the earnings of the companies they follow.

Keep in mind that an earnings report rarely comes as a surprise for those who closely track the company. First, there is an entire industry of earnings watchers and forecasters. Pros with a lot of experience tend to be right about their forecasts. Those who pay them for their research usually buy and sell ahead of the actual reports. Stocks seldom jump on earnings reports because the smart bulls have already bought or the clever bears have already sold. The pros pretty much know what to expect, and the price tends to reflect the mass expectation of what the earnings report will bring. When the report hits the newswires, there is rarely much of a surprise.

The other reason why stocks seldom jump on earnings reports is that the drift of those reports is often leaked in advance of their official release. I think that the volume of insider trading in the stock market is much greater than most people think. When the SEC catches some slob and puts him behind bars for insider trading, that action only shaves the

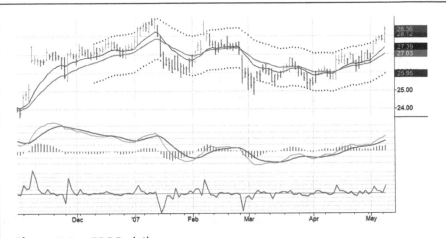

Figure 6.9 CSCO daily

Take a look at this chart of CSCO one day prior to the release of its earnings report. A slow but steady uptrend is in progress, with higher highs and higher lows. At the right edge of the chart, prices have risen into the overvalued zone above the upper channel line. Suppose you're holding a long position. What would you do at the right edge—sell or hold through the earnings?

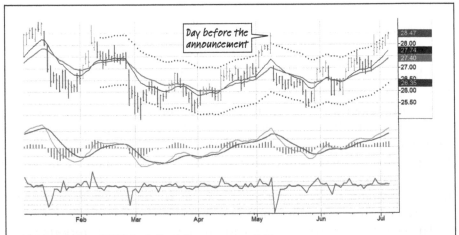

Figure 6.10 CSCO daily follow-up (to 7/8)

As the earnings report was released, the stock initially sank, then recovered. Looking at it two months later, one message is clear—it pays to sell in the overvalued zone above the upper channel line, earnings or no earnings.

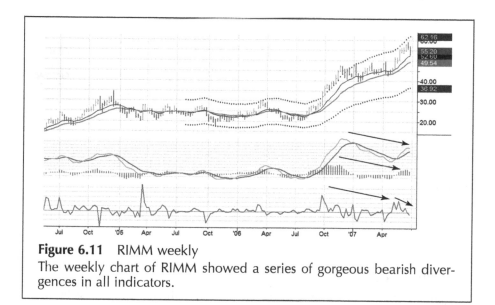

Figure 6.11   RIMM weekly

The weekly chart of RIMM showed a series of gorgeous bearish divergences in all indicators.

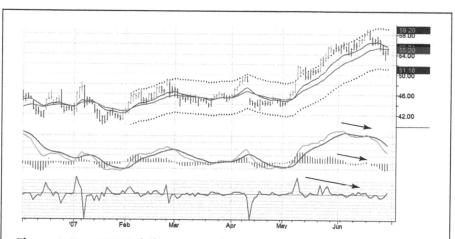

Figure 6.12   RIMM daily

The daily chart confirmed the message of the weekly with its own bearish divergences. A short trade was working beautifully, accumulating profits. At the right edge of the chart, on Thursday, it was hard to make a decision—to cover shorts or take the short trade over the earnings announcement, due after the market close on Thursday. On the one hand, the trade has not yet reached its profit target at the lower channel line but seemed on track to do so. On the other hand, the stock appeared to have recoiled from its Wednesday low.

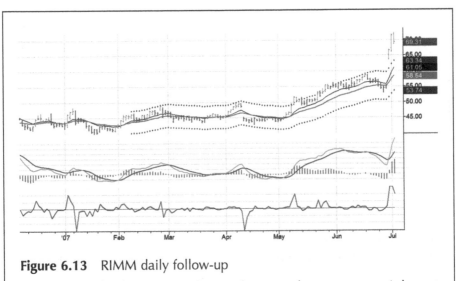

Figure 6.13   RIMM daily follow-up

"Ouch!" It is shocking to see what can happen when a company is honest and does not leak! RIMM came out with a triple whammy—it beat projected earnings, raised its projection for the next quarter, and announced a 3:1 stock split. The market was truly surprised—it roared. The stock exploded on a gap, negating bearish divergences and rising to new record highs.

tip of the iceberg. Greedy and stupid guys get caught. The slick types who trade friendly tips in country clubs can benefit from inside information throughout their careers. I learned this when, after only a few years of trading, I was befriended by a man who was on the boards of two listed companies. He boasted to me of trades based on the inside information passed among corporate buddies, making me very skeptical about market news. News for the masses, not for the classes.

Pascal Willain, a Belgian trader, spoke about insider trading in his interview for *Entries & Exits:* "A tiger does not change its stripes. I believe that insider trading is linked to the way the company is managed and its type of business. Large contracts involve multiple participants and take weeks to negotiate, creating more chances for information leaks. A company cannot change the way it does business or its management method—if it leaked information in the past, it will leak in the future. Because of this I like to look at a company's news for the past year to see whether there was a signal prior to its moves."

Those of us who take a skeptical view of companies' ability to keep secrets tend to hold positions, either long or short, through the earnings reports (see Figures 6.9 and 6.10). Since the earnings news has already probably been leaked and discounted by the markets, we can expect the pre-earnings trends to continue. On the other hand, those traders who have a greater trust in the system tend to be more cautious and close out their positions in advance of earnings reports.

In my experience, it pays to be skeptical about the impact of earnings reports. Companies leak, insiders trade, and earnings reports come and go. Still, once in a while a skeptic gets burned. Take a look at Figures 6.11 through 6.13, charts of RIMM (Research in Motion), which provided powerful shorting signals shortly before its recent earnings report.

Dishonesty is more widespread than many people think but honesty is a more powerful force. The lesson is that if you want to be on the safe side, close out your position prior to an earnings report.

THE MARKET RINGS A BELL

Once in a blue moon, the market rings a bell to let you know that a long-term trend is coming to an end. The sound of the bell is hard to recognize amidst the roar of the markets. Most people do not hear it, and only savvy traders respond to it.

You need a great deal of experience to hear the market bell, and you need a great deal of confidence to act on that signal. You need to be attentive and alert because the market rings the bell very seldom. Your ears and your mind must be open to recognize those signals. This is not a task for beginners. When you hear the sound of the market bell and act on it, it means you are becoming a serious trader.

The first time the market rang its bell in front of me I realized it only after the fact. A major money-making opportunity had slipped away, but it sensitized my ears for the future.

In 1989 I flew to Asia. The upper deck of the Boeing 747 felt clubby and comfortable. The lights went out after dinner and most passengers drifted off to sleep, but I felt keyed up on my first flight across the Pacific. I walked over to the galley and fell into a long friendly conversation with a Japan Airlines steward, a man of about 50. He told me how he grew up in poverty after the war, with little education. It took a great deal of hard work to rise to his position as the chief steward in

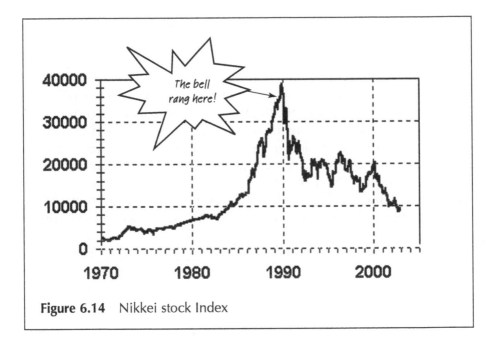

Figure 6.14   Nikkei stock Index

the business class of the national airline. He was very proud of his accomplishment.

As we continued to chat, he told me he was very active in the Japanese stock market, which had been rising for two decades. He said he was making more money in stocks than from his salary and was planning to take an early retirement. He had already selected a Pacific island where he was going to build his villa. There was only one thing that made him angry: the office girls who lived at home with their parents and did not have the family responsibilities of a married man could put even more money into the stock market, making even greater profits!

Several months later the Japanese stock market keeled over and crashed (Figure 6.14). It lost half its value in the first year, and that was just the beginning of a vicious bear market. I had missed a great shorting opportunity right near the top. It was a great lesson that made me determined not to miss such psychological signals in the future.

You can hear the market bell when you recognize an event or a series of events so far outside the norm that it may seem as if the laws of the market have been repealed. In fact the laws of the market cannot go away, no more than the law of gravity can. They can be only temporarily suspended during a bubble, creating an illusion that normal rules no longer apply.

It is not normal for a man who knows next to nothing about the stock market—as my steward told me he did—to be making more money in stocks than from his salary at the pinnacle of a successful career. It is not normal for random office girls to be making even more money than him. The markets do not exist to put money into the pockets of amateurs. When outsiders and latecomers start making a lot of money, the market is near the top.

Today, when I think of that conversation, it feels as if someone came up to me with a bell, and rang it next to my ear—sell and sell short! Because of my lack of experience that sound went in one ear—and out the other.

Bernard Baruch was a famous stock operator in the first half of the twentieth century. He managed to sidestep the crash of 1929, which ruined so many of his peers. He described how one day in 1929 he stepped out of his office, and the man who polished his shoes gave him a stock tip. Baruch recognized the sign—if people at the lowest level of society were buying stocks, there was no one left to buy. He began selling his stocks. In a different era and in a different economy, my Japanese steward had given me an identical signal.

Here's another psychological signal. Having attended traders' expos and shows for many years, I've become aware of a strong inverse correlation between the level of the stock market and the quantity and quality of free gifts that the exhibitors hand out. When the stock market boils at the top, you need a shopping bag to hold all the goodies that vendors hand out. A month before the 1987 market top, one of the Chicago exchanges was giving away good sunglasses whose frame was engraved with the saying, "The future is so bright, I have to wear shades." On the other hand, going to an expo near the bottom of a bear market, you may not even get a free ballpoint pen.

The quantity and quality of free gifts at a trade show reflect the mass mood. When the market is up and the public is happy, people spend money, and vendors, feeling flush, hand out more goodies.

On February 24, 2007, I went to a Traders' Expo in New York. The stock market had been rising for nearly four years. It had been going straight

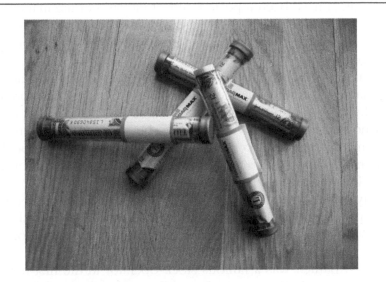

Figure 6.15   Free money at market top

They had dollar bills rolled into plastic tubes, with a little advertisement pasted to them. I could not believe my eyes and asked whether the money was real. They told me to see for myself. I opened a tube and pulled out a crisp new dollar bill. I asked whether I could take two, and they said, go ahead. My companion also got two. When I taught a class later that afternoon, I told my students that the stock market was at a top, and that a loud sell signal was being given right outside the class door, in the exhibit hall.

up for the preceding seven months with no pullbacks. The richness of the offerings at the trade show was fantastic. I picked up ski hats, baseball hats, a scarf, a stack of T-shirts, and other goodies. But the main gift awaited me at the Nasdaq booth—the exchange was giving away free money (Figure 6.15).

Monday was a holiday, but on Tuesday I began to put out more shorts. My indicators had been flashing sell signals for a month, and now this offer of free money felt as if someone was ringing a bell. The uptrend had overshot any reasonable target, and this free money proved that the uptrend had gone crazy. I exited almost all my long trades and piled on shorts. I shorted stocks and stock index futures, and even

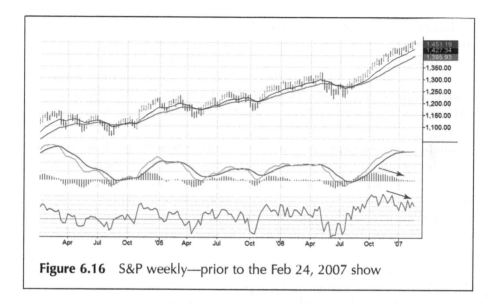

Figure 6.16   S&P weekly—prior to the Feb 24, 2007 show

bought some index puts. I did not have to wait very long. The market
went up for one day after the show and then it tanked. It was a great
time to be short (see Figures 6.16 and 6.17).

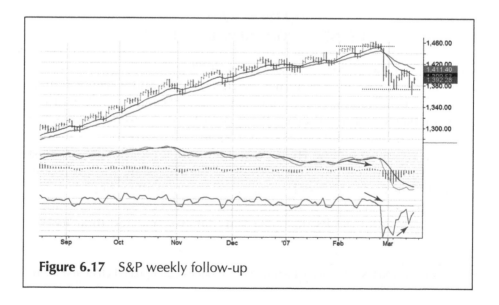

Figure 6.17   S&P weekly follow-up

Markets are like pumps that suck money out of the pockets of the uninformed majority and flow it into the accounts of a savvy minority. It is a minus-sum game in which winners receive less than what losers lose because the people who run the game siphon off huge sums of money as the cost of doing business—commissions and slippage, fees and expenses. This is why the market always has fewer winners than losers.

Amateurs profit only from long, sustained trends. Such long, one-way moves are an exception rather than the rule. When everyone becomes bullish and makes money, it is not normal. In the long run, the majority must lose, and only a minority can win. When the market rings a bell, it is telling you that an aberration has gone too far, the majority has become very big, and the mass of traders is ready for a nasty fall.

You can learn to see and hear these signals only if you are a serious student of the market and keep your mind open. When you start hearing, understanding, and acting on these signals, that will be a sign that you are no longer a beginner. When you begin acting upon these signals, you'll find yourself among the small minority of traders who are good at the market game.

TRADING WITH
THE NEW HIGH–NEW LOW INDEX

Whether you trade individual stocks or stock index futures, it pays to have an indicator that confirms market trends and warns of their upcoming reversals. When this indicator starts flashing signals that the stock market is about to turn, you should become especially alert to the technical signals in the stocks you hold.

I believe that the New High–New Low Index (NH-NL) is the best leading indicator of the stock market.[1] New Highs are the leaders in strength—they are the stocks that have reached their highest point for the past 52 weeks on any given day. New Lows are the leaders in weakness—the stocks that have on that day reached their lowest

---

[1]So important is NH-NL that every trading day we publish an updated chart and analysis on www.spiketrade.com.

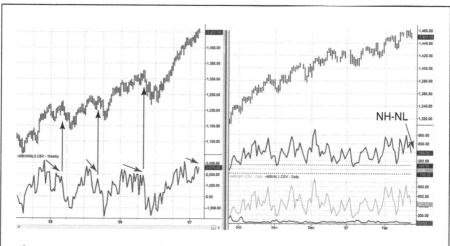

Figure 6.18 NH-NL, February 2007

Red line—new lows.
Green line—new highs.

On the left side of the chart, you can see the S&P 500 climb to a new bull market peak while the weekly NH-NL, immediately below, traced a bearish divergence (marked with a red arrow near the right edge of the chart). Similar previous divergences, marked with vertical lines, have identified important tops within the bull market. On the daily chart you can see a minor bearish divergence of the daily NH-NL. The main sell signal comes from the weekly chart.

point for the past 52 weeks. The interplay of new highs and new lows provides excellent information about the health or weakness of a trend.

NH-NL is easy to construct. Simply take the New Highs for the day, subtract the New Lows, and you'll have that day's NH-NL. Take the sum of the daily NH-NL for the past five days to find the weekly NH-NL.

When NH-NL is positive, it identifies bullish leadership. When it is negative, it indentifies bearish leadership. NH-NL confirms trends when it rallies or falls in gear with prices. Its divergences from price trends help identify tops and bottoms. If the market rallies to a new high and NH-NL rises to a new peak, it shows that bullish leadership is growing, and the uptrend is likely to continue. If the market rallies but NH-NL

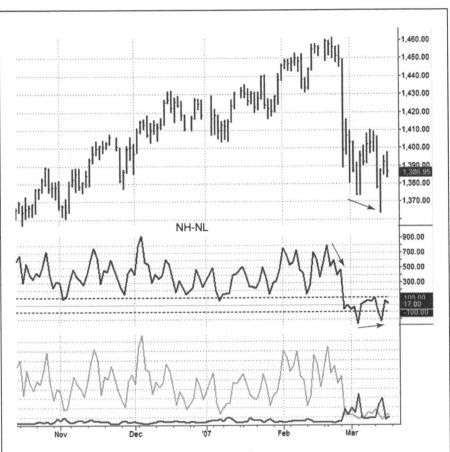

Figure 6.19 NH-NL, February 2007 follow-up

The stock market collapsed following a bearish divergence on NH-NL. It bounced, then sank to a lower low, but the daily NH-NL formed a more shallow low. This bullish divergence indicated that the downside leadership was failing and it was the time to cover shorts and buy again.

shrinks, it shows that the uptrend is in trouble. The same logic applies to the new lows in downtrends.

I like to view NH-NL on a split screen—the weekly chart on the left, the daily on the right. The weekly chart shows NH-NL as a line, while the daily chart has an additional pane showing New Highs as a green line and New Lows as a red line. Figure 6.18 shows how the chart looked during a peak in February 2007.

At the time NH-NL was flashing this sell signal, the market had rung a bell, as illustrated in Figure 6.19. When various indicators, based on different principles, give the same signals, they reinforce each other's messages.

While the timing of NH-NL signals is not as precise as MACD or the Force Index, it is very useful because it helps us recognize when it is a good time to accumulate stocks and when to unload them.

THE DECISION TREE FOR SELLING

A serious professional in any field, has a decision-making tree. It is rarely written down, as the pro usually keeps it in his head. In fact, it is probably somewhere even deeper—in his bones.

A decision-making tree is a set of rules that helps you decide what to do or not to do in any given situation. Professionals develop their decision-making trees in the course of their training, education, and practice. The best of us continue to develop our decision-making trees as long as we live. As my late great friend Lou Taylor joked in his late 70s—"If I become half a percent smarter each year, I'll be a genius by the time I die."

Few of us write down our decision-making trees. We tend to develop them in bits and pieces that gradually merge into a coherent whole. I grin remembering how, as a greenhorn trader, I decided to write down my decision-making tree during a five-hour flight from New York to Los Angeles. A month later I was still scribbling on a table-sized sheet of paper, crisscrossed with arrows and splattered with whiteout.

The only professionals who always carry printed decision-making trees are airline pilots. They are given manuals that show how to troubleshoot any problem on the plane. If a pilot thinks he smells smoke in the cockpit, he does not just wrinkle his nose and say "Geez, smoke. I wonder what I should do...." Instead of scratching and thinking, he opens his manual to the Smoke page and, with his co-pilot, goes through clearly defined "if–then" questions and answers, which lead to specific actions. An excellent recent book on developing a checklist is *The Checklist Manifesto* by Dr. Atul Gawande.

Still, even a printed decision-making tree, approved by the best airline, can never be complete. In his fascinating book *The Black Box*, Malcolm MacPherson serves up dozens of transcripts from the black boxes of crashed airliners. A trader can learn a great deal from watch-

A Decision-Making Tree

Since market conditions always change, all automatic systems eventually self-destruct, which is why an amateur with a mechanical system must lose money in the end. A pro who puts his system on autopilot continues to monitor it like a hawk. A professional system trader can afford to use a mechanical system precisely because he is capable of discretionary trading.

A trading system is an action plan for the market, but no plan can anticipate everything. A degree of judgment is always required, even with the best and most reliable plans. A system automates routine actions and allows you to exercise discretion when needed. And that's what you need in the markets—a system for finding trades, setting stops, establishing profit targets.

Adapted from *Come into My Trading Room* by Dr. Alexander Elder,
John Wiley & Sons, Inc., 2002

ing how some pilots fall apart under pressure while others rise up to the challenge. My favorite chapter is the recording of the black box of a plane whose tail engine had exploded, cutting all hydraulic lines. The onboard manual does not tell the pilot how to control a plane whose controls had been cut; and when he calls the plane manufacturer, they tell him that his plane cannot possibly be flying. The pilot hangs up and then figures out how to land by the seat of his pants. His discretionary, as opposed to systematic, flying saved him, his crew, and most of his passengers.

Still, 99 times out of a 100, it is useful to write down your decision-making tree. This is why we will discuss several points that must go into a decision tree for selling.

Before we focus on selling, just a brief reminder about the decision-making tree for buying. It must begin and end with money management. Your first question must be: *Does the 6% Rule allow me to trade?* Your last question before putting on a trade must be what size the 2% Rule allows you to trade. We discussed these rules earlier in this book, including the Iron Triangle section.

Buying well makes it easier to sell well. If you buy in accordance with your money management rules, you will not be stressed by carrying a size that is too large for your account.

To draft a decision tree for selling you need to consider several questions:

1. **Is this a short-term or a long-term trade?**
   If this is a short-term trade, you would need a nearby target in the vicinity of a channel or an envelope. If it is a long-term trade, you can set the profit target farther away, in the vicinity of major support or resistance. Trend traders tend to be long-term oriented and swing traders short-term oriented.

   Sohail Rabbani, a trader interviewed in *Entries & Exits*, compared the two types of traders to elephant hunters and rabbit hunters. One shoots rarely, at a big target, while the other shoots often at a small target. There are vast differences between the two hunters' equipment, as well as their entire hunting process. Many beginners go out into the bush with some random guns, sold to them by some fast-talking dealers. They have a vague idea of shooting something—maybe an elephant, maybe a rabbit—but they are most likely to shoot themselves in the foot.

   Have you set the target for your trade? Have you written down at what level you expect to take profits? Have you written down for how long, approximately, you expect to be in this trade? A short-term trader must keep especially close track of his trade grades and be quick to exit soon after his stock hits an A level, after traveling 30% of the channel on the daily chart. A longer-term trader needs to hold his position until the trade hits a much more remote profit target.

2. **Where will you place your stop?**
   In short-term trading, not only will you have a nearby profit target—you will also have a reasonably tight stop. With trend trading, the target is farther away, the estimated time to the target is measured in months if not years. Since an elephant may meander, hunting him requires much wider stops.

   As a general rule, stops should be tighter for short-term trades and more relaxed for long-term trades. Occasionally you may be lucky to find a stock that sits very quietly on rock-solid support. You may acquire a large long-term position with very low dollar risk. Still, the majority of long-term trades require more leeway. A long-term trader may well consider a fairly loose stop on his position, while shorter-term traders tend to use tighter stops on their trades.

Since the iron triangle limits your total risk per trade, the greater the distance to the stop, the fewer shares you may carry. As the risk per share goes up, the number of shares you buy must come down, keeping your total risk within your money management limits.

If you trade a small account, you pretty much have to go to the maximum 2% risk limit on most trades. A trader with a large account might limit his risk on short-term trades to 0.25% of trading capital, but go up to 1% on long-term trades. This means that even though his risk per share is greater on long-term trades, his position size can still be fairly large.

3. **Listen to different types of "engine noise" for short-term or long-term trades.**
   When a trade starts sputtering and jerking instead of moving towards the target, a discretionary trader might decide to hop off. He does not have to wait until the trend turns on him and hits his stop. He may well grab a small profit and move on. The type of noise that causes alarm is different for short-term and long-term traders.

   A short-term trader may watch the daily charts and indicators for any signs that his trade is becoming overbought and topping out. He would almost certainly run from a bearish divergence of daily MACD-Histogram, but he might also scramble after seeing a fairly minor sign, such as a bearish divergence of the Force index or even a simple downturn of daily MACD-Histogram. With his short-term outlook, any subtle sign of tiredness, the slightest engine noise may be a signal to hop off while there is still a good profit on the table.

   A long-term trader has to be more tolerant of minor noises. He should not jump in response to signals on daily charts. If he does, he is almost certain to lose his grip on a long-term trade. He needs to focus on the weekly charts and wait for much louder "engine noise" before getting out of his trade. He may look for signals on the weekly charts rather than on the dailies. It is not a good idea for a long-term position trader to keep too close an eye on the daily charts.

   An experienced trader can combine both approaches in a single campaign. He or she may use short-term trading skills by trading around a core position. You can maintain a core long-term position through thick and thin but keep trading shorter-term in the direction of that trade with a portion of your account.

Let's say you are trying to hold 1,000 shares of an $8 stock with a target in the low 20s. You may want to consider 500 shares of that position as a core hold. The rest may depend on the behavior of your stock. You may build up your position to 1,500 when the stock pulls back to a moving average, sell down to 500 on a rally above a channel. You may keep buying and selling while holding your long-term core position.

Whatever you do, keep a diary of your decisions and actions. Keeping good records will help you accelerate your learning, survive the inevitable hard times, and claw your way to profitability.

HOW TO SELL

You have bought a stock, and now it shows a profit. Now you need to decide when is the right time to sell your position and convert paper profits into real money. Should you sell right now, and take your money off the table? Should you let your trade ride and maybe make more money later? What if you let your trade ride but the stock reverses and your profits melt away?

Selling—the essential step of taking profits or cutting losses—must be done in a serious and businesslike manner. You need to know how to set profit targets for the stocks you buy. You need to know how to set protective stops. There is no guarantee that the stock you bought will go up, which is why you need to decide when to dump it; this decision must be made before you get into a trade. You need to know how to set protective stops.

After buying a stock, you need to bracket it with profit-taking and stop-loss orders. You have to be prepared to adjust both with the passage of time. You also need to decide whether to sell your entire position at once or take partial profits and let the rest of the position ride.

As you work through the questions in this section, please be sure to link every answer to your own experiences as a trader. Keep referring to your diary, which you should be keeping by now. Selling is the longest part of this *Study Guide*, with the largest number of questions. The topic is so important that you must make sure you earn a high score, taking and retaking this test if necessary.

Please go through all questions in this section and record your answers prior to turning to the Answers section.

Answer Sheet

Questions	Max. Pts. Available	Trial 1	Trial 2	Trial 3	Trial 4	Trial 5	Trial 6
34	1						
35	1						
36	1						
37	1						
38	1						
39	1						
40	1						
41	1						
42	1						
43	1						
44	1						
45	1						
46	1						
47	1						
48	1						
49	1						
50	1						
51	1						
52	1						
53	1						
54	1						
55	1						
56	1						
57	1						
58	1						
59	1						
60	1						

(continues on next page)

Answer Sheet, *continued*

Questions	Max. Pts. Available	Trial 1	Trial 2	Trial 3	Trial 4	Trial 5	Trial 6
61	1						
62	1						
63	1						
64	1						
65	1						
66	1						
67	1						
68	1						
69	1						
70	1						
71	1						
72	1						
73	1						
74	1						
75	1						
76	1						
77	1						
78	1						
79	1						
80	1						
81	1						
82	1						
83	1						
84	1						
85	1						
86	1						
Total points	53						

Question 34—A Plan for Selling
Find the incorrect statement about a written plan for selling:
1. It guarantees success.
2. It reduces stress.
3. It allows you to separate analysis from trading.
4. It makes you less prone to react to the market's zigzags.

Question 35—The Three Types of Selling
The three logical types of selling do not include which of the following?
1. Selling at a profit target above the market
2. Selling on a stop below the market
3. Selling in response to the "engine noise" of changing market conditions
4. Selling after feeling impatient about the trade

Question 36—Planning to Sell
Prior to buying a stock, serious traders ask themselves all of the following questions except:
1. How high is the stock likely to rise—what is the profit target?
2. How low does the stock have to fall to activate a protective stop?
3. What is the stock's reward-to-risk ratio?
4. Should I move my target farther away after the stock reaches it?

Question 37—Targets for Selling
Which of the following tools can help set targets for selling?
   A. Moving averages
   B. Envelopes or channels
   C. Support and resistance zones
   D. Other methods
1. A
2. A and B
3. A, B, and C
4. All of the above

Question 38—A Stock Below Its Moving Average

Find two correct statements about a stock that trades below its moving average:

    A. The stock is trading below value.
    B. It is definitely headed lower.
    C. It is definitely headed higher.
    D. If the indicators are pointing higher, the first target is the moving average.

1. A and D
2. B and D
3. A and C
4. A and B

Question 39—Moving Averages as Selling Targets

Find the incorrect statement about using moving averages as targets:

1. Selling at a moving average works especially well on weekly charts.
2. Prices tend to oscillate above and below their moving averages.
3. It is highly desirable that the distance to the target be longer than the distance to the stop.
4. When you sell at a target, the sell grade is unimportant.

Question 40—Regrets About Selling

A trader feels intense regret after he sells at an EMA but prices continue to rise. Which of the following statements is correct?

1. Regret is good because it motivates you not to exit the next trade too soon.
2. A strong feeling of regret about exiting early can lead to overstaying the next trade.
3. If your analysis is good, you should know not to sell early.
4. Leaving money on the table is a sign of a poor trader.

Question 41—EMA as a Profit Target

What is the best time to use an EMA as a target for a rally?

1. When prices rally from bear market lows
2. In the midst of an ongoing uptrend
3. When prices are near their historic highs
4. All of the above

Question 42—Channels as Price Targets

Find the correct statement about using channels as price targets:

1. A powerful upmove on the weekly charts is the best time to target channels on the dailies.
2. Uptrends rarely show an orderly pattern of tops and bottoms.
3. The best time to go long in an uptrend is when prices hit the upper channel.
4. It does not pay to sell at a channel because prices may rally higher.

Question 43—Measuring Performance Using Channels

Measuring the percentage of a channel height captured in a trade can help a swing trader:

    A. Focus on points rather than dollars.

    B. Provide a yardstick for measuring performance.

    C. Set a realistic profit target.

1. A
2. A and B
3. All of the above

Question 44—Selling Targets

Please find statements that match among the following two pairs of statements:

    A. The first target for selling into a rally off the lows

    B. The first target for selling in an ongoing uptrend

1. At or below value, as defined by moving averages
2. Near the overvalued zone, as defined by the upper channel line

Question 45—Reaching for More

Always reaching out for a greater profit makes a trader:

    A. More relaxed

    B. More stressed

    C. More successful

    D. More hyperactive

1. A and B
2. A and C
3. B and D
4. B and C

Question 46—The Top of a Rally

Find the correct statement about the top tick of a rally:

1. Forecasting it will provide a reasonable target for selling.
2. It can be forecast with a good degree of consistency.
3. Trying to sell at the top tick tends to be a very expensive undertaking.
4. If one can sell consistently at the absolute top, one can also sell short there.

Question 47—Prices above the Upper Channel Line

Prices have rallied above the upper channel line; find the correct statement among the following:

1. A trader must immediately take profits.
2. When prices close above the upper channel line for two days in a row, a trader must take profits.
3. When prices close above the upper channel line, it means the rally will continue.
4. When prices close above the upper channel line but then fail to reach a new high, the trader should consider selling that day.

Question 48—Profit Targets

Find the correct statement about setting profit targets:

1. Let the trade run as far as it will without worrying about targets.
2. There is a perfect profit target for any market.
3. The longer your time horizon, the farther away the profit target.
4. A moving average provides the best profit target for any trade.

Question 49—Support and Resistance Zones

Support and resistance zones provide attractive price targets for long-term trades for all of the following reasons, except:

1. Congestion zones show where the masses of market participants are prepared to buy or sell.
2. A trading range represents a general consensus of value among huge masses of traders.
3. The duration of trading ranges tends to be longer than that of price trends.
4. A trend always stops at the edge of a trading range.

Question 50—A Protective Stop

Using a protective stop makes sense for all of the following reasons, except:

1. It is a reality check, reminding you that prices can move against you.
2. It works against the ownership effect, when people fall in love with their stocks.
3. It reduces the emotional stress of making decisions in open trades.
4. It puts an absolute limit on the amount of dollars you can lose in any given trade.

Question 51—Breaking through Resistance

If a stock rises to its resistance level, pauses, and then rallies and closes above that level, it gives us a signal to:

    A. Go long immediately.

    B. Get ready to sell short if the stock sinks back into its resistance zone.

    C. Sell short immediately.

    D. Get ready to buy if the stock declines towards its resistance zone.

1. A or D
2. A or B
3. B or C
4. C or D

Question 52—A Trade without a Stop

A trade without a stop is:

1. Permitted only for experienced traders
2. A gamble
3. A way to be more flexible
4. A realistic approach to trading

Question 53—Changing Stops

Which of the following are allowed during a trade?

    A. Raising stops on longs

    B. Raising stops on shorts

    C. Lowering stops on shorts

    D. Lowering stops on longs

1. A and B
2. B and C
3. A and C
4. C and D

Question 54—Re-entering a Trade

Buying a stock, getting stopped out, and then re-entering the trade by buying that stock back is:

1. A common tactic among professionals
2. Throwing good money after bad
3. A sign of stubbornness
4. A waste of time and money

Question 55—Deciding Where to Set a Stop

The single most important question in setting a stop is:

1. What is the volatility of the market you are trading?
2. How much money are you prepared to risk?
3. What is your profit target?
4. How many shares are you planning to buy?

Question 56—The Impact of the Last Trade

What impact should the size of your latest profit or loss have on your plans for the next trade?

1. Trade a bigger size after a profitable trade.
2. Trade a smaller size after an unprofitable trade.
3. Trade a bigger size after an unprofitable trade.
4. None of the above

Question 57—"The Iron Triangle"

Please match the components of "The Iron Triangle" of risk control with their descriptions:

    A. Money management
    B. Stop placement
    C. Position sizing

1. Set it on the basis of chart analysis.
2. Decide how much money you will risk in this trade.
3. Divide one of the three factors by another.

Question 58—A Limit Order

A limit order is preferable to a market order for all of the following reasons except:

1. It prevents slippage.
2. It guarantees execution.
3. It works best for entering trades.
4. It is useful for taking profits at target levels.

Question 59—Soft Stops

Which of the following statements about soft stops is correct?

1. They are useful for system traders.
2. They offer a good way to get started in the markets.
3. They help avoid whipsaws.
4. They are easier to set than hard stops.

Question 60—A Stop One Tick below the Latest Low

Putting a protective stop on a long position one tick below the latest low is problematic for all of the following reasons, except:

1. Even a small sell order thrown at the market near the lows can briefly push it below the latest low.
2. A bullish pattern occurs when a market takes out its previous low by a small margin and reverses.
3. Professionals like to fade (trade against) breakouts.
4. Once the low is taken out, prices are likely to decline much lower.

Question 61—A Stop at the Level of the Previous Low

Placing a stop exactly at the level of the previous low can be good for all of the following reasons, except:

1. A downtrend often slows down as it approaches the level of the previous low.
2. If the stock declines to its previous low, it is likely to go even lower.
3. Stocks often accelerate immediately after taking the previous low.
4. Slippage tends to be higher when the stop is at the level of the previous low rather than one tick below that low.

Question 62—A Stop That Is "Tighter by a Day"

Find the correct statement about a stop that is "tighter by a day" ("Nic's Stop"):

1. Examine the bars that bracket a recent low and place your stop a little below the lower of those two bars.
2. Using a tight stop is not suitable for short-term trading.
3. This method is especially useful for long-term position trades.
4. A tight stop like this one eliminates slippage.

Question 63—Trade Duration

The outcome of a trade depends in part on the duration of that trade. Find the incorrect statement about the impact of trade duration:

1. Longer-term trades give you the luxury of time to think and make decisions.
2. If a day-trader stops to think, he loses.
3. The more time a stock has, the farther it can move.
4. Long-term position trades provide the best learning experience.

Question 64—Wider Stops

Find the correct statement about using wider stops:

1. A major uptrend is less volatile than a minor one.
2. The wider the stop, the greater the risk of a whipsaw.
3. A stop belongs outside of the zone of the normal chop of prices.
4. The wider the stop, the larger position you can carry.

Question 65—Moving Stops

Which of the following statements about moving stops is incorrect?

1. You may move stops only in the direction of the trade but never against it.
2. When you switch to a trailing stop after the prices reach their target you increase your risk.
3. When prices hang just above your stop, it makes sense to lower it to reduce the risk of a whipsaw.
4. When prices move in your favor, it makes sense to raise your stop to protect a part of your paper profit.

Question 66—The SafeZone Stop

Find the correct statement about the SafeZone stop:

1. It acts as a filter that suppresses the signal of the trend.
2. Noise is any part of today's range that protrudes outside of the previous day's range.
3. SafeZone tracks Average Upside Penetration in uptrends and Average Downside Penetration in downtrends.
4. SafeZone works best during trends and worst during trading ranges.

Question 67—Trading with the SafeZone

Which of the following statements about SafeZone stops is incorrect?

1. SafeZone is a mechanical trading system.
2. You have to establish the lookback period for the SafeZone.
3. You need to choose the coefficient by which to multiply the normal noise to obtain the SafeZone stop.
4. Usually, a coefficient between two and three provides a margin of safety.

Question 68—The Volatility-Drop Method

Which of the following statements about the Volatility-Drop method is incorrect?

1. A Volatility-Drop ensures getting greater profit from every trade.
2. This methods allows a trader to start out with a modest target, but reach out for more while in the trade.
3. Using a Volatility-Drop stop involves risking some of the paper profit.
4. Using this method helps automate profit-taking decisions.

Question 69—"Engine Noise" in the Markets

Selling "engine noise" refers to selling when:

1. Your target is reached.
2. Your stop is hit.
3. You want to take partial profits.
4. You do not like how the market is acting.

Question 70—Selling "Engine Noise"

Which statement about selling "engine noise" is incorrect?

1. A system trader may not sell "engine noise."
2. A discretionary trader may exit the market sooner or later than planned.
3. Selling "engine noise" is especially well suited for beginning traders.
4. Selling "engine noise" carries a risk of cutting profits.

Question 71—New High–New Low Index

Find the incorrect statement about the New High–New Low Index:

1. NH-NL confirms uptrends by reaching new highs; it confirms downtrends by falling to new lows.
2. The signals of NH-NL are symmetrical at tops and bottoms.
3. Bearish divergences of NH-NL warn of impending market tops.
4. Downspikes of NH-NL often identify important market bottoms.

Question 72—Not Liking Market's Action

You are holding a long position but do not like the toppy signals of indicators. Which statement about your choice is incorrect?

1. If you are a system trader, you must hold your position as planned.
2. If you are a discretionary trader, you may sell your position.
3. If you are a system trader, you may switch to a different system that allows an earlier exit.
4. If you are a discretionary trader, you may take partial profits but retain the core position.

Question 73—Earnings Reports

Which statement about the impact of earnings reports is incorrect?

1. Prices are largely driven by the anticipation of future earnings.
2. An earnings report never changes a long-term stock trend.
3. Earnings reports rarely come as a surprise to professional watchers.
4. Insider trading is usually linked to the way a company is managed.

Question 74—The Market "Rings a Bell"

The market "rings a bell" when:

1. It makes a multiyear high.
2. It falls to a multiyear low.
3. An event occurs far outside the norm for this market.
4. The market flashes a signal anyone can recognize.

Question 75—Trading with the New High–New Low Index

Which statement about the New High–New Low Index (NH-NL) is incorrect?

1. When NH-NL is above zero it shows that bulls are stronger than bears.
2. New Highs are the leaders in weakness and New Lows are the leaders in strength.
3. Bearish divergences are commonly seen near the ends of bull markets.
4. A severe downspike of weekly NH-NL usually signals a market bottom.

Question 76—A Decision-Making Tree vs. a Trading System

The key difference between a decision-making tree and a trading system is that only one of them includes:

1. The rules for entering a trade
2. The rules for exiting a trade
3. The permission to bend your exit rules
4. The parameters for trade sizing

Question 77—A Decision-Making Tree

Which of the following questions does not belong in a decision-making tree:

1. Is this a short-term or a long-term trade?
2. Where will you place your stop?
3. What kind of "engine noise" will you listen to while in a trade?
4. What kind of record-keeping will you perform for a trade?

Question 78—Value Buying and Selling Targets

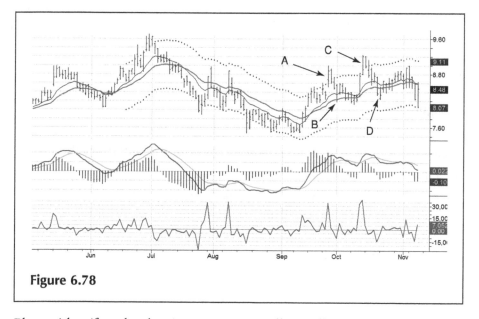

Figure 6.78

Please identify value buying zones as well as selling targets among the points on this chart marked by letters:

1. Value buying zones
2. Selling targets in overvalued zones

Question 79—Support, Resistance, and Targets

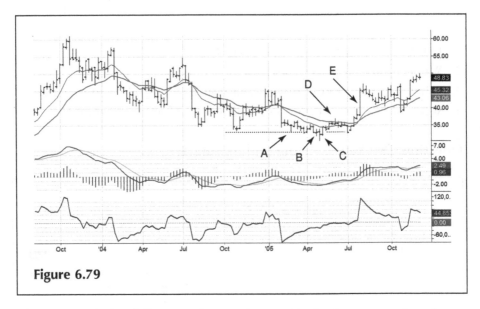

Figure 6.79

Please match the following descriptions with the letters on the chart:

1. Line of support broken
2. Prices close above support, giving a signal to buy
3. Support established
4. Second selling target at the upper channel line
5. First selling target at the EMA

Question 80—Multiple Targets

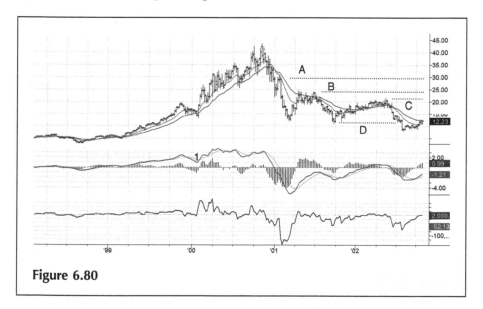

Figure 6.80

Please match the following descriptions with the letters on this monthly chart:

1. The minimal price target
2. Support
3. The bull market target

Question 81—Holding, Adding, or Profit-Taking

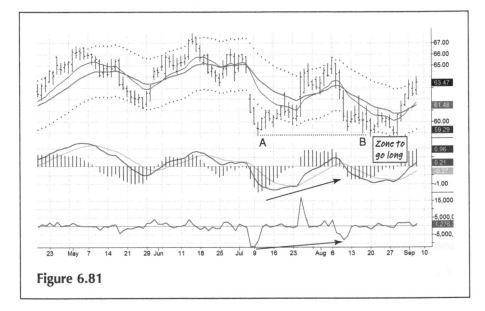

Figure 6.81

At point A the stock declined to 58.78. At point B it fell to 58.71 but recoiled from its new low. This false downside breakout was accompanied by bullish divergences in several indicators. If a trader went long with a target near the upper channel line, which of the following actions are legitimate at the right edge of this chart?

    A. Sell and take profits.

    B. Sell half, hold half.

    C. Continue to hold, tighten the stop.

    D. Add to the winning position.

1. A
2. A or B
3. A, B, or C
4. All of the above

Question 82—Handling a Profitable Trade

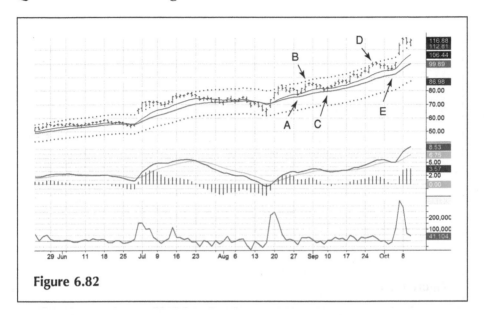

Figure 6.82

A trader recognizes an uptrend and starts buying the stock near value, selling near the upper channel line. He goes long at point A and sells at B, long at point C and sells at D, long again at point E. When prices gap above the upper channel line he decides to hold for a greater gain. What is the wise course of action at the right edge of this chart?

1. Sell and take profits.
2. Sell half the position.
3. Hold the position.
4. Add to the position.

Question 83—Placing a Stop

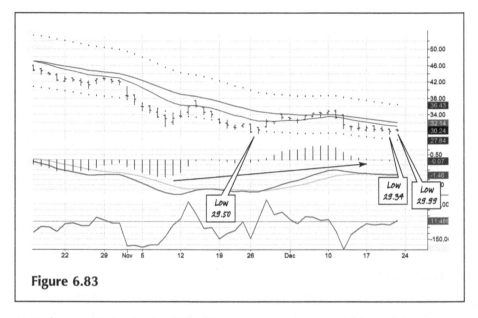

Figure 6.83

A trader recognizes a bullish divergence accompanied by a false down-side breakout. He decides to go long, but needs to place a stop. At which of the following levels would he be advised to place it?

1. 29.49
2. 29.33
3. 29.34
4. 29.98
5. 28.99

Question 84—The Impulse System

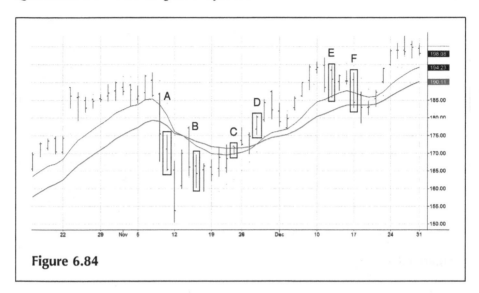

Figure 6.84

The Impulse system tracks both the inertia and the power of market moves. Some software packages allow traders to color price bars in accordance with the Impulse reading. Even on a black-and-white chart, a trader can tell what color any of the bars should be in accordance with the Impulse rules. Please match the following comments on the Impulse system with the letter bars on the chart:

1. Impulse Green—buy or stand aside; shorting not permitted
2. Impulse Red—sell short or stand aside; buying not permitted
3. Impulse Blue—no position is prohibited

Question 85—The Signals of NH-NL

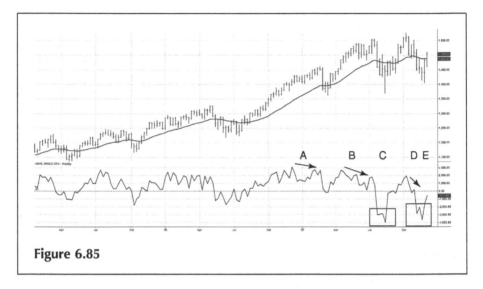

Figure 6.85

The weekly chart of New High–New Low Index (NH-NL) can help traders anticipate important turns in the stock market. Please match the following comments on NH-NL with the letters on the chart:

1. A spike identifies an unsustainable extreme and calls for a reversal.
2. A divergence identifies the weakness of the dominant crowd and calls for a reversal.

Question 86—The Decision at the Right Edge of the Chart

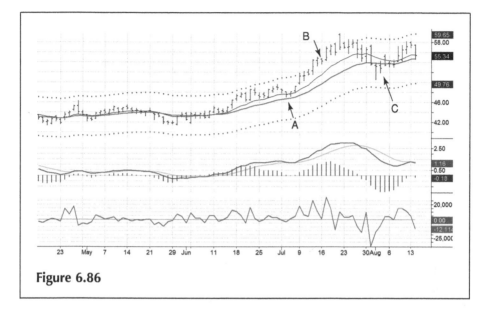

Figure 6.86

A trader recognizes an uptrend and goes long at point A. He sells at point B, after prices blow out of their channel but then fail to make a new high. He buys again at point C, after prices decline below value and stop making new lows. What would be the reasonable course of action at the right edge of this chart?

1. Continue to hold.
2. Add to long position.
3. Sell.

Answers to Questions

Part Two: How to Sell

Question 34—A Plan for Selling

Answer 1 Selection "It guarantees success" is incorrect.

Putting a plan on paper has a powerful psychological effect on most people, making them feel less dependent on the whims of the market. Writing down a plan and executing it from a sheet of paper helps you reduce tension by separating the jobs of analysis and trading. Still, nothing guarantees success in the financial markets.

Question 35—The Three Types of Selling

Answer 4 Selection "Selling after feeling impatient about the trade" is incorrect.

Every trading plan should include a profit target and a stop. Furthermore, an experienced discretionary trader may exit a trade in response to "engine noise"—a perception that the market conditions have changed. On the other hand, selling in response to feeling impatient is amateurish.

Question 36—Planning to Sell

Answer 4 Selection "Should I move my target farther away after the stock reaches it" is incorrect.

Buying a stock is akin to applying for a job—you want to know your responsibilities and rewards, and decide whether the pay is worth the work. The time to think about moving a target will come later in a trade, and even then only for experienced traders.

Question 37—Targets for Selling

Answer 4 All of the above

You can use a great variety of methods for setting profit targets. While the range of choices is virtually limitless, two factors are most important. First, you must understand the logic of your target-setting process, and avoid impulsive behavior. Second, you must keep records to help evaluate the quality of any method.

Question 38—A Stock Below Its Moving Average

Answer 1 **A** and **D**

A moving average represents an average consensus of value. It indicates the level of value in the current market, and its slope shows whether that value is increasing or declining. Nothing is definite in the stock market (except for commissions, slippage, and the fact that an unprepared trader will suffer losses). When the indicators are bullish and price is below the EMA, that EMA becomes the first target for a rally.

Question 39—Moving Averages as Selling Targets

Answer 4 Selection "When you sell at a target, the sell grade is unimportant" is incorrect.

Time and again, the weekly charts trump the dailies. As a rule, you want to put on trades with attractive reward-to-risk ratios. The quality of entry and exit must be graded for every trade, whatever the reason for the exit.

Question 40—Regrets About Selling

Answer 2 A strong feeling of regret about exiting early can lead to overstaying the next trade.

Regret is a corrosive force in trading. If you kick yourself today for leaving some money on the table, you will reach out too far tomorrow and probably overstay your next trade. A mature trader creates a plan and follows it. He grades his performance and strives to improve it. He does not allow the outcome of a trade he made today to impact his behavior in a new trade tomorrow. Leaving some money on the table is an inevitable part of the game; only a paper-trader or a liar catches every bottom and sells at every top.

Question 41—EMA as a Profit Target

Answer 1 When prices rally from bear market lows

The time to use an EMA as a price target is when prices are below that EMA. This is unlikely to happen in an uptrend or near the highs. When prices rally from bear market lows, an EMA serves as a reasonable target for the first rally.

Question 42—Channels as Price Targets

Answer 1 A powerful upmove on the weekly charts is the best time to target channels on the dailies.

An orderly pattern of rallies and declines is fairly typical during major uptrends. This is why it makes sense to trade by going long whenever prices drop to or below value and take profits whenever they rise to or above an overvalued zone, as identified by the upper channel line. It pays to sell when and where you plan to sell. You may plan to sell a short-term trade at the channel line or hold a smaller position for a longer, trend-following trade. Whatever your plan, do not change it in the middle of the game!

Question 43—Measuring Performance Using Channels

Answer 3 All of the above

Focusing on money gained or lost in any given trade tends to distract traders. It is important to focus on the quality of trading decisions; paying too much attention to money leads one towards thinking about what that money will buy, and then the trader loses his focus. The goal is to become the best trader you can be—the money will follow.

Question 44—Selling Targets

Answer 1. A
        2. B

The first rally from bear market lows tends to run into great resistance; it makes sense to set a modest profit target near the EMA. Prices seldom fall to the lower channel line in an ongoing uptrend; it makes sense to buy near the EMA and be prepared to take profits near the upper channel line.

Question 45—Reaching for More

Answer 3 More stressed and more hyperactive

One of the great psychological problems in trading is that the markets offer endless temptations. With thousands of dollars flashing on every screen, many traders lose self-control and reach for more than they can catch, before losing balance and suffering losses. The power word in trading, as in life, is "enough." Using a trading channel to set profit targets can help establish realistic goals for trades.

Question 46—The Top of a Rally

Answer 3 Trying to sell at the top tick tends to be a very expensive undertaking.

The top tick of a rally is the most expensive tick in the market—fortunes have been lost hunting for it. Here, as with everything else in trading, it is important to avoid reaching for extremes. It is much safer and more practical to try and take a chunk out of the middle of a price move. The less you stress yourself, the better results you're likely to get.

Question 47—Prices above the Upper Channel Line

Answer 4 When prices close above the upper channel line but then fail to reach a new high, the trader should consider selling that day.

Envelopes or channels provide good targets for short-term trades. Still, occasionally a rally rockets higher, tempting us to hold on for a bit longer than initially planned. A very powerful rally may cause a stock to "walk its channel line," rising along that line for days and sometimes weeks. Still, a short-term swing trader would be well advised to sell when that rally stumbles and fails to reach a new high after having risen above the upper channel line.

Question 48—Profit Targets

Answer 3 The longer your time horizon, the farther away the profit target.

A market can move much farther in the long run than in the short run—a short-term swing trade needs a close-by target, while a long-term trend trade needs a target farther away. There is no universal method that will set a price target for every trade.

Question 49—Support and Resistance Zones

Answer 4 Selection "A trend always stops at the edge of a trading range" is incorrect.

A price range represents a huge financial and emotional commitment by masses of buyers and sellers. The composition and the attitude of the market crowd keep shifting, which is why the edges of congestion zones tend to be ragged rather than straight.

Question 50—A Protective Stop

Answer 4 Selection "It puts an absolute limit on the amount of dollars you can lose in any given trade" is incorrect.

Prior to entering a trade you need to examine the chart and decide where you want to get out if that trade starts going against you. Your decision is likely to be much more objective if you make it before entering a trade. Every trade deserves a protective stop—but a stock may gap across that level. A stop is not a perfect defense but it is our best defense against damaging losses.

Question 51—Breaking through Resistance

Answer 2 A or **B**

Prices breaking out above resistance may either signal the beginning of a new uptrend or the first step in a fakeout move. If the breakout is for real, there is no time to waste. It does not pay to wait for a pull-back—a rocket that has left its launching pad has no business sinking back to it. If, on the other hand, your long-term studies point to a top and you think this is a false breakout, it makes sense to wait for a con-firmation from prices sinking back into the range. A breakout alone does not provide a clear signal—it pays to view it within the frame-work of your longer-term studies.

Question 52—A Trade without a Stop

Answer 2 A gamble

A stop is every trader's link with reality. There are many types of stops and many methods of using them, but even the most experi-enced professional trader knows at what level he will exit a trade that is going against him.

Question 53—Changing Stops

Answer 3 **A** and **C**

You may move a stop only in the direction of a trade—up for longs or down for shorts. Moving a stop in the opposite direction to give a trade gone bad "more room to work out" is a loser's game. You created your plan before you entered the trade, when you were more objective than during the trade. Once you are in a trade, you are allowed to reduce your risk level but never to increase it.

Question 54—Re-entering a Trade

Answer 1 A common tactic among professionals

Beginners usually take a single stab at a stock and move on to the next trade after a loss. A professional knows that a good stock is hard to find. He or she uses a tight stop and is not afraid to make several stabs at a stock before catching an important trend.

Question 55—Deciding Where to Set a Stop

Answer 2 How much money are you prepared to risk?

Setting stops is an integral part of risk control and money management. Prior to entering a trade you must decide how much money you are trying to make and how much you are prepared to risk in reaching your goal. Gauging possible profits and current volatility is very important but all questions ultimately boil down to defining what risk you'll be ready to accept.

Question 56—The Impact of the Last Trade

Answer 4 None of the above

Allowing the results of your latest trade to influence your plans for the next is amateurish behavior. There is a fair degree of randomness in the market, making the outcome of any single trade difficult to predict. A professional puts his trust not in any individual trade but in his or her ongoing performance over a period of time. The pros do not let something as relatively minor as the outcome of the latest trade make them deviate from their thought-out plans.

Question 57—"The Iron Triangle"

Answer 1. **B**
     2. **A**
     3. **C**

Stops are set on the basis of chart analysis. Your money management rules will give you the maximum amount of dollars you may risk in this trade, although you may want to risk less. Dividing this number by the dollar risk per share gives you the size of the trade.

Question 58—A Limit Order

Answer 2 Selection "It guarantees execution" is incorrect.

Only a market order guarantees an execution. A limit order, on the other hand, demands a fill at a specific price or better—or no execution at all. It helps you avoid slippage, one of the major but seldom recognized causes of poor performance among traders. The only time not to quibble about slippage is when you are trying to get out of a trade that is going against you. That's why it pays to use market orders for stops.

Question 59—Soft Stops

Answer 3 They help avoid whipsaws.

A hard stop goes into the market as a specific order. A soft stop is the number you keep in your head. System traders must use hard stops, as do all beginning traders. Experienced discretionary traders may use soft stops in order to reduce whipsaws. Both hard and soft stops take the same amount of work and belong on the same level—their placement is identical, only the execution is different.

Question 60—A Stop One Tick below the Latest Low

Answer 4 Selection "Once the low is taken out, prices are likely to decline much lower" is incorrect.

The trouble with putting a stop a penny below the latest low is that markets very often trace out double bottoms, with the second bottom slightly lower than the first. The level immediately below the latest low is where amateurs cut and run and where professionals tend to buy. Once in a while prices take out the previous low and go into a waterfall decline—but that is an exception rather than a rule. It is essential to use stops, but there are much better ways to place them than one tick below the latest low.

Question 61—A Stop at the Level of the Previous Low

Answer 4 Selection "Slippage tends to be higher when the stop is at the level of the previous low rather than one tick below that low" is incorrect.

If you put a stop at the exact level of the previous low and that stop gets hit, your slippage is likely to be lower than in the case of a stop a tick below that low. Stocks often accelerate after taking out their previous low, causing greater slippage on stops below. Your risk of a whipsaw increases only very slightly—if the stock falls to that level, it is virtually certain to go a tick lower.

Question 62—A Stop That Is "Tighter by a Day"

Answer 1 Examine the bars that bracket a recent low and place your stop a little below the lower of those two bars.

Placing a stop inside the recent trading range is designed for short-term swing trading. It tells the market to "put up or shut up." Still, no stop order can ever completely eliminate slippage.

Question 63—Trade Duration

Answer 4 Selection "Long-term position trades provide the best learning experience" is incorrect.

Time is a hugely important factor in trading. The more time a market has, the farther it can move, increasing both the profit opportunities and the risk of an adverse move. A trader with a longer-term orientation can stop to think, unlike a day-trader who must react almost automatically. The best way to learn to trade is by making many small trades; the slower pace of long-term trading does not provide as good a learning experience as shorter-term swing trading.

Question 64—Wider Stops

Answer 3 A stop belongs outside of the zone of the normal chop of prices.

Prices meander, and the more time they have, the wider their swing. The tighter the stop, the greater the risk of a whipsaw. The whole point of using wider stops is to put them outside the zone of the normal chop of prices. The downside of using a wider stop is that by accepting greater risk per share you reduce the size of the position you may carry.

Question 65—Moving Stops

Answer 3 Selection "When prices hang just above your stop, it makes sense to lower it to reduce the risk of a whipsaw" is incorrect.

No matter how strong the temptation to make your stop wider, you must stick with your original decision. If prices move your way, you may adjust your stop to protect a part of your paper profit. If prices reach your target but you want to stay in the trade, you may switch to a trailing stop; reaching for a greater profit means accepting the risk of giving back some of the existing profit if the trend reverses on you.

Question 66—The SafeZone Stop

Answer 4 SafeZone works best during trends and worst during trading ranges.

The purpose of SafeZone is to suppress noise so that the signal of the trend can come through. The noise is that part of the day's range which protrudes outside of yesterday's range but only in the direction opposite to the trend. For example, when the trend is up, upside penetrations are normal, while downside penetrations are considered noise. When the trend is down, downside penetrations are normal while upside penetrations are considered noise. SafeZone tracks Average Downside Penetrations during uptrends and Average Upside Penetrations in downtrends and sets up stops outside of the noise level. Like many other methods, it works best during trends but leads to whipsaws during trading ranges.

Question 67—Trading with the SafeZone

Answer 1 Selection "SafeZone is a mechanical trading system" is incorrect.

To use SafeZone one must establish its lookback period and the coefficient by which to multiply the normal noise to obtain the SafeZone stop. Setting that coefficient must be done individually for every market—hardly a mechanical approach to trading.

Question 68—The Volatility-Drop Method

Answer 1 Selection "A Volatility-Drop ensures getting greater profit from every trade" is incorrect.

Kerry Lovvorn, the author of this method, says "I do not think of using a trailing stop until my target is hit. At that time the trade has fulfilled its duty, but the market may be moving in a way that seems to have potential for an additional reward." The Volatility-Drop method puts some of the existing profit at risk to squeeze more money out of the trade, but it does not guarantee that every trade will become more profitable as a result.

Question 69—"Engine Noise" in the Markets

Answer 4 You do not like how the market is acting.

A discretionary trader does not have to hold every trade to its planned target. Perhaps the market wants to give you less than you initially expected. If you see signals of the trend weakening, it could be a wise decision to sell sooner than originally planned.

Question 70—Selling "Engine Noise"

Answer 3 Selection "Selling 'engine noise' is especially well suited for beginning traders" is incorrect.

While selling at profit targets or using protective stops works for traders at all levels, selling in response to "engine noise" requires a much greater level of experience. There is a very real risk that a trader, especially an inexperienced one, will sell too soon out of boredom or anxiety.

Question 71—New High–New Low Index

Answer 2 Selection "The signals of NH-NL are symmetrical at tops and bottoms" is incorrect.

NH-NL may be the best leading indicator of the stock market, but it behaves differently at tops and bottoms. The emotions of the market crowds are different in those areas. Tops are formed by greed, which tends to last a lot longer than fear, the dominant emotion at market bottoms. This is why the best signals of the tops are longer-lasting divergences, while the best signals of the bottoms are brief and violent downspikes.

Question 72—Not Liking Market's Action

Answer 3 Selection "If you are a system trader, you may switch to a different system that allows an earlier exit" is incorrect.

A system must be followed. Deciding to change to a different system in the middle of a trade means that you are no longer a system trader. Exiting a trade or reducing its size in response to "engine noise" is the privilege and the responsibility of a discretionary trader. A system trader may anticipate some of the "noises" and incorporate them into his system—but not change that system while in an open trade.

Question 73—Earnings Reports

Answer 2 Selection "An earnings report never changes a long-term stock trend" is incorrect.

When we buy a stock, we are paying for future earnings and dividends. Insiders have the best knowledge of those factors, and many of them profit from it. Stocks seldom jump on earnings reports because smart bulls have already bought or clever bears have already sold. Still, the stock of an honestly run company can change its trend following a surprising earnings report.

Question 74—The Market "Rings a Bell"

Answer 3 An event occurs far outside the norm for this market.

You hear the market bell when you recognize an event so far outside the norm that it may seem as if the laws of the market have been cancelled. In fact, the laws of the market cannot go away, any more than the law of gravity can. An extraordinary event is a sign of a bubble ready to burst. This behavior is very clear only in retrospect, but during the bubble it seems perfectly normal; only a cool and objective trader can hear this bell.

Question 75—Trading with the New High–New Low Index

Answer 2 Selection "New Highs are the leaders in weakness and New Lows are the leaders in strength" is incorrect.

New Highs are the leaders in strength—they are the stocks that have reached their highest point for the past 52 weeks on any given day. New Lows are the leaders in weakness—the stocks that have reached their lowest point for the past 52 weeks on that day. Tops and bottoms in the stock market tend to be asymmetrical. Tops are formed more slowly and often show bearish divergences of NH-NL. Bottoms are formed faster and often marked by panicky downspikes of NH-NL, as losers dump their shares on the market, creating an opportunity for savvy bulls.

Question 76—A Decision-Making Tree vs. a Trading System

Answer 3 The permission to bend your exit rules.

A good trading system is totally objective—if you give it to two different traders, both should come up with the same entries, exits, and trade sizes. The decision-making tree of a discretionary trader also addresses entries, exits, and trade sizing, but it permits some flexibility in applying those rules.

Question 77—A Decision-Making Tree

Answer 4 Selection "What kind of record-keeping will you perform for a trade?" is incorrect.

Good record-keeping is extremely important—it is the foundation of successful trading. The records of a serious trader must address the issues of record-keeping, choice of software, and psychology. Decision-making trees are built on this foundation but deal with specific trading issues, such as entries, exits, and position sizing.

Question 78—Value Buying and Selling Targets

Answer 1. **B** and **D**
    2. **A** and **C**

In a steady uptrend, it pays to go long near value, as defined by moving averages, and take profits in the overvalued zone, above the upper channel line. Note that markets have quite a bit of noise, and the best signals are clearly visible only in retrospect. For example, after buying at point D, prices never reached the upper channel line and eventually slid lower. People who seek perfection feel overwhelmed by such turns, while mature traders protect themselves with good money management and charge ahead.

Question 79—Support, Resistance, and Targets

Answer 1. **B**
    2. **C**
    3. **A**
    4. **E**
    5. **D**

A false downside breakout, accompanied by a bullish divergence is one of the strongest signals in technical analysis. Once prices break below an important support line, you need to watch very closely what happens next: Will the decline accelerate or will the break fizzle out? When a price bar closes above the previously broken line of support it gives a powerful buy signal. Here this signal was reinforced by a bullish divergence of MACD-Histogram. Notice the pullback to support between points D and E, which provided an excellent opportunity to hop aboard the long trade. You cannot count on such pullbacks happening very often; they are an exception rather than the rule.

Question 80—Multiple Targets

Answer 1. **B**
    2. **D**
    3. **A**

Line D identifies the zone of major support, the floor of a vicious bear market. Near the right edge of the chart, prices broke below support but then, instead of falling any lower, reversed and closed above support. A false downside breakout, coupled with a bullish divergence of MACD, provided a major buy signal. Since we are looking at a monthly chart, it is reasonable to expect a major move—the longer the timeframe, the greater the forecast. If we expect a new bull market to begin, then line C, drawn across the top of the most recent rally, is not even a target—it is too close. Line B, drawn across the top of the previous major rally, provides a minimal measurement for the upmove. Line A, drawn across the bottom area of the all-time top, provides a more reasonable target for the bullish move, although reaching that height will require patience. The stock eventually exceeded its previous peak, rising to a new all-time high.

Question 81—Holding, Adding, or Profit-Taking

Answer 3 **A**, **B**, or **C**

A false downside breakout, coupled with a series of bullish divergences provides a powerful buy signal. A system trader or a beginning discretionary trader must take profits at the target, in this case the upper channel line. A more experienced discretionary trader is allowed to hold out for more, depending on his judgment. It would make no sense for a value trader to add to his position near the upper channel line, in the overvalued zone.

Question 82—Handling a Profitable Trade

Answer 1 Sell and take profits.

When a rally goes vertical, it is extremely difficult to forecast where it will end. At the rightmost bar on the chart we see that, for the first time since the stock blew through its upper channel line, it failed to reach a new high. This reduction of momentum flashes a signal to take your money and go home. Additional support for this decision is provided by MACD-Histogram which has reached a level consistent with tops. Also, you can see here that the tall peaks of the Force Index are usually followed by a period of flat prices rather than a continuation of an uptrend.

Question 83—Placing a Stop

Answer 3 29.34

A stop needs to be placed fairly close to prices, but not so close as to get into the zone of normal market noise; 29.34 marks the lowest point of the latest downmove. Putting a stop at this level tells the market to "put up or shut up"—a strong buy signal should lead to a quick rally; if the signal fails, there is no reason to give that stock extra time. Putting the stop a penny lower, at 29.33 would risk slippage—once the bottom tick is taken out, prices tend to go flying, leading to gaps and slippage. Placing the stop below the low of the last trading day in such a flat market would mean getting into the zone of normal market noise.

Question 84—The Impulse System

Answer 1. C and **D**
       2. A and **F**
       3. B and **E**

The primary purpose of the Impulse system is that of censorship. It keeps traders out of trouble by telling them what they are prohibited from doing at any given time.

Question 85—The Signals of NH-NL

Answer 1. C and **E**
         2. A, B, and **D**

Divergences are more often seen at market tops, as the trend keeps rising out of inertia while its leadership becomes weaker. Spikes are much more common at stock market bottoms, where they identify zones of panic liquidation. Whenever NH-NL declines to several thousand below zero, a bottom is close at hand.

Question 86—The Decision at the Right Edge of the Chart

Answer 3 Sell.

At the right edge of the chart, the trade continues on track, showing a small profit. There are, however, disturbing technical signs. The primary sign of danger for the bulls is a severe bearish divergence of MACD-Histogram. At point A, the indicator rallied in gear with price, confirming the upmove. At point B prices returned to the top area, but the indicator barely rose above the zero line, pointing to a severe weakness of the bulls. This kind of "engine noise" coming from the market provides a signal that the uptrend is weak and it is better to get out of a long trade.

GRADING YOUR ANSWERS

46–53: Excellent. You have a good grasp of selling. Now is the time to turn your attention to selling short.

38–45: Fairly good. Successful trading demands top performance. Look up the answers to the questions you've missed, review them, and retake the test in a few days before moving on to the next section.

Below 38: Alarm! Not being able to perform in the top third may be acceptable in many professional fields, but not in trading. The competition is just too intense to accept this result. Before you go into the markets, you must bring yourself up to speed. Please study the second section of *The New Sell and Sell Short* and retake the test. If your grade remains low on the second pass, look up the books recommended in that section and study them before retaking the test.

PART THREE

HOW TO SELL SHORT

Pssst! Want to hear a secret?

Here it is, but please keep very quiet: Stocks sometimes go down.

Yes, really! Everybody keeps buying them but sooner or later every stock price drops.

If living well is the best revenge, then one of the sweetest things you can do in the markets is to take something that hurts everybody—price drops—and turn that into a source of profits. Think of all those times you bought a stock and it cratered. Had you been on the opposite side of that trade, you'd be making money instead of losing on every downtick.

If you would like to profit from price declines, we need to talk about selling short.

Everybody understands how to make money from buying low and selling high, but many have no concept of how to profit from price drops. To make sure we are on the same page, let's run through a basic explanation.

Suppose you look at IBM, trading at $90, and decide it is going to $99. You buy a hundred shares, hold, and sell when the stock reaches your profit target. You make $9 per share, for a total of $900 on 100 shares, minus commissions and fees. This is so simple, a child could understand it. But what if you look at IBM at $90 and conclude that it is overvalued and likely to drop to $80? How can you possibly profit from that?

A short-seller enters a trade by borrowing someone else's shares and selling them in the market. Later on he buys back the same number of shares and returns them to his lender. This is possible because one share of IBM is just like any other share. It does not matter which shares you borrow, sell, and return—as long as the numbers match. If you can sell borrowed shares today and buy them back at a lower price later, you'll make money.

Your friendly broker will handle the entire transaction. If you tell him to sell short 100 shares of IBM, currently trading at $90, he'll begin by making sure you have $9,000—the cost of 100 shares—in your account. He'll set that money aside as a security deposit (for simplicity's sake we will not discuss margin here). Then he will put on shirt-sleeve protectors and shuffle into the back office where he keeps rows of folders with clients' stock certificates. As he goes through those folders, he finds that Aunt Millie has a few hundred shares of IBM that she inherited and not touched in years. He borrows 100 shares from her folder, leaving a note that you owe her those 100 shares. He then turns around, sells 100 borrowed shares in the market, and puts the proceeds into his safe deposit box with a note about the transaction. Now you owe Aunt Millie 100 shares, while the proceeds from selling them are sitting in your broker's safe. You can always use that money to buy back IBM and return shares to Aunt Millie.

Suppose your analysis was on target and IBM declines to $80. You call your broker and tell him to cover your short position. He takes the envelope with $9,000 cash from the safe and buys 100 shares of IBM. Now, with the share price down to $80, he needs only $8,000 to buy those 100 shares. There will be $1,000 left over. That money, minus commissions and fees, will be your profit. Your broker will put it into your account and release your security deposit that he held during the short trade. With 100 shares of IBM in hand, he will shuffle into the back room, find Aunt Millie's folder, put 100 shares back, and remove the note that you owe her those shares.

Now the transaction is over—you have your profit as well as your security deposit, the broker has his commission, and Aunt Millie has her shares back. Why would she lend them out to you? A standard agreement for a margin account in the United States automatically gives a broker the right to lend out your shares. Or maybe Aunt Millie was savvy enough to negotiate a small fee with the broker for giving him the right to lend out her shares. There is really no risk to her because the money from the sale is held by the broker and that, plus your security deposit, is enough to buy her shares back at a moment's notice.

Of course, this is a cartoon-like simplification. There are no shirt-sleeve protectors or back rooms with dusty share certificates. Every step of selling short is performed electronically.

What can go wrong with selling short? When you buy a stock, it can go down instead of up. Just as the stocks you buy can go down, the stocks you sell short can rally. For example, IBM, instead of declining from $90 to $80 might rally to $95. If you decide to cover your short at that point, it will cost you $9,500. Since the proceeds of the short sale brought only $9,000, the broker will take an additional $500 from your security deposit to buy back enough shares to make Aunt Millie whole. Also, if IBM declares a dividend, Aunt Millie will expect to receive it because she owns the stock. Since you borrowed her shares and sold them, you'll have to pay that dividend to her out of your own pocket.

These two risks—the price risk and the cost of the dividend—pretty much cover the waterfront. You can evaluate your risks in advance and decide whether you can live with them. People are usually much more afraid of fantasy than reality—and the scariest fantasy in shorting is the idea of unlimited risk.

If you buy IBM at $90, the worst thing that could happen would be for it to drop to zero, wiping out your investment. That would be bad, but you know your maximum risk before putting on a trade. If, on the other hand, you short IBM at $90, and it begins to rise, your loss would be unlimited. What if it went up to $1,000 per share? $2,000? You could be financially wiped out.

Right, and a meteorite could also fall on your head while you're walking down the street.

It is a well-known fact of human psychology that people underestimate common dangers and overestimate unusual dangers. In the city of New York, where I live, a murder on the subway becomes front-page news. It obscures the fact that many more people get killed by slipping and falling in their own bathrooms. A zoo animal that mauls its keeper makes national news, while thousands of fatal auto accidents pass virtually unnoticed.

Every serious trader must have an action plan. An important part of that plan is to define your risk and set a stop-loss order. The stops on purchases go below the market, on short sales above the entry price.

Occasionally you will encounter a fast market. There will be slippage and your loss may be bigger than anticipated. Still, if you short large, liquid, actively traded stocks, such unpleasantness rarely will occur.

For any person who can imagine shorting IBM at $90, not using a stop, and then watching it climb to $1,000, I have only one piece of advice. It is the same advice I'd give to his counterpart who buys IBM at $90 without a stop and watches it slide down to zero, wiping out his investment: "Don't be an idiot. Use stops."

Instead of shivering and imagining fantastic risks of shorting without stops, let us discuss the practical dos and don'ts of shorting stocks, futures, and options. Let us discuss real risks, as well as very real opportunities.

All stock market beginners buy stocks. Most short-sellers are pros. Why do you think they keep shorting, year after year? Do they do it out of civic-mindedness, as a public service? Do they do it because they like to gamble? Or do they sell short because the money can be much better there than in buying? Think about it.

Let us now take a closer look at shorting.

CHAPTER 7

SHORTING STOCKS

There is one common prejudice from which you must free your-self in order to sell short. Most people feel comfortable buying but feel uneasy profiting from declines. I think they acquire this preju-dice as young adults. When I taught a class on trading at a local high school, the kids took to shorting like fish to water. They had to bring in trading ideas, and we would discuss them in class and trade them in the account I had opened for that class. On any given day the kids would make as many suggestions to sell short as to buy. Often the same kid would bring in both a long and a short.

The kids got it. They understood that trading means betting on the direction of moving objects. It matters little whether you bet on a rise or a decline. You only need to get the direction right and determine the most promising entry point, profit target, and a protective stop. The kids came to the market without prejudices and had no inhibitions against shorting. The class bagged some profits on the way up and on the way down. It also took some losses, but we made sure they were smaller than our wins. We played the game in both directions.

It is my belief that short-sellers, while pursuing their own self-interest, provide an important public service in the markets. First of all, by selling overvalued shares, we increase their supply and dampen excessive market volatility. Selling more stock when prices are high tends to smooth out wild peaks. Second, when a stock is in a severe decline, short-sellers are among the first to step in and buy, cushion-ing that decline. Buyers tend to grow skittish and hang back during severe drops. It is short-sellers, flush with profits, who step in to buy in order to cover and turn paper profits into real money. Their covering slows down the decline, and that's when the bargain hunters step in. Next thing you know, a bottom is in place and the stock is rising again. Short-selling dampens excessive price swings and benefits the public.

I do not want to imply that short-sellers are a bunch of social workers. We aren't. But as the great economist Adam Smith showed two centuries ago, people in the free market help others by doing what is best for themselves. Bears help the markets, as long as there is no collusion between them—no "bear raids." This caveat applies equally to buying, to manipulating stocks upward.

While the government has a legitimate role in policing the market, in its zeal, it slapped several illogical restrictions on short-sellers. The worst of them was "the uptick rule," which said you may only sell short if the previous tick—a minuscule price change—was an uptick. In other words, you may only sell short a rising stock. Ostensibly this was done to protect buyers from the packs of short-sellers hammering their stock with an avalanche of sell orders. I have only one question for these protectors of the public—why not have a downtick rule as

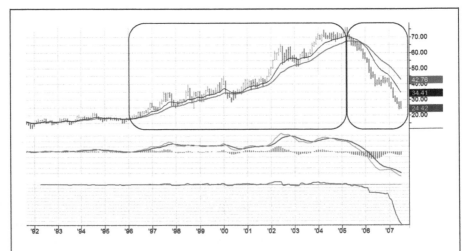

Figure 7.1   MNI monthly

Downhill faster than uphill: from 23 to 76 in 10 years, from 76 back down to 23 in 2.5 years.

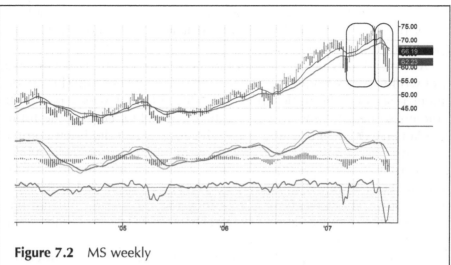

Figure 7.2 MS weekly

Downhill faster than uphill: from 58 to 75 in 14 weeks, from 75 to 58 in 8 weeks.

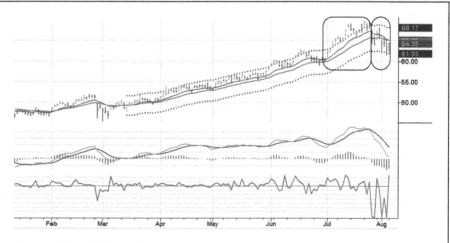

Figure 7.3 EWY daily

Downhill faster than uphill: from 59 to 69 in 19 days, from 69 to 60 in 12 days.

well, to protect the innocent from being swept away in a bubble? To carry the uptick rule to its logical conclusion, a downtick rule would permit buying only on a downtick, when prices decline.

A tremendously positive development occurred in the U.S. stock market while I was working on the first edition of this book. The government rescinded the uptick rule. The silly rule that was a part of the trading scene for some 70 years is finally gone! Of course, the futures markets never had a downtick rule. The government did briefly prohibit shorting of several groups of stocks during the crash of 2008–2009.

Shorting has one great advantage over buying and one massive disadvantage. The big advantage of selling stocks short is that they tend to go down about twice as fast as they rise. This applies to all time-frames—to monthly (Figure 7.1), weekly (Figure 7.2), and daily (Figure 7.3), as well as intraday charts.

It takes buying to put the stocks up but they can fall under their own weight. The greater speed of declines creates a real advantage for experienced traders. The faster the trade, the less time you spend exposed to market risk.

The one great disadvantage of selling stocks short is that the broad stock market has a centuries-old tendency to rise over time (Figure 7.4).

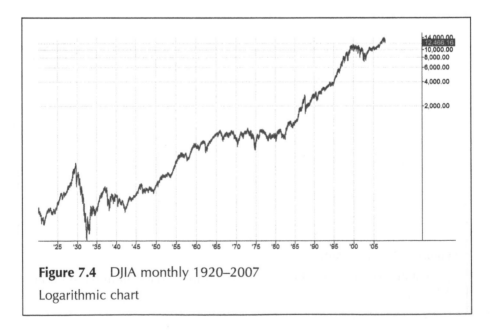

Figure 7.4   DJIA monthly 1920–2007

Logarithmic chart

The estimates of this so-called "secular rise" vary, clouded by many old stocks disappearing and new stocks being listed. Still, an average 3% rise per year seems like a reasonable estimate. This means that in shorting you are swimming against a gently rising tide.

Every action in the stock market has two angles—one helpful, the other dangerous. You can never fully separate the two or have one without the other. It is essential that you keep your eyes open to both sides of the coin and be realistic. What should we do in response to the advantage and disadvantage we just discussed?

In general, you want to be more short-term oriented in shorting than in buying. You are surfing against the gently rising tide, the downtrends are faster, and there is no point in giving a short trade too much time to "work itself out." Give the short trade less time to put up or shut up than you would give to a long trade.

YOUR FIRST SHORTS

Beginners often ask how to find stocks to short. I suggest thinking of all those stocks you bought and lost money on. Think of the stocks you expect to decline. Find the stock you hate the most—and sell it short.

A friendly reminder: do not try to make a lot of money on your first short, or on the second short for that matter. Sell short just a few shares.

Take your first baby steps without having to worry about money. You'll have plenty of other things to think about—selecting a stock, choosing a profit target, setting a stop, as well as learning the mechanics of placing an order. Be sure to work out these and other issues while trading a size so small that neither gain nor loss will get you emotionally involved.

Trade size serves as a huge emotional amplifier. The bigger the size, the greater the stress. To reduce stress, especially early in the game, when you are still learning to short, trade a small size. There will be plenty of time to increase the size of your trades once you grow more comfortable with shorting.

Several weeks prior to writing this chapter, I was trading from home one morning in front of a live screen. My laptop beeped, signaling an incoming e-mail. It came from Zvi Benyamini, a recent Traders' Camp graduate who wrote that he was ready to begin shorting. I suggested that he write up his analysis of the stock he wanted to short, using the format we discussed in the Camp. Several minutes later an e-mail came in (Figure 7.5):

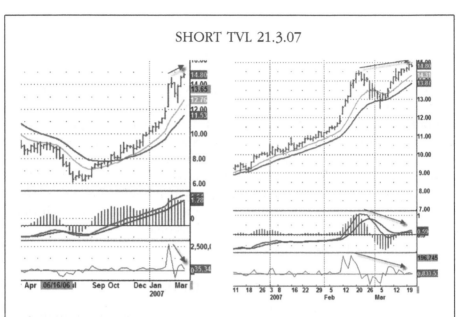

Figure 7.5 TVL entry

Weekly double top, blue for a while, diverging FI. Daily major MACD divergence, FI major divergence from a month ago, this peak also losing force. Ticked blue today.

Shorted 100 @ 14.79
Stop: hard at 15.2, bail if turns green.
Target: 12.77 weekly fast MA. Partial around 13–13.5 if stalls.
Note—Alex's warnings: strong MACD-Histogram on the weekly chart, and stock visibly strong (not affected by the recent crash).

This is a good example of how an intelligent person learns to short and how little he pays for his lessons. This camper found a stock and worked it up independently. He created a good Trader's Diary entry and documented his decision-making process. He even wrote down my objections to his trade. As an independent man, he put on the trade anyway, but made its size very small. His loss cost him 20 cents per share on 100 shares, or $20 plus commissions. Yet he received a lot of educational value from this trade, with tiny financial risk. He can afford many such lessons, without becoming stressed by losses.

I did not like TVL as a short pick that day. First of all, the time was not right for shorting. The stock market had just established an important double bottom and rallied from it. The tide of the market was moving up, and I had already covered almost all of my own shorts. Furthermore, it did not feel right to short a stock that kept reaching new highs almost every day for several weeks.

When you go long, it is not a good idea to buy a stock that keeps making new lows. It is OK to buy low, but not OK to buy down. Similarly, when you want to go short, it is not a good idea to sell short a stock that keeps making new highs. You want to see some evidence that the uptrend has hit the ceiling, stopped rising, and is ready to turn down.

My camper made two mistakes by shorting a rising stock in a strong market. At the same time, he got two important things absolutely right. He made excellent notes and he traded a very small size, so that his mistakes cost him next to nothing. He paid cheap tuition for a lot of serious learning.

After the market closed for the day, I received a follow-up (Figure 7.6):

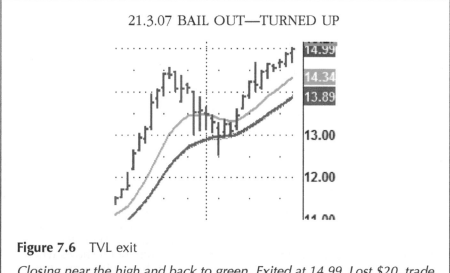

Figure 7.6 TVL exit

Closing near the high and back to green. Exited at 14.99. Lost $20, trade grade D.

THE ASYMMETRY OF TOPS AND BOTTOMS

When we talked about buying stocks, we focused on two main approaches—value buying and momentum buying. When we look for stocks to sell short, we cannot simply flip these methods. Shorting is different from buying because mass psychology is different at tops and bottoms, in uptrends and downtrends. Stock market bottoms tend to be narrow and sharp, while the tops tend to be broad and uneven.

Stock market bottoms are built on fear. When longs can no longer take the stress of losing, they panic and dump their shares with little regard to price. Their fingers have been caught in the door, and the pain is so bad that they want to get out at any price.

Fear and pain are sharp and powerful emotions. A selling panic shakes out weak holders, and once they are out, the stock is ready to

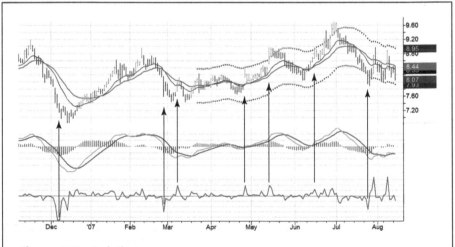

Figure 7.7 F daily

The asymmetry of tops and bottoms is clearly reflected by the Force Index. Its downspikes tend to serve as good markers of public panics that clear the air and augur new advances. A downspike of the Force Index does not necessarily nail the exact day of the bottom, but it shows where the weak holders are dumping their shares, and the buying opportunity tends to come within days.

rise again. As long as you do not buy prematurely and then panic and sell at the bottom, buying tends to be fairly permissive (Figure 7.7).

Tops are built on greed, a happy emotion that can last a long time. As bulls make money, they call their friends and tell them to buy, even after their own money runs out. That's why the tops tend to last longer and be more irregularly shaped than the bottoms. You can see that the upward spikes of the Force Index do not identify tops but rather confirm the ongoing uptrend.

While the bottoms tend to stand out clearly on the charts, the tops tend to be broad and less defined, with many false breakouts. Whenever the bulls find more money, they toss it at their favorite stock, making it rise above a seemingly well established top. Those brief, upward fake-outs are very typical of market tops.

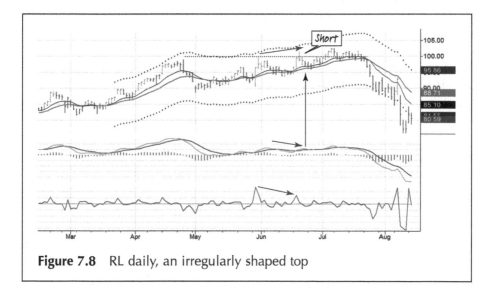

Figure 7.8 RL daily, an irregularly shaped top

Figure 7.8 comes from my trading diary. I shorted RL in June, after it staged a false upside breakout that was accompanied by a slew of bearish divergences. I thought that the false breakout had cleared the air for the decline, but it was slow in coming. Instead of collapsing, the stock continued to percolate at a high level, sorely testing my patience, before it finally did what I expected it would. It stayed up like a bull with a sword plunged through its heart that still continues to run during a bullfight.

This kind of behavior at the tops makes shorting much harder than buying. Tops demand wider stops, increasing the risk per share. If you use tight stops, your risk of a whipsaw is much greater when shorting than buying.

Let us zoom in on some of the major opportunities and dangers of shorting.

SHORTING TOPS

Shorting near the top tends to be harder than buying near the bottom. At the end of a downtrend, markets often appear exhausted and listless, with low volatility and tight price ranges. On the other hand, when prices are boiling near the top, you can expect high volatility and wide price ranges. If buying can feel like climbing on a horse that is standing by a fence, shorting can feel like trying to mount a horse running in the field.

One of the key solutions for this problem is money management. You need to short smaller positions and be prepared to reenter if stopped out. If you commit all your permitted risk to one entry, a single false breakout will kick you out of the game. It pays to trade a size smaller than the maximum permitted by your money management rules. It makes

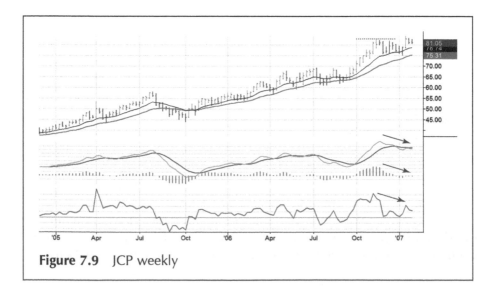

Figure 7.9   JCP weekly

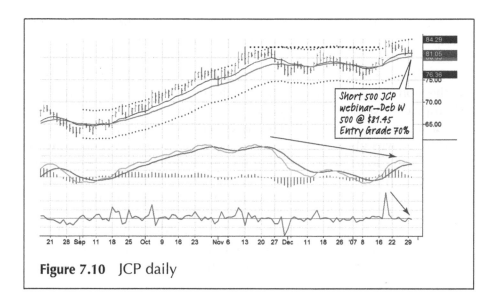

Figure 7.10 JCP daily

JCP	short	Date	Upchannel	Downchannel	Day's High	Day's Low	Grade
Entry	$81.45	30-Jan-07	84.09	76.56	$81.79	$80.66	70%
Exit							
P/L						Trade	

sense to keep some risk capital in reserve. You need to be able to hold on to your bucking horse (Figure 7.9).

During a webinar in January 2007 a trader named Deborah Winters asked me to analyze JCP. I had not looked at the stock in years but became very excited once I saw its chart. Against the background of a toppy stock market, the weekly chart of JCP looked like a screaming short:

- The stock was expensive, just below its all-time high.
- It had broken out to a new high two weeks earlier; that break-out failed and the stock fell back into the trading range. A false breakout to a new high provides a strong shorting signal.
- The weekly price was above value—above both moving averages.
- There were clear bearish divergences in MACD Lines and the Force Index; MACD-Histogram, while not diverging, was declining.

The daily chart of JCP confirmed the message of the weekly, suggesting that the stock was near its top (see Figure 7.10). It showed a false upside breakout—a sharp spike to a new high, followed by a slide back into range. There were bearish divergences of MACD Lines and the Force Index, but not MACD-Histogram. Whenever a webinar pick appears especially attractive, I announce to the group that I might trade it in the days to come. That is exactly what I did with JCP. My profit target was about $75, in the value zone on the weekly chart. I was not going to continue holding the stock much above $88. It was not a very appealing reward-to-risk ratio, but the technical signs told me that the likelihood of a price break was much greater than that of a rally.

The ideal place to sell or sell short is near the upper channel line on the daily chart. I avoid shorting below value, below the daily EMAs. I refuse to sell short at or below the lower channel line, where

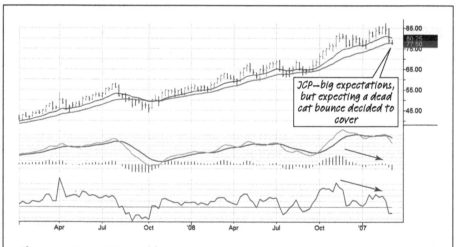

Figure 7.11 JCP weekly exit

This weekly chart reflects profit-taking. Prices fell below the fast red EMA and even the slower yellow EMA, but their decline appeared to have slowed down. At the same time, the weekly Force Index had produced a downspike, a likely sign of a bottom. Weekly MACD-Histogram fell to the level at which it could be expected to make a bottom. The sweet part of a downmove appeared to be over; there was no point waiting for prices to hit the initial $75 target.

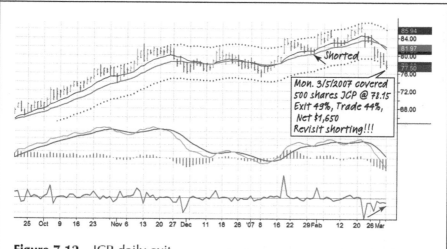

Figure 7.12 JCP daily exit

While my exit grade was a reasonable 49% and the trade grade of 44% well above the "A level," I took less profit from this trade than was available. By shorting too early, less profit and more stress.

JCP	short	Date	Upchannel	Downchannel	Day's High	Day's Low	Grade
Entry	$81.45	30-Jan-07	84.09	76.56	$81.79	$80.66	70%
Exit	$78.15	5-Mar-07			$79.05	$77.21	49%
P/L						Trade	44%

prices are overextended to the downside. Here I was so bearish that I shorted near value, a little low for my liking. It was not a very good entry, because near the EMA you get no help from the rubber band effect that can help snap prices down from the upper channel. Still, it was a nice entry—selling closer to the day's high than to its low, scoring a 70% sell grade.

The daily chart helps you understand some of the psychological pressure associated with shorting. The exit charts (Figures 7.11 and 7.12) show that my shorting was quite premature, and there were several weeks when holding short felt stressful. There were two strong reasons why I was able to hold. One was that I was extremely bearish on the market and was heavily short across the board. Many of my shorts were turning out a lot better than JCP, reinforcing my confidence in the bearish view.

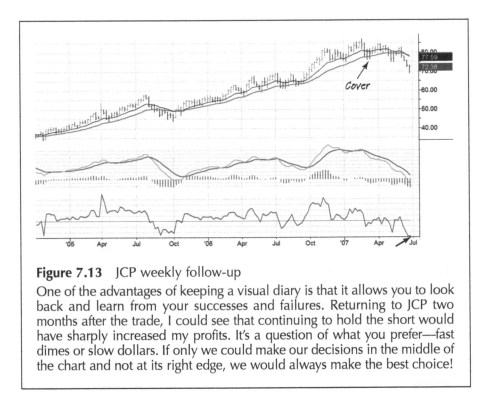

Figure 7.13 JCP weekly follow-up

One of the advantages of keeping a visual diary is that it allows you to look back and learn from your successes and failures. Returning to JCP two months after the trade, I could see that continuing to hold the short would have sharply increased my profits. It's a question of what you prefer—fast dimes or slow dollars. If only we could make our decisions in the middle of the chart and not at its right edge, we would always make the best choice!

The second reason was that the size of my short position was min-uscule relative to the size of my trading account. If I had to use a tight stop, I would have been stopped out of this trade. A trader who is not greedy and has a bigger account has an advantage. If you risk only 0.25% of your capital on a trade, and it starts going against you, you may increase your risk to 0.5% and still be well within the 2% maxi-mum risk limit. A small trader who throws a full-size position at the market has no such option. Having a large account is like driving a power-ful car—you do not want to put the "pedal to the metal" all the time, but it is comforting to know that you have a power reserve.

Throughout this trade I remained in touch with Deborah, who had brought JCP to my attention. I encouraged her to hold, especially when she felt like throwing in the towel several times during the trade. One of my rules is that when I trade a friend's pick, I tell that friend when and where I get in and out. Sharing a trade is like shar-ing a meal or going on a trip together (Figure 7.13).

SHORTING DOWNTRENDS

Several years ago, at a dinner in Sydney held by the Australian Technical Analysts Association, I found myself sitting next to an architect who told me that every year he flew to Spain and ran with the bulls in Pamplona. As a herd of bulls destined for bullfights are released from their pens, they run to the bull ring through the narrow streets of this medieval town. A crowd of men race in front of the bulls, taking the risk of getting gored or trampled if they do not run fast enough. I asked him why he did it, and he said that nothing else made him feel as alive as flirting with mortal danger.

I sometimes wonder whether trying to short market tops is similar to running in front of a thundering herd. This pursuit attracts us not only with its great profit potential, but also with the emotional satisfaction of having challenged and outrun the crowd.

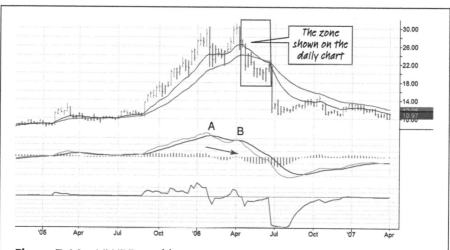

Figure 7.14 NWRE weekly

This weekly chart of NWRE shows a terrific opportunity to sell short near the top in early 2006. A false breakout to a new high, accompanied by a bearish divergence A-B, rang the bell for short-sellers. The wonderful thing about the middle of any chart is that trading signals stand out so clearly. The problem is that the closer we get to the right edge, the foggier the market becomes. I have not yet found a broker who will take my orders in the middle of the chart—they all want me to trade at the right edge.

There is another approach to shorting. Instead of tangling with a running bull you can wait until a bull is going down the chute at a slaughterhouse. Men stand by the side of that chute, zapping bulls dead. Their level of emotional satisfaction is probably a lot lower than that of those who run in front of the herd in Pamplona, but their success rate in bringing home a steady paycheck is a lot higher.

Let us keep in mind that the slaughterhouse job is not without its risks. A bull can lurch and crush a worker. We need to position ourselves outside of that chute and zap the bull with the least risk. Let us now take a look at shorting stocks that are already in downtrends (Figure 7.14). Let us zoom into the area highlighted on the weekly chart and examine it using a daily chart.

That chute is the envelope on the daily chart (Figure 7.15).

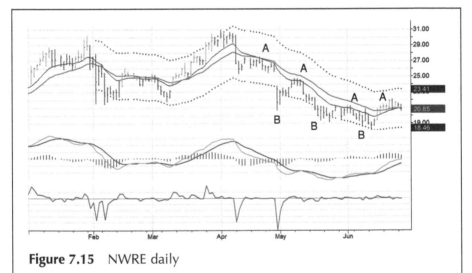

Figure 7.15   NWRE daily

A. Value—short   **B.** Oversold—cover

The false breakout to a new high that we saw on the weekly is also clearly visible in the middle of the daily chart. What is extremely useful about the daily chart is that it allows us to see the chute through which the bulls are going to their slaughter.

The idea is to sell short when prices are near value, in the middle of the chart. The time to cover shorts and take profits is when prices fall to or below the lower channel line. We want to short value and cover in the undervalued zone.

After NWRE collapsed from its top in early April, it pulled back up to value. The space between the two moving averages is the value zone. That pullback provided a shorting opportunity. NWRE gapped down and fell below its lower channel line. In May, prices pulled back up to value again, creating another shorting opportunity. By mid-May prices slid into the oversold zone below the lower channel line, giving the signal to cover. This pendulum-like motion—the rise to the value zone, followed by a drop to the over-sold level below the lower channel line—continued up to the right edge of the chart and beyond.

Selling short within a channel provides a series of clearly defined trading opportunities. Still, nothing in the markets is completely sim-ple; there are always hidden dangers. For one thing, the depth of the penetration of both the value zone and the oversold zone varies from week to week and from month to month. You cannot afford to be greedy inside the chute. You must be satisfied with grabbing a quick profit and moving on.

This is where the practice of grading your trades by the percentage of the envelope you capture in your trade becomes extremely useful. Remember, an A trade captures 30% or more of the envelope height. A third of any envelope equals two-thirds of the distance from the EMA to the channel line. This is the distance you must consistently catch to consider yourself an A trader. Technically, this is not such a hard task. Psychologically, it tends to be excruciatingly difficult. Your two enemies here are greed and perfectionism—both of which cause you to overstay your trade and miss an exit.

To trade successfully within a channel, you must set a realistic goal, take your profit, and be satisfied with it. Kicking yourself when you occasionally miss an opportunity to catch a bigger move is absolutely forbidden.

To summarize the lessons from this trade:

- Make a strategic decision on the weekly chart, tactical plans on the dailies.

- A divergence of MACD-Histogram is one of the strongest signals in technical analysis.

- Trading within a channel lowers risk but also reduces potential rewards.

- You must rate all your short-term trades by the percentage of the channel captured in that trade.

- Trading within a channel, you must have your finger on the trigger, ready to exit with a realistic profit.

SHORTING FUNDAMENTALS

Fundamentalists explore supply-demand relationships in futures and the financial data for companies whose shares they want to trade. Technicians follow the trails left by buyers and sellers on their charts. A savvy trader can rely on both types of analysis and profit from both.

You cannot become an expert in both fields—you will always be stronger in one than the other. Your guiding principle when using both fundamentals and technicals should be to make sure that their signals do not contradict one another. If one screams to buy while the other yells to sell, the safest course of action is to step aside.

You can apply the same technical tools to stocks and futures, to indexes and forex. Fundamental analysis is the more narrow. A fundamental analyst cannot possibly be an expert on both bonds and crude oil, or on biotech stocks and defense.

There are two main approaches to using fundamental analysis in trading—one broad, the other narrow. First of all, it pays to have a general understanding of the major fundamental trends that affect your market. For example, if you are looking for stocks to buy, you want to know that biotech or nanotechnology have greater potential for new advances than commodity chemicals or household appliances. This basic understanding can help you focus on the more promising areas of the market.

A more focused approach is to take a specific trading idea from fundamental analysis and put it through the filter of technical analysis. The key principle is to use fundamental information as an idea generator and

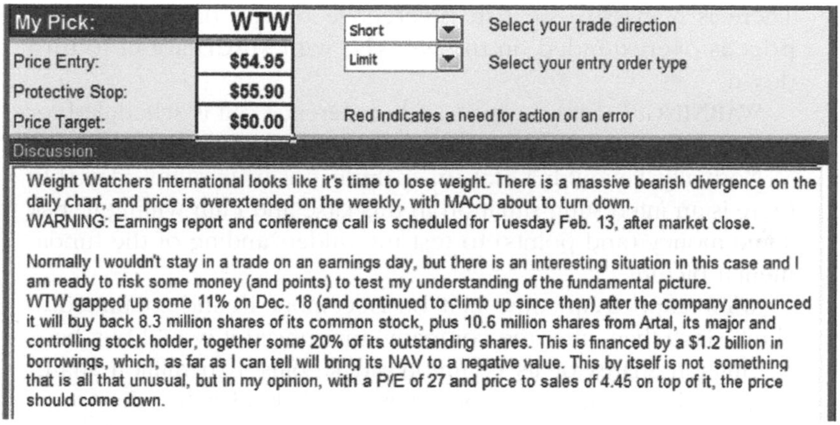

My Pick:	**WTW**	Short ▼	Select your trade direction
Price Entry:	**$54.95**	Limit ▼	Select your entry order type
Protective Stop:	**$55.90**		
Price Target:	**$50.00**	Red indicates a need for action or an error	

Discussion:

Weight Watchers International looks like it's time to lose weight. There is a massive bearish divergence on the daily chart, and price is overextended on the weekly, with MACD about to turn down.
WARNING: Earnings report and conference call is scheduled for Tuesday Feb. 13, after market close.

Normally I wouldn't stay in a trade on an earnings day, but there is an interesting situation in this case and I am ready to risk some money (and points) to test my understanding of the fundamental picture.
WTW gapped up some 11% on Dec. 18 (and continued to climb up since then) after the company announced it will buy back 8.3 million shares of its common stock, plus 10.6 million shares from Artal, its major and controlling stock holder, together some 20% of its outstanding shares. This is financed by a $1.2 billion in borrowings, which, as far as I can tell will bring its NAV to a negative value. This by itself is not something that is all that unusual, but in my opinion, with a P/E of 27 and price to sales of 4.45 on top of it, the price should come down.

Figure 7.16   WTW weekly

technical studies as a trigger. The technicals can either release you to pursue that trade or stop you from going any further.[1]

No matter how good a fundamental story, if the technical factors do not confirm it, there is no trade. This rule applies to both bullish and bearish signals. When the fundamentals suggest a trade and technical factors confirm that signal, you have a very powerful combination. Here is an example of a trade that illustrates this approach.

During the weekend of February 10, 2007, I received an e-mail from Shai Kreiz, a member of our Spike group (Figure 7.16). The group's members compete for prizes each weekend by sending in their best picks for the week ahead. On most weekends I select a favorite and trade it myself.

Many picks are technical, but this one had an unusually high volume of fundamental information. Shai wrote:

---

[1] I believe in this idea so strongly that for years I have been telling friends who like to buy stocks without any knowledge of technical analysis: "Go to a free website like www.stockcharts.com, pull up a weekly chart of your stock and overlay it with a 26-week moving average; do not buy a stock whose slow moving average is pointing down, indicating a downtrend."

Weight Watchers International looks like it's time to lose weight. There is a massive bearish divergence on the daily chart, and price is overextended on the weekly, with MACD about to turn down.

WARNING: Earnings report and conference call is scheduled for Tuesday, February 13, after the market close.

Normally I wouldn't stay in a trade on an earnings day, but there is an interesting situation in this case and I am willing to risk some money (and points) to test my understanding of the fundamental picture.

WTW gapped up some 11% on December 18 and continued to climb since then, after the company announced it would buy back 8.3 million shares of its common stock, plus 10.6 million shares from Artal, its major and controlling stock holder, together some 20% of its outstanding shares. This is financed by $1.2 billion in borrowings, which, as far as I can tell, will bring its NAV to a negative value. This by itself is not something that is all that unusual, but in my opinion, with a P/E of 27 and price-to-sales of 4.45 on top of it, the price should come down.

Shai wrote that he was going to short at $54.95, with a stop at $55.90 and a profit target of 50. I understood his fundamental note as saying that this bird was flying higher and higher despite a major bloodletting of capital; a further flight would be unsustainable. Technically, the weekly chart looked awful (Figure 7.17).

The amount of money a trader commits to a trade can stress him and impair his decision-making. As noted above, I carried double my normal position size in WTW. I was still well under the 2% Rule risk limit, but at double the normal risk this trade certainly had more than its share of my attention. The money was clouding my judgment.

Normally, when prices open down on a severe gap, there is no great rush to cover shorts. Prices tend to hang around the gap level for a while, testing lower ground and giving plenty of opportunity to cover. But here, trading a double position size, I had a quick $10,000 profit within 48 hours of entering the trade. I felt anxious not to let it slip away, and as soon as prices began to rally from their gap opening, I felt jittery and covered.

It was a fairly sloppy exit, with only a 42% rating. The trade itself had an excellent 79% rating, but it could have been higher had I let it run a little longer (Figure 7.23).

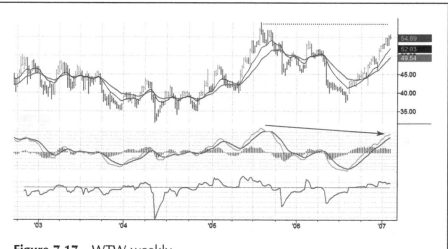

Figure 7.17 WTW weekly

WTW was approaching major resistance in the vicinity of its 2005 top while MACD Lines were tracing a bearish divergence and the Force Index was sagging.

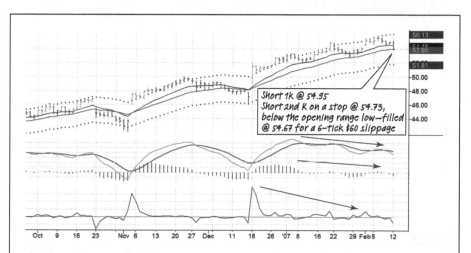

Figure 7.18 WTW daily entry

The daily chart showed massive bearish divergences of MACD Lines, MACD-Histogram, and the Force Index. The stock appeared poised at the edge of a cliff, ready to tumble down.

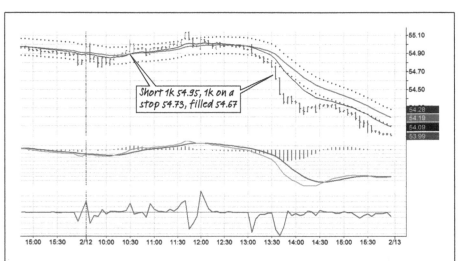

Figure 7.19   WTW entry, 5 minute chart

This combination of ominous fundamental and technical signs looked so bearish that I decided to double the size of my short position. After shorting 1,000 shares at the level recommended by Shai, I placed another order to short 1,000 shares at $54.73, at the low of the opening range. WTW had opened flat, tried to rally but then reversed, and accelerated on its way down. My second order to short was filled at $54.67, suffering $60 worth of slippage, six times greater than the commission cost.

WTW	short	Date	Upchannel	Downchannel	Day's High	Day's Low	Grade
Entry 1	$54.95	12-Feb-07	56.85	51.09	$55.14	$53.95	84%
Exit							
P/L						Trade	

WTW	short	Date	Upchannel	Downchannel	Day's High	Day's Low	Grade
Entry 2	$54.67	12-Feb-07	56.85	51.09	$55.14	$53.95	61%
Exit							
P/L						Trade	

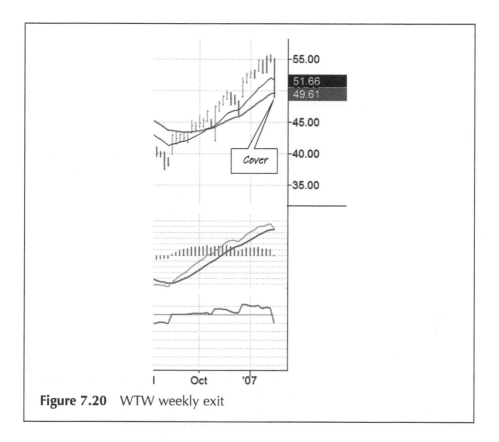

Figure 7.20   WTW weekly exit

WTW	short	Date	Upchannel	Downchannel	Day's High	Day's Low	Grade
Entry 1	$54.95	12-Feb-07	56.85	51.09	$55.14	$53.95	84%
Exit	$50.39	14-Feb-07			$51.38	$49.03	42%
P/L						Trade	79%

WTW	short	Date	Upchannel	Downchannel	Day's High	Day's Low	Grade
Entry 2	$54.95	12-Feb-07	56.85	51.09	$55.14	$53.95	61%
Exit	$50.40	14-Feb-07			$51.38	$49.03	42%
P/L						Trade	79%

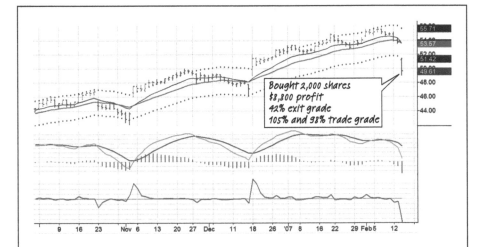

Figure 7.21   WTW daily exit

WTW closed near the low of the day after I shorted on Monday. It stayed near that level on Tuesday. On Wednesday the market did not like what management had to say in their earnings report and conference call. The stock gapped down, hitting Shai's target for the trade.

The price of WTW on the weekly chart stabbed down, below the slow yellow EMA. For me, the trade had completed what it was supposed to do. Just a few days prior, WTW was above value on the weeklies. It made sense to sell short an overvalued stock for a trip down into the value zone. Now that the destination had been reached, it made little sense to stick around. Yes, of course, the stock could continue even lower and become undervalued, but that would be a different trade. There are many concepts for trading the markets, and you have to choose the ones with which you are comfortable. This trade was based on a concept I liked—shorting above value and covering at value. My choice was to exit and take profits.

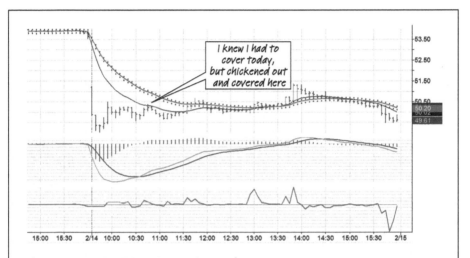

Figure 7.22   WTW exit, 5-minute chart

As a discretionary trader, I did not have a standing order to cover shorts. When WTW overshot Shai's target at the opening, I waited to see whether the downmove would continue. When WTW began to rally, I covered both positions in two separate trades, within a penny of each other.

To summarize the lessons from this trade:

- Fundamental information can provide useful trading signals, as long as technical analysis confirms them.
- The value zone between two moving averages serves as a magnet for prices—they tend to return to it from above and below.
- The amount of money we have riding on a trade tends to negatively impact our decisions.
- It pays to keep good records.

A visual diary is a valuable learning tool. If you keep records like these and return to review them, you will profit from your experience. Reviewing your diary will help you become a better trader.

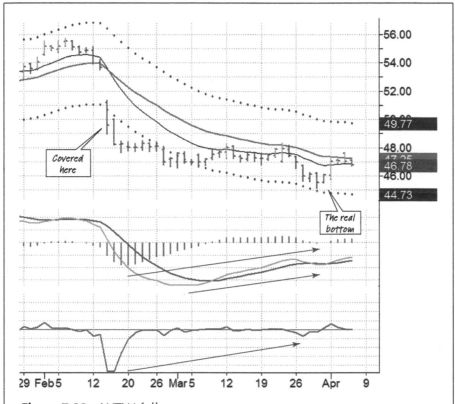

Figure 7.23 WTW follow-up

Keeping a visual diary encourages you to return to completed trades and learn with the benefit of hindsight. This follow-up chart, from some 8 weeks later, shows that the profit per share could have been doubled by a patient trader. I did not need to carry a double-sized position to make more money. Normal size, coupled with peace of mind, would have worked just as well.

FINDING STOCKS TO SHORT

I have two main ways of searching for stocks to short—one is easy and the other is hard.

The "easy" way is not all that easy, of course. It involves looking at short candidates from the Spike group, as well as other sources. I have already described my approach to trading tips. They provide ideas for possible trades which I analyze using my system and make my own decision whether to trade them or not. My own trading system, described earlier in the book, must confirm the tip in order for me to trade it. Still, with dozens of smart people scanning and researching the stock market, and sending in their picks, there are often attractive short candidates. I put them through the Triple Screen and Impulse systems to decide whether to trade those picks and what parameters to use.

The "hard work" approach involves looking at the entire universe of stocks. I begin by scanning stock industry groups and subgroups, looking for those that look attractive for shorting (Figure 7.24). If you

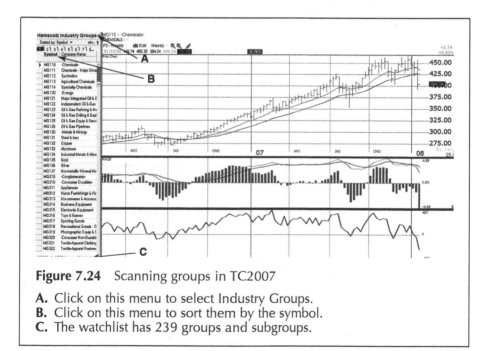

Figure 7.24   Scanning groups in TC2007

A. Click on this menu to select Industry Groups.
B. Click on this menu to sort them by the symbol.
C. The watchlist has 239 groups and subgroups.

like to short the tops, look for the groups that appear toppy. If you like to short the downtrends, look for the groups that are already moving within established downtrends. Once you find an attractive group or subgroup, open up the list of its component stocks and look for shorting candidates among them.

Looking at a hundred or more stock industry groups keeps you in touch with the entire stock market. Analyzing individual stocks within selected groups allows you to efficiently allocate your time. Several friends have offered to automate the entire process for me, but I want to look every group and subgroup in the face, so to speak. I try to go through this scanning process twice a month.

The program I like to use for this is TC2007[2] (www.tc2000.com). I like how it breaks the entire stock market into 239 industry groups and subgroups and makes it easy to switch from any group or subgroup to its component stocks. Chart 7.24 shows the beginning of a scan. Select

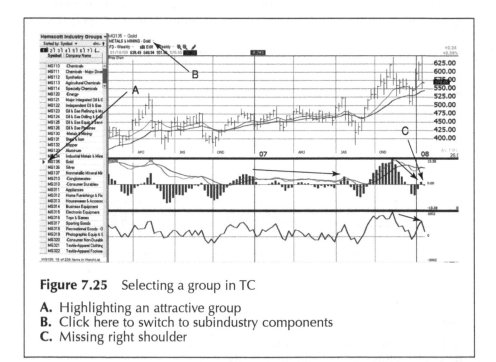

Figure 7.25   Selecting a group in TC

A. Highlighting an attractive group
B. Click here to switch to subindustry components
C. Missing right shoulder

"Industry Groups" from the directory of securities. Then select "Symbol" from the list of sorting options. Since I run these scans on weekends, I want to look at the weekly charts whose template includes my favorite indicators: two moving averages, MACD Lines and Histogram, and the Force Index. Of course you can implement these ideas in many other software programs.

During today's scan we find an attractive group, MG135—Gold (Figure 7.25). The weekly chart had recently broken out to a new high but could not hold that level and sank back below resistance, leaving behind a false upside breakout—a great sign of weakness. MACD-Histogram traced out a bearish divergence. That was another great sign of weakness, marking an attractive subgroup in which to look for shorting candidates.

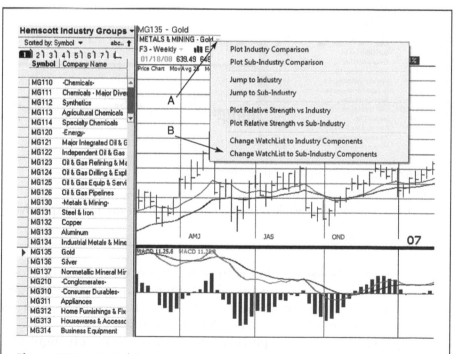

Figure 7.26 Switching to component stocks

A. Right-click here to open a menu
B. Click here to switch from the group to the list of stocks that make up this group

Two clicks take us from the selected subgroup (which TC calls Sub-Industry) to its component stocks (Figure 7.26). Here we will look for a shorting candidate.

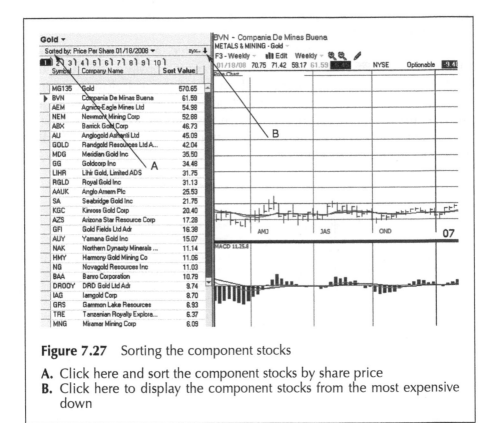

Figure 7.27   Sorting the component stocks

A. Click here and sort the component stocks by share price
B. Click here to display the component stocks from the most expensive down

First, a bit of housekeeping is in order. We need to sort the stocks within a group or subgroup by price rather than by symbol (Figure 7.27). When looking for stocks to sell short, I want to look at the most expensive stocks first. When looking for stocks to buy, I want to begin with the least expensive stocks. Buy low, sell high! (See Figure 7.28.)

At this point I like to switch from TC to TradeStation (www. tradestation.com). The first has a much better scanning capability, while the latter has more technical tools. Again, the sequence of steps is more important than any specific software. The search process

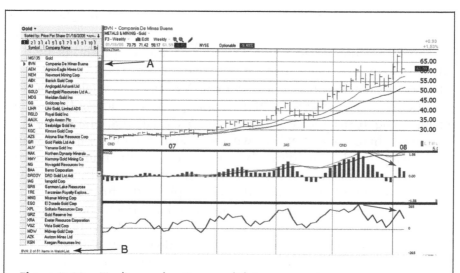

Figure 7.28 Finding a shorting candidate

A. BVN is the most expensive stock in this subgroup.
B. There are 50 stocks in this subgroup.

The pattern of BVN—Compania de Minas Buena—appears remarkably similar to that of the entire subgroup. You can see several strong sell signals on this weekly chart. Now is the time to switch to the daily chart and make tactical decisions on where to enter, where to set a target, and where to place a stop. Now is also the time to use money management rules to decide on position size. Finally, you should create a visual diary for your planned trade.

we've just discussed allows you to keep tabs on the entire stock market but zoom in on specific stocks and dedicate the bulk of your time to them.

SHORT INTEREST

If misery loves company, what does happiness love? Solitude, perhaps?

We know that most traders lose money, and only a minority makes steady profits. A successful trade is likely to run in the direction opposite to that of the majority of traders. This is why it pays to know how much or how little company you will have when you short a stock.

Very few people sell short, and the total number of shares shorted is usually a tiny percentage of any company's shares. If you want to measure the intensity of short-sellers' involvement in any given stock, you have two indicators—the Short Interest Ratio and Days to Cover.

The Short Interest Ratio compares the number of shorts held by the bears with the "free float" in any given stock. The free float is the number of shares available for shorting. You find it by taking the total number of shares issued by the company and deducting three share groups: the restricted stock granted to executives, shares held by "strategic shareholders" who own more than 5% of company shares, and, finally, insiders' holdings. When you subtract the number of shares that cannot be easily sold from the total number issued by a company, you find the number of shares that are in play—the free float.

Brokers report the number of shares that have been shorted and not covered to the exchanges, which summarize this information for every stock and disclose it to the public. If you divide the total number of shares that are being held short by the total free float, you'll have the Short Interest Ratio. It reflects the intensity of shorting in any given stock.

When the Short Interest Ratio rises, it shows that the bears are becoming more numerous. You must keep in mind that every short position must eventually be covered. When shorts become scared and run, they run fast. Short-covering rallies are notorious for their speed. A growing Short Interest Ratio delivers a warning that a stock is subject to a violent upmove.

There is no clearly defined safe or dangerous level of the Short Interest Ratio. It varies from stock to stock, especially in optionable stocks, where speculators may sell the stock short and at the same time write a put, in effect balancing the two, trading a spread rather than expressing any great bearishness. As a rule of thumb, a Short Ratio of less than 10% is likely to be tolerable, while a reading of over 20% marks a suspiciously large crowd of short-sellers.

Another useful measure of bearishness is the Days to Cover indicator. To calculate it, divide the total short interest in a stock by its average daily volume. It shows how many days it would take for all the short-sellers to cover their positions.

When someone yells "Fire!" in a crowded movie theater, it matters little whether there is in fact a fire, as people rush for the exits. It takes little to touch off a panic in the stock market—either up or down. The shorts may become lazy and complacent on the way down, but they are prone to dash for the exit in a wild short-covering rally, creating a panic rally that feeds on itself.

When a crowd panics in a movie theater, people get trampled. If the number of Days to Cover is less than one, you have a small crowd at a wide door, and a panic is unlikely. If Days to Cover rises above 20 (it sometimes goes above 50), it tells you that the stock has become a safety hazard for the bears—it would take that many days for them to escape, and some of them are sure to get killed, as they try to push through the narrow doors.

Keep in mind that the door can quickly become wider, making it easier to escape and reducing the number of Days to Cover. For example, if there are 10 million short shares outstanding while the average daily

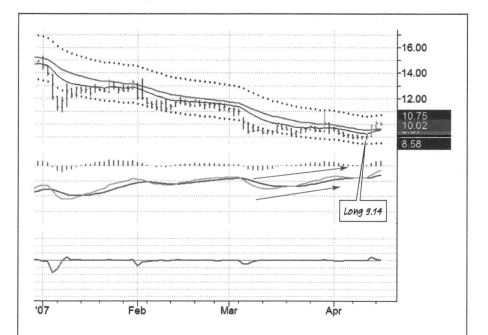

Figure 7.29 NURO daily

"I traded NURO from the long side because I liked the divergences and the fact that the stock was in a tight price squeeze. Still, there were other attractive stocks at the same time. What clinched the deal for me was that NURO had a very high level of shorts, with a Short Interest of 50% of the float and 20 Days to Cover. Needless to say, the first lit- tle strength in the stock triggered massive short-covering, and there was a very satisfying price pop."

volume is 1 million, then Days to Cover equals 10. If the volume zooms up to 2 million, Days to Cover will drop to 5. As a rule of thumb, when the Days to Cover indicator is below 10, the danger of a squeeze is low, while a reading above 20 sends a definite warning.

There are several ways to obtain the Short Interest Ratio and Days to Cover for most stocks. For example, you can go to the popular Yahoo Finance website, type in a symbol and click "Get quotes." Scroll down the page and click on "Key statistics." There you will find "Shares short" and "Short ratio."

Kerry Lovvorn, a trader mentioned earlier in this book, has said:

> I do not trade specifically on short interest. I work up all my trades the way I usually do, but then look at Short Interest to help rule trades in or out. Given two trades of equal attractiveness, I am more apt to buy a stock with a higher Short Interest Ratio. I know that the people who are short will have to come in and buy it— that there will be willing buyers. But I will not buy a stock simply because it has a high Short Interest Ratio (see Figure 7.29).

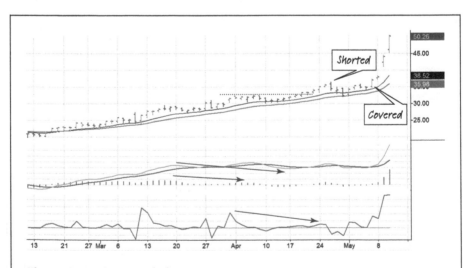

Figure 7.30   HANS daily

The divergence looked beautiful, and the stock started curling down. What we overlooked at the time was its high short interest. The stock just started going up and up, and we had to cut losses. Then it gapped up on a major distribution agreement with an industry leader.

I also pay attention to short interest when looking at potential shorts. Here I primarily use the Short Interest Ratio as a filter to help me stay away from certain stocks. I do not want to be a part of the crowd, trying to pass through that door. Remember when both you and I were shorting HANS? (See Figure 7.30.)

Misery loves company and happiness loves solitude. The Short Interest Ratio and Days to Cover help you find stocks whose short side is not overcrowded.

CHAPTER 8

SHORTING NON-EQUITY INSTRUMENTS

While there are some restrictions on shorting stocks, we are free to short futures, options, and forex. Those markets simply could not exist without shorting.

As a stock trader, you must learn to buy and sell, but shorting is optional. Even in bear markets, where buying opportunities are few and far between, a savvy bull can find an industry group that rises while others sink. Still, a stock trader who knows how to sell short has a definite advantage over a perma-bull, especially during bear markets. This is why I encourage you to learn to sell short.

While only a small minority of stock traders ever sell short, a vast amount of shorting takes place in forex, futures, and options. As a matter of fact, the volume of shorting in futures or forex is exactly equal to that of buying! For every contract bought there is a contract sold short.

Shorting is an integral part of the derivatives markets. Instead of teaching you the A-to-Z of futures, options, and forex, I will begin each section by referring you to what I think are the best books on that market. They will help you learn the basics of futures, options, or forex before delving into how to sell them short. Then, as we get into a discussion of each market, we will jump right into shorting.

SHORTING FUTURES

When you buy a stock, you buy a share in an existing business. When you go long a futures contract, you buy nothing but simply enter into a binding contract for a future purchase of a commodity. The person on the opposite side of your trade enters into a contract for a future sale. This means that for every long there is a short, for every promise to buy

Futures: Recommended Literature

Winning in the Futures Markets by George Angell is the best introductory
book for futures traders (and the only book by that author I recommend).
The Futures Game by Teweles and Jones is a mini-encyclopedia that has
educated generations of futures traders (be sure to get the latest edition).
Economics of Futures Trading by Thomas A. Hieronymus is a profound
book, but it's long been out of print—try finding a used copy. Last but not
least, there is a chapter on futures in my book *Come into My Trading Room.*

a promise to sell. Those promises are backed by margin deposits on
both sides.

Nobody expressed the basic principles of futures trading better than
the late Thomas Hieronymus in his *Economics of Futures Trading.* One of
the deepest and wisest books on futures, it unfortunately has been out
of print for many decades. Probably because this is not a "how to" book,
nobody cares to reprint it, with only an occasional used copy turning up
on book-selling websites. Leafing through my old copy, I want to share
with you several quotes, before we turn to the topic of shorting futures.

Of course, in shorting futures there is no silly "uptick rule." When you
place an order to sell a future, it makes no difference whether it is an
order to sell a long position or to open a new short trade.

There is no prohibition against insider trading. You can track the behavior of the insiders through the "commitments of traders" reports regularly published by the CFTC (Commodity Futures Trading Commission).

Most shorts in most futures markets are held by the commercials or
hedgers who are the true insiders. For example, a major agribusiness
may sell futures to lock in a good price for a harvest that has not yet
been gathered. But that is only part of the game. Any hedger worth its
salt runs its futures division as a profit center and not merely as a price
insurance office. They expect to make money on those shorts.

As futures prices swing, a hugely important factor, pointed out by
Hieronymus, comes into play. Commodities incur carrying charges, as
the cost of storing, financing, and insuring them gets worked into their
price. If this process were to continue unabated, month after month,
prices would gradually climb to dizzying heights. What happens instead
is that relatively slow and steady price increases get punctuated by brief
violent drops, returning prices to realistic levels—and then the process
begins again.

Hieronymus on Futures

- The market is a balance of judgments, so that for every good judgment there is a poor judgment. Futures trading is an exciting game, the score of which is kept with money.
- A commodity contract has a short life span. Thus, speculative fictions in securities can be long perpetuated but speculative excesses in commodities, up or down, are soon pricked by the test of the first delivery day.
- The supply harvested during a short period of time must be made to last until the next crop is available. There is one and only one average price that will make the supply just clear the market.
- The current price reflects the composite judgment of the traders in forecasting the equilibrium price. The composite judgment of all the market participants is that the equilibrium has been found and that prices will not change. But none of the individuals who make up the composite think that the equilibrium has been reached, else they would not have a position. Obviously, the composite is always wrong.
- To take a position in a market is to challenge the aggregate judgment—to say that the market is in error.
- Each speculator must identify and do his own thing. Perhaps more importantly, he must stay out of someone else's game. The market will tell its own story and your only task is to hear it fast.
- To try to squeeze out the last bit of opportunity is to get too cute with the market; to be too disdainful of the intelligence of the market. The locals are in the business of fine-tuning.
- In the aggregate, the participants break even gross and lose net by the amount paid in commissions, brokerage, and clearing fees.
- The big contributors to the game are the people who badly overstay positions.
- The people who do not trade regularly and consistently are among the biggest contributors to the game.
- The existence of inventories creates a carrying charge. The effect is to force a continually rising price of futures. But if the basic value is unchanged over time, a continual rise in futures is not possible. Accordingly, the total price structure must periodically collapse.

As the waves pound the sand at an ocean shore, they build up the dunes. At some point the dunes fall under their own weight, and the whole process begins anew. This is exactly what you see in most futures markets—slow build-ups followed by quick collapses.

On Futures

Buying a stock makes you a part-owner of a company. When you buy a futures contract you don't own anything, but enter into a binding contract for a future purchase of merchandise, be it a carload of wheat or a sheaf of Treasury bonds. The person who sells you that contract assumes the obligation to deliver.

Each futures contract has a settlement date, with contracts for different dates selling for different prices. Many professionals analyze the spreads between the months to predict reversals.

Futures can be very attractive for those who have strong money management skills. They promise high rates of return but demand ice-cold discipline. When you first approach trading, you are better off with slower-moving stocks. Once you have matured as a trader, take a look at futures. They may be right for you if you're very disciplined.

Futures, unlike stocks, have natural floors and ceilings. Those levels are not rigid, but before you buy or sell, try to find out whether you're closer to the floor or the ceiling. The floor price of futures is their cost of production. When a market falls below that level, producers start quitting, supply falls, and prices rise. If there is a glut of sugar, and its price on the world markets falls below what it costs to grow the stuff, major producers are going to start shutting down their operations. There are exceptions, such as when a desperately poor country sells commodities on the world markets to earn hard currency while paying domestic workers with devalued local money. The price can dip below the cost of production, but it cannot stay there for long.

The ceiling for most commodities is the cost of substitution. One commodity can replace another, if the price is right. For example, with a rise in the price of corn, a major animal feed, it may be cheaper to feed animals wheat. As more farmers switch and reduce corn purchases, they take away the fuel that raised corn prices. A market in the grip of hysteria may briefly rise above its ceiling, but cannot stay there for long. Its return to the normal range provides profit opportunities for savvy traders. Learning from history can help you keep calm when others are losing their heads.

Adapted from *Come into My Trading Room,*
by Dr. Alexander Elder, John Wiley & Sons, Inc., 2002

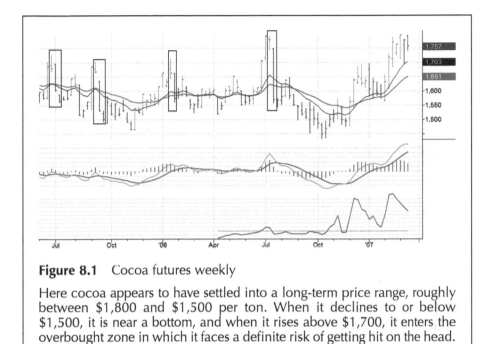

Figure 8.1 Cocoa futures weekly

Here cocoa appears to have settled into a long-term price range, roughly between $1,800 and $1,500 per ton. When it declines to or below $1,500, it is near a bottom, and when it rises above $1,700, it enters the overbought zone in which it faces a definite risk of getting hit on the head.

While there are many great opportunities for buying in the futures markets, this is a book about selling and selling short. This is why we will bypass buying and take a closer look at shorting futures. Let us see how we can take advantage of their propensity for relatively slow and steady rises and sharp declines.

Cocoa is a notoriously difficult market to trade. An American journalist who used to write under the pseudonym of Adam Smith in the 1970s quipped that if you ever feel a desire to trade cocoa futures, just lie down and wait until the feeling passes. Cocoa is notorious for its brief violent moves. As you can see on this chart, most of its violence is to the downside (Figure 8.1).

Even in a relatively peaceful stock market, rallies tend to last longer than declines. Here, in futures, declines tend to be compressed into sharp shakeouts. Even during this fairly flat range in cocoa, you can see that most rallies take several weeks or even months, while most declines are over in a single week. They cover great distances and terminate old bulls, clearing the path for a new gradual advance.

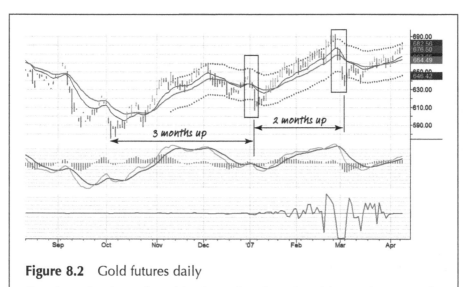

Figure 8.2   Gold futures daily

Crawl up slowly and tumble down fast: it took gold over three months to rise from $575 to $660—but only three days to slam down to $606, retracing 64% of the price increase. The next rise, from $607 to $692, went on for over two months—followed by a drop to $635, a 67% decline, in only four days. Those long, gradual rises lull most traders into a false sense of security, prepairing the ground for successful shorts.

Slow and shallow rises make beginners think that their longs are safe. Then a sudden event, like an unexpected blow, punctures their balloon, and the air escapes with a great *whoosh!* The shorts, many of them professional traders, clean up while public traders get taken out feet first, and the next round of the game is ready to begin. At the right edge of Figure 8.2, gold is in the midst of a slow and steady rise, looking very peaceful, as if saying to bulls "everything's nice, come here to play."

A savvy trader looks at the time scale at the bottom of the daily chart (Figure 8.2) and notices that the rise has been going on for a month and a half and covered a distance of $42. He knows that if he buys gold here he absolutely must use stops—and hard stops at that. Furthermore, it may make sense to use stop-and-reverse orders. I am not a huge fan of such orders, but they can make sense during slow rallies, since they

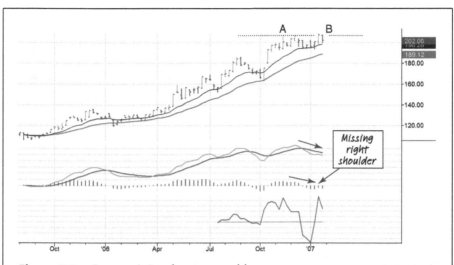

Figure 8.3   Orange juice futures weekly

The weekly chart of OJ showed a false breakout to a new high accompanied by a bearish divergence—one of the most attractive patterns in technical analysis. At point B, OJ broke above the level of the top A but could not hold the altitude and dropped back into range. MACD Lines traced a bearish divergence. MACD-Histogram showed an extremely powerful pattern that Jackie Patterson, a member of the Spike group, has named "a missing right shoulder" (actually, Jackie used a more colorful term that I slightly toned down).

   In area A, MACD-Histogram rallied well above the zero line, creating a left shoulder. Then it cracked below zero, "breaking the back of the bull." Later, at point B, MACD-Histogram could not lift itself above the zero line. It just pulled up towards zero and then ticked down. This weekly chart was a screaming sell. The rally had been going on for a while, and the clock was ticking for one of those downdrafts that occur when the bubble gets pricked.

can help you get stopped into a short position simultaneously with the closing of the long one.

   In conclusion, let me pull up a record of a futures trade from my diary (Figure 8.3). This trade shows how a trader can capitalize on futures' tendency for quick deflationary moves.

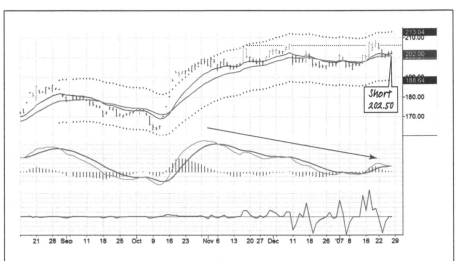

Figure 8.4   Orange juice futures daily, entry

The daily chart also showed a failed upside breakout accompanied by a bearish divergence of MACD Lines. While this signal was not as strong as on the weekly charts, it certainly did not contradict the weekly. It is quite normal for either the weekly or the daily to send a better signal—and whenever that happens, the weekly trumps the daily. I decided to short OJ soon after the opening on Monday, unless there was an extremely strong rally at the open or if the price collapsed before I could get in.

OJ 3/7	short	Date	Upchannel	Downchannel	Day's High	Day's Low	Grade
Entry	$202.50	29-Jan-07	212.50	188.25	$203.80	$195.25	85%
Exit							
P/L						Trade	

OJ drew my attention while doing my weekend homework. On most weekends, I take about an hour to review all the major U.S. futures markets. One of several advantages of futures is that there are so few of them. It is easy to keep track of all futures, unlike the many thousands of stocks.

The price balloon got pricked soon after the opening on Monday. The slow sluggish uptrend was punctured, letting out the hot air that had held up OJ (Figure 8.4).

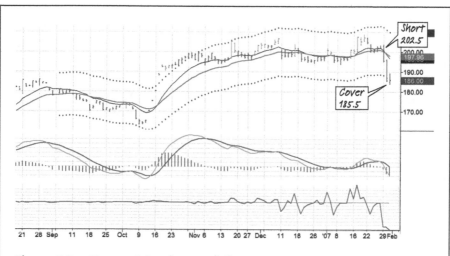

Figure 8.5 Orange juice futures daily, exit

When prices stabbed below their lower channel line on the daily charts, my target was reached and I covered shorts in OJ. The trade was over and done within two days. Perhaps the collapse would continue, but with the profit target already hit, I had no further reason to stay in the trade.

OJ 3/7	short	Date	Upchannel	Downchannel	Day's High	Day's Low	Grade
Entry	202.50	29-Jan-07	212.50	188.25	$203.80	$195.25	85%
Exit	185.50	31-Jan-07			$189.25	$184.20	74%
P/L					Trade		70%

This was an emotionally as well as financially satisfying trade—I wish more of my trades were like this (Figure 8.5). The entry made logical sense and the exit signals were very clear. It pays to be aware of the fact that futures tend to have long slow rises and quick violent declines that hurt slow bulls and offer fantastic rewards to quick bears.

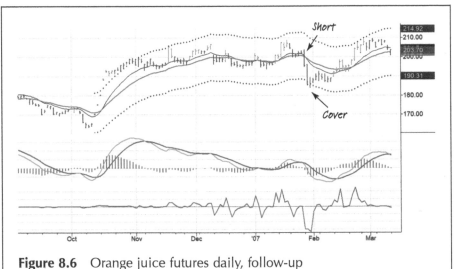

Figure 8.6 Orange juice futures daily, follow-up

Looking at OJ almost two months later, both the entry and the exit made a lot of sense. At the right edge of the chart, OJ is starting to sink again, after a false upside breakout indicating another likely spell of trouble.

WRITING OPTIONS

In options, there is a sharp dividing line between two groups of people. On the one side are the beginners and gamblers who lose money year after miserable year. On the other side are the pros, making a steady living in the options market.

Do you know where that line is drawn?

The great dividing line in options is between the buyers and the writers. On the one side of the line are the winners who write options. On the other are the losers who buy them.

Options: Recommended Literature

Every options trader should own Lawrence McMillan's *Options as a Strategic Investment.* You will probably use it as a handbook rather than read it from cover to cover. Many professionals read Sheldon Natenberg's *Option Volatility and Pricing Strategies.* Harvey Friedentag's *Options: Investing Without Fear* has a nice angle on covered writing.

I have never in my life met a person who built equity buying options.

Almost every option buyer can tell you about a successful trade or even a few trades in the options market. But those are merely flashes in the pan—totally different from having a long-term positive equity curve. Those occasional wins are like payouts from a slot machine—enough to keep losers motivated to throw more money away.

Options tend to attract poor beginners because the game is cheaper than stocks. Many buy options as a substitute for stocks, and I always tell such folks that they are chasing a deadly illusion. The key difference between options and stocks is that options are wasting assets. When you buy an option, you have to be right on the stock, right on the extent of its move, and right on your timing. This would be like trying to toss a ball through three moving rings at an amusement park.

A beginner can be bullish on a stock, buy its calls, watch that stock go up, and still lose money. He might be right on the trend, but if the stock takes longer than expected to hit his target, the option will expire worthless. After taking his lumps a beginner may decide to shop for a longer-term option next time. Then he discovers that longer-term options are ruinously expensive.

A woman who was a market maker on the floor of the American Exchange once said to me: "Options are a hope business. You can buy hope or sell hope. I am a professional—I sell hope. I come to the floor in the morning, find out what people hope for, price that hope, and sell it to them."

Profits in the options business are in the writing, not in buying.

When you write options, you begin every trade by taking in someone else's money. A hopeful buyer forks over some money to a writer who is almost always a much more experienced trader. As lawyers say, possession is 90% of the law. The job of options writers is to hang on to buyers' money and not let it slip away.

Poor option buyers are twisting in the wind, trying to convert hope into money. Meanwhile, options sellers lean back and enjoy the passage of time. An options writer has shorted a wasting asset, and as time chips away at its value, it will cost him less and less to cover his short. Its value might even go down to zero, and then he will not have to pay a commission to cover his short position.

It is easy for a successful option writer to feel magnanimous and give a little money back to the poor buyer. If he has sold an option for a dollar and now that option is quoted for a dime, there is not much reason to hold it to expiration. He has already earned the bulk of what was available from that trade and there is no need to try and squeeze out the last cent. If he buys the option back for ten cents, he will close the trade, escape any future risk, and will have the peace of mind to look for another option to write.

In options, as in so many things in life, it pays to do things differently from the crowd. Since most traders are heavy buyers of options, it is a good idea to take a contrary tack and write options. As you become more experienced, it will feel very sweet to take what kills most options traders—time—and convert it into a source of profit.

The main choice in selling options is whether to write them covered or naked. In covered writing, you write options against the stocks you own. In naked writing, you create options out of thin air, backing them with the capital in your trading account.

Covered Writing

If you hold a stock whose upside potential appears limited, you may sell calls on your shares. You will immediately collect cash from the sale and then wait for one of three things to happen:

- If the stock stays relatively flat and does not reach the option's exercise price, you will pocket the premium, boosting your total return.

- If the stock falls, you will also pocket the premium, cushioning the fall in your stock.

- If the stock rises above the option exercise price, it will be called away. You'll keep the premium in addition to the capital gain on the stock. Since there is a big universe of interesting stocks out there, you take your freed-up capital and look for new opportunities.

After you sell a stock short, you can sell puts against your short position. If the stock stays flat, you keep the option premium. If it rises, you also keep the premium, reducing your loss on the short position. If the stock falls below the exercise level for the put, your position will be called away. You'll keep the premium and also pocket the capital gain.

The main use of covered writing is to boost returns and reduce losses in a large stock portfolio. It is a labor- and capital-intensive business. It is not enough to go out and write covered calls on a single stock—that would be too much work for a small reward. To make economic sense, covered writing needs to be done for a large number of stocks. As your stock portfolio gets bigger, covered writing makes more and more sense. The manager of a multimillion-dollar diversified stock portfolio owes it to his investors to explore putting that portfolio into a covered writing program.

Naked Writing

The edgy, promising, but dangerous area of the options business is writing naked options. While conservative investors write covered calls against their stocks, naked writers create options out of thin air. They are protected only by their cash and skill and need to be absolutely disciplined in taking profits or cutting losses.

When I began working on this chapter, I called Dr. Diane Buffalin in Michigan, an experienced writer of naked options, and asked for a few examples of her trades. Diane sounded bubbly when she talked of her love of writing options.

> I am doing lots of boring options trades. It's so simple, I could teach my granddaughter to do it. I said to her—you go to an art high school, you can recognize lines. I can show you—when those lines stop going down, it is time to sell a put.
>
> I like taking money in and do not like paying it out. Happiness is selling an option that expires worthless. I had taken my Schedule D to several accountants who said there was a problem with it; buy prices were missing. I had to explain to them that I had sold options and they expired worthless.
>
> I love naked selling. The problem with covered selling is that to make money on an option you have to lose some on a stock, and I don't like that. I look for stocks that I would like to own which are declining. When they stop going down I sell their puts and collect a 10% premium.
>
> I feel like a dealer in a casino, making money off the players' egos. Those flashy guys keep coming in, wearing gold chains. They throw hundreds of dollars on my table for some plastic yellow chips. The wheel keeps spinning and they have fun, but on the third Friday of the month the wheel stops, and that's when I collect. I try not to smile too much, not to show them how happy I am to have their business.
>
> I am a professional psychologist, but the insurance company pays the same rate whether I give a patient good advice or not.

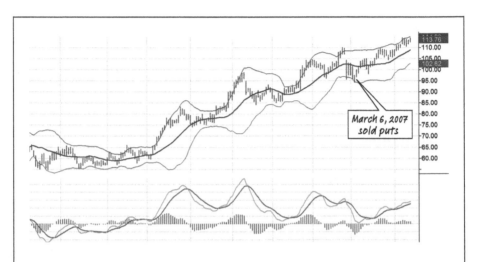

Figure 8.7   ATI daily

ATI hit the bottom of the Bollinger band on March 5th and was rebounding: The MACD had stopped going down—that was my trigger. At that time I had two choices. I could buy 1,000 shares of the stock at 97, but that would put $97,000 of my money at risk after a precipitous drop in the market. Alternatively, I could sell a put and take in about $4,800 for my promise to buy a good stock at a $2 discount from its current price. I sold the April 95 put for $4.80, taking in $4,800. It is now worth only 5 cents, and I will let it expire and have another zero in my "Paid" column.

Trading is the only business where you get paid in proportion to how smart you are. But you have to work hard. People keep asking me to teach them to write options. I give them a few stocks to follow and tell them to keep a daily list of their prices, along with several options prices. Not one person who came to me could keep that list up for a month. Lazy.

A stock can go up, down, or sideways. If you buy a stock or an option, you have one way to make money and two ways to lose. When I sell an option, I have two ways to make money, and sometimes even three. The time to sell an option is when a stock stops moving, and the sharper its move has been, the more they will pay you for the option.

Here are two simple current option trades on two popular stocks: ATI (Allegheny Technologies) and CHL (China Mobil). On March 6,

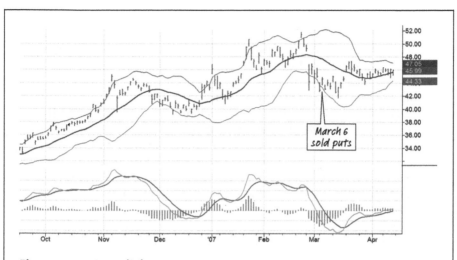

Figure 8.8 CHL daily

Initially, it appeared I was wrong about this stock, as it fell further during the Asia sell-off. It dropped to $41.70 a week later, but I didn't fold my position. The option was showing a $300 loss, but the stock was still above my break-even point and time was definitely on my side. Currently, the stock is at $45.90, the option shows about $1,500 profit, and it still has two more months to make the other $1,500. It looks as if the only thing better than being right and making money, is being wrong and making money anyway!

2007, both stocks showed a pattern I like. I visually scan my charts for this pattern because I am not computer-savvy enough to create an electronic scan.

The stock market had dropped precipitously on February 27 and was still forming a bottom. Because of the high volatility, puts had a bit more of a premium. That was good. Better to sell more expensive merchandise than cheap merchandise—there is more profit built into the price (Figure 8.7).

The downside was that I could have made a lot more money buying the stock, which is now at 113, but then I would have had to put $97,000 of capital at risk, and I like to sleep at night and not live on antacids. Actually, I did make a lot more money on the stock by continuing to sell puts at higher strike prices, much the way you would add to a stock position.

I also sold the puts on China Mobil on the same day, for the same reason (Figure 8.8). The stock was at $44.5, and its June 45 put was at $4.80. I selected June because that's how far I had to go to make 10%, which is what I like to get. I'm really selling time, thinking that in three months the stock will not drop below 45. If it drops and I have to buy it, I'll receive a 10% discount.

People ask me all the time, "If selling options is so great, how come more people don't do it?" I think it's because most options traders like to gamble. They look for tips, but have little patience to play options like chess. Buying options takes little money (about 10% of the stock price), but selling them takes considerable cash. Most brokerage houses won't let you sell puts unless you have at least $100,000; some require $250,000 and two years' experience. Brokerage houses say they are trying to protect you, but they let you buy options which have a high probability of losing money; they won't let you sell options, which have a much lower probability of losing money.

If you sell a put, the worst thing that can happen is that you will buy a stock at a predetermined price. How awful is that? Don't millions of investors and traders do exactly that every day? So I just sell puts on stocks that I would buy anyway, at a price that I would gladly pay. The only difference is that I get to make the profit without putting my capital into the market. I actually have it in secure bonds, earning interest. And what is the worst thing that can happen if you sell a naked call? You end up with a short position on a volatile stock. Isn't that exactly what many professional traders do anyway? I love options because I get my profit up-front. And "the worst thing that could happen" is just fine with me.

FOREX

Whereas the sections on futures and options began with lists of recommended books, I cannot offer such a list here. There is not a single book on trading forex that I can confidently hand to you and say "It is good; read it." You will have to pick bits and pieces from among the stacks of books on forex.

The forex market has several distinct segments, and your choice of where to trade will have a huge impact on your chances of winning or losing. The differences between traders in the forex market remind me of the class system in a Third World country. There are a few rich citizens, the great unwashed masses of poor people who are not likely to ever get a fair shake, and a tiny middle class, trying to hold on to its tenuous gains.

The big money plays in the interbank market, where dealers trade tens of millions of dollars at a clip. The middle class is in forex futures, getting battered by gap openings because futures trade almost 24/7. Down at the bottom of the pyramid are the poor folks with small trading accounts at forex houses.

Gamblers, losers, and poorly capitalized beginners are always on the lookout for the next big chance to get rich quick. Years ago they used to trade odd lots on the stock exchange, and then moved to buying options. After they lost their shirts and many other garments, the get-rich-quick crowd migrated into the forex market.

The trouble with forex is that most forex houses operate as bucket shops. When you place an order to buy or sell, they give you what they call a confirmation. In fact, there is not a real trade, merely a bookkeeping entry. Whatever you want to trade, the forex house will take the opposite side of your trade, knowing full well that the clients will lose on balance. They hit starry-eyed dreamers with multiple charges to help them go down faster.

Forex houses offer wild margins, as high as 400:1. Remember, you need to pay 50% as a margin in stocks, perhaps as low as 5% in futures. The 0.2% margin in forex ensures that no meaningful money management is even remotely possible.

Aside from charging you a spread when you buy or sell, a forex house charges interest on your nonexistent "position." In fact there is usually no real position, only a bookkeeping entry, since your order has not gone anywhere. When you trade a cross, a forex house will pay less than base rate on the long leg of the currency trade and charge more than the base rate on the short leg of the trade.

When you trade stocks, a brokerage house does not care whether you make or lose money. They merely execute your orders and collect commissions. In most forex houses, instead of transmitting orders to the markets, the brokers simply play against their customers. The forex shops are betting against you on every trade. This means that in order for you to make money, the broker has to lose. This is a deeply flawed system. The stock market was purged of this malignancy nearly a century ago, but the broom has not yet reached the forex shops.

The proprietors of forex houses know that customers are doomed because of lack of skill, and poor capitalization. Why transmit an order to the market and share the money with someone else?

Spreads, commissions, and interest charges on non-existent positions drive the nails into gamblers' coffins.

Savvy dealers monitor their clientele's total positions, and when those become too one-sided in any given market, say by $1 million, they lay off that risk in the interbank market. Some houses go a step further—when clients' positions reach an extreme, they trade against them.

A really honest house, transmitting trades for execution, would suffer from a terrific competitive disadvantage in comparison to the bucket shops. Bucket shops can always underprice an honest house because they do not have to pay the execution costs. I am sure there are some decent and properly run forex houses, but the deck is stacked against them.

Governments around the world have failed to clean up the forex business. I hope that in the future some private entrepreneurs using Internet technology will create a more even playing field for small forex traders. Until such a transparent system emerges, I have only two words for you—buyer beware!

If you do not have millions of dollars to play the interbank market and are too smart to use a bucket shop, you're left with only one choice —forex futures. These were first traded in the pits of the Chicago Mercantile Exchange in the 1970s. Now, of course, forex futures trade in many countries on different continents. More importantly, they trade electronically, providing access to a well-established and transparent business virtually around the clock.

Why would anyone go to a bucket shop instead of forex futures? To trade a forex future, you might need to lay down a couple of thousand dollars margin. At the same time, some forex shops allow you to open an account with as little as $50, while offering a "shoulder" of 100:1, meaning you can buy $5,000 worth of forex with your measly deposit. Of course, you "buy" nothing except for a receipt from that bucket shop which then charges you interest on the entire $5,000.

Needless to say, to trade forex futures you must understand how to trade futures in the first place. There are many books on this topic, and my favorites are listed in the previous section. My goal here is merely to point out the differences between shorting forex and shorting stocks.

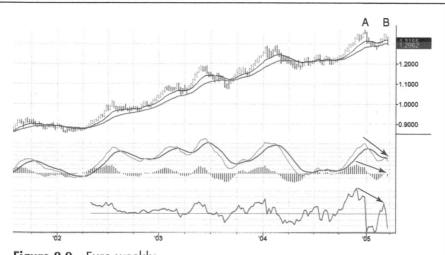

Figure 8.9 Euro weekly

This chart shows a four-year upmove in the euro against the U.S. dollar. The trend, driven by economic fundamentals, appeared unstoppable. One could buy and hold or try to play the swings At the right edge of the chart there are multiple severe bearish divergences. The bulls are healthy and powerful at peak A, which was followed by a normal pullback to the value zone. The rally to peak B was accompanied by prominent bearish divergences in MACD Lines and the Force Index; the divergence of MACD-Histogram was of a particularly ominous type—a missing right shoulder. The signals to sell and sell short were loud and clear.

Shorting is an integral aspect of forex because whenever you buy one currency, you automatically go short another. Buying forex without shorting at the same time is impossible, like finding a coin with only one side.

All trades are measured in money. Depending on where you live, you deal in dollars or pounds or yen, and so on. If your trading account is in dollars and you buy the euro, then as you go long the euro, you automatically go short the dollar. If you short the Swiss franc in that same dollar account, you automatically go long the dollar.

A forex trader can go outside of his home currency by trading the so-called "crosses." For example, EURAUD means long the Euro, short the Australian dollar. SWFJPY means long Swiss, short Yen. Every forex

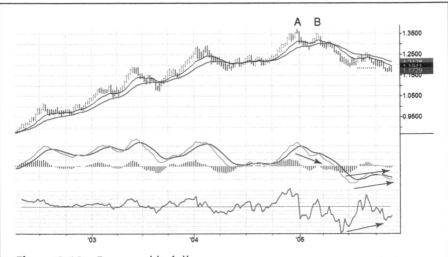

Figure 8.10   Euro weekly follow-up

The euro's downward reversal was initially pooh-poohed by the bullish crowd. As the downtrend deepened, the crowd woke up and started looking for a bottom, to load up for the next upleg. When the euro fell below its latest bottom, they threw in the towel. That's where the buy signal emerged, almost a mirror image of the sell signals at the top: a false downside breakout, with bullish divergences in all the indicators. One could not hope for a better set of signals to cover shorts and go long.

trade is a spread trade. When you speak of buying forex it automatically means shorting some other forex—you cannot buy or sell just one side of a coin.

Study after study has confirmed that the forex market is among the most trending in the world (Figures 8.9 and 8.10). Once a currency gets into a major trend, whether up or down, it might stay in it for years. This is due to the fact that in the long run, the value of a country currency depends on government policies. When a new government comes to power and starts implementing its economic policies, a currency is likely to enter into a long-term trend. No trend, of course, proceeds in a straight line. In the short and intermediate term, there is a lot of backing and filling. Those counter-trend moves are frequent enough and large enough to provide short-term trading opportunities.

Keep in mind that one type of trading that works well in the stock market is likely to be very problematic in the forex market. Swing trading, which involves holding a position from several days to a couple of weeks, is much more prone to whipsaws in forex than in the stock market.

The reason for this difficulty is that forex trades essentially 24/7, and what you see on the charts in your time zone is just a segment of total worldwide activity. The bulk of trading takes place while you are asleep or away from the screen. It is hard to bet on a horse that keeps running around the track while you're dreaming in your bed.

To sidestep this problem you can move into either very long-term or very short-term trading. You can open a small position with a very wide stop and try to hold it through thick and thin, riding a long-term trend. Alternatively, you can zoom into the right edge of the chart and day-trade forex, closing your positions at the end of the day and avoiding overnight risk.

HOW TO SELL SHORT

As markets rise and fall, the vast majority of traders and investors miss half of the action. They try to profit from going long. Every beginner buys something, but it takes an experienced trader to recognize an overvalued market and sell it short.

Shorting—profiting from market declines—is one of the favorite games of market professionals. They account for the bulk of shorting in most markets. Whenever you see a situation in which the mass of amateurs is crowding one side, while the more experienced and better capitalized professionals are on the opposite side, ask yourself—which side is more likely to win?

It pays to run your trading account like a hedge fund, with some long and some short positions at any given time, shifting their balance as your view of the market changes. Being comfortable with selling short allows you to wrestle with the market while standing on both feet. This is much better than standing on just one foot, only going long.

Selling short has its own challenges, which you must master. This chapter will test your knowledge of the basic concepts of shorting tops and downtrends. It will quiz you on the pluses and minuses of shorting, on short interest, and on selecting stocks for shorting. It will also ask you about shorting non-equity instruments.

**Please go through all questions in this section and record
your answers prior to turning to the Answers section.**

Answer Sheet

Questions	Max. Pts. Available	Trial 1	Trial 2	Trial 3	Trial 4	Trial 5	Trial 6
87	1						
88	1						
89	1						
90	1						
91	1						
92	1						
93	1						
94	1						
95	1						
96	1						
97	1						
98	1						
99	1						
100	1						
101	1						
102	1						
103	1						
104	1						
105	1						
106	1						
107	1						
108	1						
109	1						
110	1						

(continues on next page)

Answer Sheet, *continued*

Questions	Max. Pts. Available	Trial 1	Trial 2	Trial 3	Trial 4	Trial 5	Trial 6
111	1						
112	1						
113	1						
114	1						
115	1						
Total points	29						

Question 87—Shorting a Stock

Selling a stock short means:

1. Selling an overvalued stock from your portfolio
2. Selling a borrowed stock
3. Selling a stock in a severe downtrend
4. Selling a stock you expect to be delisted

Question 88—Risk Factors in Shorting

The major risk factors in selling short include all of the following, except:

1. A stock might rally.
2. A stock might issue a dividend.
3. A stock might be called back by the owner.
4. A stock might crash.

Question 89—The Impact of Shorting

People who sell stocks short help create a more orderly market through all of the following, except:

1. Dampening price increases
2. Cushioning price declines
3. Increasing price swings
4. Dampening volatility

Question 90—Short vs. Long

The main advantage of shorting over buying is that:

1. Tops are easier to recognize than bottoms.
2. Stocks fall faster than they rise.
3. It is easier to sell into a rally than buy into a decline.
4. Stocks rise faster than they fall.

Question 91—Disadvantages of Shorting

The greatest disadvantage in shorting stocks is that the stock market:

1. Keeps fluctuating
2. Has relatively slow rises and fast declines
3. Rises over time
4. Has an uptick rule

Question 92—Learning to Sell Short

Which statement about learning to sell short is incorrect?

1. Find a stock you'd hate to own.
2. Trade a large size to make the experience worthwhile.
3. Avoid shorting stocks making new highs.
4. Look for expensive stocks.

Question 93—Shorting vs. Buying

Find the correct statement among the following comparisons of buying and shorting:

1. Tops take longer to form than bottoms.
2. Stock bottoms are built on hope and greed.
3. Precise timing is more important in buying than shorting.
4. Fear is the dominant emotion of stock tops.

Question 94—Shorting Stock Market Tops

Which statement about shorting stock market tops is incorrect?

1. Stops need to be placed relatively farther away, due to high volatility.
2. Wider stops require larger positions.
3. There is nothing wrong with trying to re-enter a trade after getting stopped out.
4. Trading positions smaller than the maximum allowed by money management rules increase holding power.

Question 95—Shorting in Downtrends

Find the correct statement regarding shorting in downtrends:

1. Shorting in the middle of a channel means shorting above value.
2. Covering near the lower channel line means buying below value.
3. There is only one good shorting opportunity within a channel.
4. Grading your trades by the percentage of a channel does not work for shorting.

Question 96—The Tactics of Shorting Downtrends

Find the incorrect statement about shorting in downtrends:

1. Make a strategic decision on the weekly chart, tactical plans on the daily.
2. Shorting within a channel lowers both the risk and the rewards.
3. Shorting within a channel increases the risk of a whipsaw.
4. A single short within a channel will not catch a major move.

Question 97—Shorting the Fundamentals

Find the correct statement about shorting on the basis of fundamental information:

1. A fundamental analyst can cover more markets than a technician.
2. One can use technical studies as an idea generator and fundamentals as a trigger.
3. Fundamental information overrides technical factors.
4. The most powerful situation exists when the fundamentals suggest a trade and technical factors confirm that signal.

Question 98—Looking for Shorting Candidates

Which of the following is not a valid method of looking for shorting candidates?

1. Looking at the weakest stock industry groups
2. Listening to rumors and tips, then checking them using your analytic method
3. Looking for the weakest stocks among the Nasdaq 100
4. Selling short stocks that are being upgraded by major analysts

Question 99—The Short Interest Ratio

The Short Interest Ratio reflects the intensity of shorting by measuring:

1. The number of shares held short by the bears relative to the "free float."
2. The number of stocks shorted by a trader relative to the number of shares he bought.
3. The number of traders holding shorts relative to the number of traders holding longs.
4. The number of traders whose accounts are set up for shorting relative to the total number of traders.

Question 100—Trading the Short Interest Ratio

Tracking the Short Interest Ratio can help a trader in all of the following ways, except:

1. A rising Short Interest Ratio confirms a downtrend.
2. A Short Interest Ratio over 20% warns that the stock is liable to have a sharp rally.
3. A Short Interest Ratio under 10% means that shorting is relatively safe.
4. A falling Short Interest Ratio calls for a break in the stock.

Question 101—Markets Need Shorting

Which of the following markets could exist without shorting?

1. Stocks
2. Futures
3. Options
4. Forex

Question 102—Who Shorts Futures

Most shorts in the futures markets are being held by:

1. Public speculators
2. Commercials or hedgers
3. CFTC
4. Hedge funds

Question 103—Shorting Futures

Find the incorrect statement about shorting futures:

1. A seller enters into a binding contract for future delivery.
2. The floor for a commodity price is defined by its cost of production.
3. Insider trading is illegal in futures.
4. The ceiling for a commodity price is defined by the cost of substitution.

Question 104—Long Rallies and Sharp Breaks

What is the main factor that makes commodities prone to sharp breaks?

1. Carrying charges
2. Manipulation
3. Seasonal factors
4. Cost of substitution

Question 105—Writing Options

What is the main reason that options writing is much more profitable than buying?

1. The time value of options
2. Most buyers are undercapitalized.
3. Options move differently than stocks.
4. Most buyers are beginners.

Question 106—Writing Covered Options

What is the main disadvantage of writing covered options?
1. If the stock stays flat, you will have no capital gain in it.
2. If the stock falls, your long position will lose value.
3. If the stock rises above the exercise price, it will be called away.
4. Covered writing requires large capital.

Question 107—Naked vs. Covered Writing

What is the main difference between naked and covered options writing?
1. Trade duration
2. How the trades are backed
3. Trade size
4. The analytic techniques

Question 108—The Demands of Naked Writing

The greatest demand that naked writing of options places on traders is:
1. Cash
2. Trading ideas
3. Discipline
4. Timing

Question 109—Brokers Against Traders

In the following list of venues for trading forex, where does a broker's profit usually depend on a trader's loss?
1. The interbank market
2. Currency futures
3. Holding foreign cash
4. Forex trading houses

Question 110—Forex Market

Which of the following does not apply to the forex market?

1. It is one of the most trending markets on a long-term basis.
2. It is largely driven by the fundamentals of government policies.
3. It is easy to plan and enter trades in forex.
4. It trades essentially 24/7.

Question 111—Learning to Become a Better Trader

The most important factor in learning to become a better trader is:

1. Researching the market
2. Keeping good records
3. Finessing your entry and exit techniques
4. Luck

Question 112—Trading Signals of the Force Index

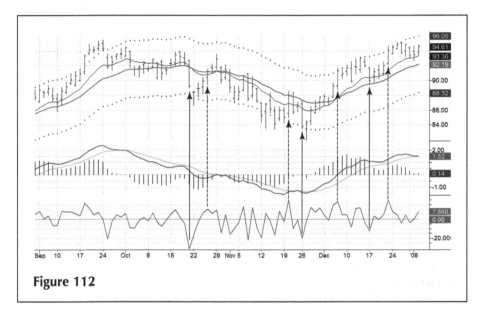

Figure 112

On the chart above, you can see that the downspikes of the Force Index (marked by solid arrows) tend to be followed by price bottoms the following day. The chart also shows that the upspikes of the Force Index (marked by dashed arrows) tend to be followed by the continuation of the uptrend rather than a top. These differences indicate that:

1. This indicator works only in downtrends.
2. This indicator works only in uptrends.
3. Uptrends and downtrends are not symmetrical and have to be traded differently.
4. One can base a trade on a single indicator in a bear market.

Question 113—False Breakouts and Divergences

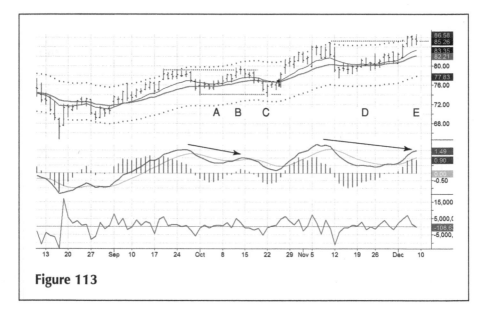

Figure 113

Please match the letters on the chart to the following descriptions:

1. False breakouts
2. Divergences

Question 114—Shorting and Covering Signals

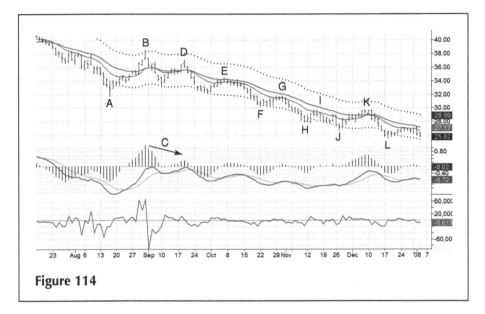

Figure 114

Please match the letters on the chart to the following descriptions:

1. Pullbacks to value
2. Undervalued zone
3. Kangaroo tails
4. Divergences

Question 115—Shorting Tactics

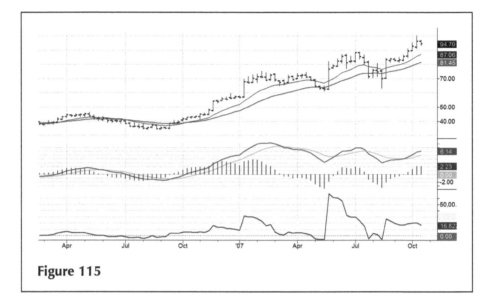

Figure 115

Please select the tactic to follow for the next few weeks at the right edge of the chart:

1. The trend is up—buy here, near $94.95.
2. The trend is up—buy on a breakout above the recent peak of $100.50.
3. The Impulse system turned Blue with the downtick of MACD—sell short, with the target of $87, near the fast EMA.
4. The Impulse system turned Blue—sell short with a target of $81, near the slow EMA.

ANSWERS TO QUESTIONS

PART THREE:
HOW TO SELL SHORT

Question 87—Shorting a Stock

Answer 2 Selling a borrowed stock.

There are many reasons to sell a stock—you may think that it is overvalued or about to decline. While these reasons can apply to any stock, there is only one way to sell a stock short—by borrowing its shares. People who sell short reverse the standard process of buying first and selling later. Shorts begin by selling borrowed shares in order to buy them back later. This allows them to profit from stock declines rather than rallies.

Question 88—Risk Factors in Shorting

Answer 4 Selection "A stock might crash" is incorrect.

A crash is profitable for shorts, whereas a rally leads to a loss. If the company whose stock a trader sold short declares a dividend, it goes to the person who bought that stock. Now the short-seller must reimburse the owner, whose shares he borrowed, for the cost of that dividend. If the owner decides to sell his stock and the broker cannot find another owner willing to lend his stock to a short-seller, that short-seller will be forced to cover earlier than planned in order to return the borrowed shares.

Question 89—The Impact of Shorting

Answer 3 Selection "Increasing price swings" is incorrect.

Short-sellers sell into rallies, increasing supply when prices are high. They cover during price breaks, thus cushioning them. By trading against the crowd, which is almost uniformly long, short-sellers help dampen excessive price swings.

Question 90—Short vs. Long

Answer 2 Stocks fall faster than they rise.

The great advantage of selling stocks short is that they tend to go down about twice as fast as they rise. This applies to all timeframes—to monthly, weekly, daily, as well as intraday charts. It takes buying to put the stocks up, but they can fall under their own weight. Nothing is really "easy" in the markets, whether selling tops or buying bottoms.

Question 91—Disadvantages of Shorting

Answer 3 Rises over time.

The one great disadvantage of shorting stocks is that the broad stock market has a centuries-old tendency to rise over time. The estimates vary, but an average 3% rise per year above the rate of inflation seems like a reasonable estimate. This means that in shorting you are swimming against a gently rising tide. To deal with this, you want to be more short-term oriented in shorting than in buying. The uptick rule is no longer in effect in the United States.

Question 92—Learning to Sell Short

Answer 2 Selection "Trade a large size to make the experience worthwhile" is incorrect.

When learning to short, think of the stocks you expect to decline and zero in on those you would hate to own. If it makes sense to buy low and sell high, then more expensive stocks are likely to produce good shorting candidates. When you go long, it is not a good idea to buy a stock that keeps making new lows. Similarly, when you want to go short, it is not a good idea to sell a stock that keeps making new highs. Trade size serves as a huge emotional amplifier—the bigger the size, the greater the stress. Make your first baby steps while trading a size so small that neither gain nor loss will matter much at all—this will allow you to focus on quality.

Question 93—Shorting vs. Buying

Answer 1 Tops take longer to form than bottoms.

Stock market bottoms tend to be narrow and sharp, while the tops tend to be broad and uneven. Stock market bottoms are built on fear, a sharp and powerful emotion. Tops are built on greed, a happy emotion that can last a long time. Since the declines tend to occur faster than rallies, precise timing is more important in shorting.

Question 94—Shorting Stock Market Tops

Answer 2 Selection "Wider stops require larger positions" is incorrect.

When prices are boiling near the top, you can expect high volatility and wide price swings. As a result, stops are hard to place. The wider the stops, the greater your risk per share. As the risk per share increases, the size of the position must be reduced. It is not uncommon to take several stabs at shorting a top before catching a big break. Reducing the size of your position below the maximum dictated by money management rules increases your holding power.

Question 95—Shorting in Downtrends

Answer 2 Covering near the lower channel line means buying below value.

In the middle of a channel prices are near value. The time to cover shorts and take profits is when prices fall to the undervalued zone near the lower channel line. Channels often provide multiple trading opportunities, as prices keep rising to value only to collapse below value again and again. Grading swing trades by the percentage of a channel captured in that trade works equally well for longs and shorts.

Question 96—The Tactics of Shorting Downtrends

Answer 2 Selection "Shorting within a channel lowers both the risk and the rewards" is incorrect.

The risk of a whipsaw is the greatest when trying to short a market top. Shorting within a channel reduces the risk of a whipsaw. Nothing is free in the markets, and one pays for reduced risk by a corresponding reduction in potential profits—those are greater when shorting tops and relatively smaller in downtrends.

Question 97—Shorting the Fundamentals

Answer 4 The most powerful situation exists when the fundamentals suggest a trade and technical factors confirm that signal.

Fundamental analysis is narrower than technical analysis because of the economic differences between various markets; a technician can apply his tools across the board. Fundamental ideas must be verified with technical analysis. No matter how good a fundamental story, if the technical factors do not confirm it, there is no trade. When both point in the same direction, they create a very powerful combination.

Question 98—Looking for Shorting Candidates

Answer 4 Selection "Selling short stocks that are being upgraded by major analysts" is incorrect.

There are just as many methods of looking for shorting as for buying candidates. The key principle is to verify any idea using your own method or system. You may do something as labor-intensive as digging through industry groups or the 100 biggest stocks on the Nasdaq; alternatively, you may do something as simple as listening to tips, rumors, or downgrade news. Anything can provide grist for the mill—as long as you test all tips and ideas using your analytic method.

Question 99—The Short Interest Ratio

Answer 1 The number of shares held short by the bears relative to the "free float."

The Short Interest Ratio compares the number of shorts held by the bears with the "free float" in any given stock. The free float is the number of shares available for shorting—the total number issued by the company minus restricted stock granted to executives, shares held by "strategic shareholders," and insiders' holdings. Brokers report the number of shares that have been shorted and not covered. If you divide that number by the total free float, you'll have the Short Interest Ratio, reflecting the intensity of shorting in any given stock.

Question 100—Trading the Short Interest Ratio

Answer 4 Selection "A falling Short Interest Ratio calls for a break in the stock" is incorrect.

When the Short Interest Ratio rises, it shows that bears are becoming angrier and louder. Every short position must eventually be covered, and those short-covering rallies are notorious for their speed. As an estimate, a Short Interest Ratio of less than 10% is likely to be tolerable, while a reading of over 20% marks a suspiciously large crowd of short-sellers. The Short Interest Ratio tends to increase as the stock slides and more bears join the party. The Short Interest Ratio tends to decline during the uptrend; such uptrends can last for a long time.

Question 101—Markets Need Shorting

Answer 1 Stocks

While only a small minority of stock traders sell short, the volume of shorting in futures, options, or forex is exactly equal to that of buying. For every contract bought there is a contract sold short—total long and short positions are absolutely equal in every trading vehicle except stocks.

Question 102—Who Shorts Futures

Answer 2 Commercials or hedgers

Most shorts in most futures markets are held by the commercials or hedgers who are the true insiders. For example, a major agribusiness may sell wheat futures to lock in a good price for a harvest that has not yet been gathered. But that is only part of the game. Any hedger worth its salt runs its futures division as a profit center and not merely as a price insurance office. They expect to make money on those positions.

Question 103—Shorting Futures

Answer 3 Selection "Insider trading is illegal in futures" is incorrect.

When you trade futures, you enter into binding contracts for a future purchase or sale of a commodity. All trades are backed by margin deposits on both sides. Futures, unlike stocks, have natural floors and ceilings. The cost of production creates a floor and the price of substitution a ceiling. Those levels, however, are somewhat flexible rather than totally rigid. In futures, there is no prohibition against insider trading because hedgers are the true insiders. You can track their behavior through "commitments of traders" reports, regularly published by CFTC.

Question 104—Long Rallies and Sharp Breaks

Answer 1 Carrying charges

Commodities incur carrying charges, as the cost of storing, financing, and insuring them gets worked into their prices. As all of these charges keep adding up month after month, prices could gradually climb to unrealistic heights. What happens instead is that relatively slow and steady price increases get punctuated by brief violent drops, returning prices to realistic levels—and then the process begins again.

Question 105—Writing Options

Answer 1 The time value of options

The key difference between options and stocks is that options are wasting assets. While all the factors listed in the question contribute to option buyers' mortality, the wasting time value of options is the most important among them. As the clock keeps ticking towards option expiration, it reduces the value of an option: the buyer keeps losing money, while the writer (seller) is more and more secure in his possession of the money received from the buyer.

Question 106—Writing Covered Options

Answer 4 Covered writing requires large capital

If the stock stays relatively flat and does not reach the option's exercise price, you will pocket the premium, boosting your total return. If the stock falls, you will also pocket the premium, cushioning the fall of your stock. If the stock rises above the option exercise price, it will be called away. You'll keep the premium in addition to the capital gain from the purchase price of the stock to the exercise level. Since there is a big universe of interesting stocks, you can take your freed-up capital and look for new opportunities. The fact that one needs substantial capital to purchase shares against which to write options in a large enough size to make financial sense, prevents most traders from getting into this business.

Question 107—Naked vs. Covered Writing

Answer 2 How the trades are backed

While conservative investors write covered calls against their stocks, naked writers create options out of thin air, backed only by their cash. This backing for the trades—either by shares or cash—is the key difference between covered and naked writing. The differences in other areas are minimal or non-existent.

Question 108—The Demands of Naked Writing

Answer 3 Discipline

Naked writers walk a narrow line, protected only by their cash and skill; they need to be absolutely disciplined in taking profits or cutting losses. You cannot write options without sufficient cash, and you need to have good ideas and good timing. Even if you are excellent in those areas, you must have perfect discipline to succeed.

Question 109—Brokers Against Traders

Answer 4 Forex trading houses

Most forex houses operate as bucket shops—rather than transmit your orders for execution, they take the opposite side of any trade, whatever you want to trade, either long or short. When you trade in the interbank market, buy or sell currency futures, or simply exchange cash, a brokerage house does not care whether you make or lose money. They execute your orders and collect commissions. On the other hand, most forex shops bet against their own customers on every trade. When their clients lose, the shops make money.

Question 110—Forex Market

Answer 3 Selection "It is easy to plan and enter trades in forex" is incorrect.

Any time a salesman tells you that something is easy in the market, run the other way! Yes, forex trades 24/7, but this means that a trade which you have carefully planned may come together on the other side of the globe while you are asleep. Once a currency gets into a major trend, whether up or down, it might stay in it for years, due to the fact that in the long run the value of a country's currency depends on government policies.

Question 111—Learning to Become a Better Trader

Answer 2 Keeping good records

The single most important factor in your long-term success or failure is the quality of your records. Keeping and reviewing them will allow you to improve your research and trading techniques. The harder you work, the luckier you'll become.

Question 112—Trading Signals of the Force Index

Answer 3 Uptrends and downtrends are not symmetrical and have to be traded differently.

Uptrends are driven by greed and tend to last longer. Downtrends are driven by fear; they tend to be more intense but last a shorter time. This essential asymmetry of tops and bottoms means that while the general principles of chart reading remain the same, selling short requires sharper timing. A single indicator is never enough; a trader must look for confirming signs—for example, a spike occurring while the price hits the channel line. A short-seller cannot afford to give his trade more time to "work out."

Question 113—False Breakouts and Divergences

Answer 1. B, C, and E
       2. A and D

Tops and bottoms tend to be asymmetrical. Technical signals, such as false breakouts and divergences can provide signals to sell short as well as to buy, but the timing is likely to be different. Notice, for example, how a false downside breakout was over in a day, while each of the false upside breakouts lasted for three days. It is harder to place stops on shorts; two days beyond the right edge of this chart the stock stabbed to a new high before collapsing; a tight stop would have led to a whipsaw.

Question 114—Shorting and Covering Signals

Answer 1. D, E, G, I, and K
       2. A, F, H, J, and L
       3. A, B, and D
       4. C

When you find a stock traveling in a well-defined down-sloping channel, you can sell short at or above value, as defined by the moving averages. You can cover whenever prices fall to or below the undervalued area, defined by the lower channel line. Like many other patterns, kangaroo tails work near the bottoms as well as near the tops.

Question 115—Shorting Tactics

Answer 4 The Impulse system turned Blue—sell short with a target of $81, near the slow EMA.

This stock is in a powerful bull market, but no trend goes in a straight line. The place to buy is near value, but now prices are over-extended above value. With the MACD-Histogram ticking down and the Impulse turning blue, while the Force Index is showing a bearish divergence, shorting becomes an attractive option. The fast EMA is a realistic target; if and when prices approach that target, a trader may re-evaluate the situation and decide whether to cover or to hold.

GRADING YOUR ANSWERS

If a question requires only one answer, you earn a point by answering it correctly. If a question requires several answers, rate your answer proportionately. If you answer both correctly, give yourself a point, but if only one, then half a point.

25-29: Excellent. You have a good grasp of selling short. The markets await you. Be sure to keep good records in order to learn from your experience.

21-24: Fairly good. Successful trading demands top performance. Look up the answers to the questions you've missed, review them, and retake the test in a few days before moving on to the next section.

Below 21:Alarm! Being below the top third in your answers is a sign of great danger in trading. Professional traders are waiting for you in the markets, ready to take your money. Before you do battle with them, you must bring yourself up to speed. Please study the third section of *The New Sell and Sell Short* and retake the test. If your grade remains low on the second pass, look up the books recommended in that section and study them. Avoid shorting until your performance on this test has improved.

PART FOUR

LESSONS OF
THE BEAR MARKET

Rising stock prices are good for expense accounts. In February 2007, as the great bull market was charging towards its final peak, my publisher invited me and two friends to dinner at an expensive restaurant in New York City.

In those happy days, my research kept warning that the bull was running out of breath. I told my publisher that the area least covered in trading literature was selling. He liked the idea and urged me to write *Sell and Sell Short*.

I promised to deliver the manuscript before the end of the year; it would take the publishing house a few more months to produce the book. I told my publisher that by then I expected the bull market to be finished—we would be releasing the book into a bear market.

Markets often overshoot their targets, both on the way up and on the way down. The 2007–2009 bear market has turned out to be

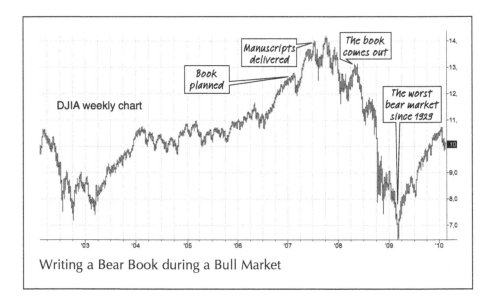

Writing a Bear Book during a Bull Market

unusually severe—but its final wash-out in March 2009 created bargains of the century.

Traders who survived this bear market learned the importance of planning when and where to sell. Many more have become interested in shorting. This is what the pros have been doing all along—the quick money tends to be on the short side of the markets.

In February 2010, my publisher called to suggest updating *Sell and Sell Short*. We discussed the project over the phone—there were no more expense account feasts. We agreed to condense Part One (on buying) because most of that information could be found in my other books. We decided to keep Parts Two and Three (on selling and selling short), because their concepts have stood the test of time and remain valid today. Last but not least, we decided to add this Part Four, showing trades that illustrate the principles of selling and shorting. Let us see how we can trade even better today, using lessons of one of the greatest bear markets in history.

CHAPTER 9

BEARS MAKE MONEY

We tend to learn more from our losses than from our wins. The 2007–2009 bear market was a demanding teacher, delivering painful losses to most traders. Now is the time to summarize its lessons. I updated my book to help you create a better trading plan for the road ahead and smooth out your journey.

THE BEAR WAS BEGINNING TO STIR IN ITS CAVE

By the middle of 2007, the bull market that began in 2003 was growing old. It is unusual for a full bull/bear cycle to last more than four and a half years, and by 2007 the clock was ticking louder and louder.

I believe that the New High–New Low Index is the best leading indicator of the stock market. The New Highs on any given day are the stocks that are reaching their highest price for the year. They are the leaders in strength. The New Lows for the day are the stocks that are falling to their lowest price for the year. They are the leaders in weakness.

If we compare all stocks listed on an exchange to soldiers in a regiment, then New Highs and New Lows are the officers. When this regiment attacks, watch whether its officers are leading the charge or running towards the rear. A well-led unit will win, and a poorly led unit will lose. Years ago, when I went through officer training, they kept telling us that there were no bad soldiers—only bad officers. I believe in that, and I always keep an eye on the New High–New Low Index.

To construct the daily NH-NL, subtract the number of today's New Lows from the New Highs. To construct the weekly NH-NL, add up the daily NH-NL numbers for the last five trading days.

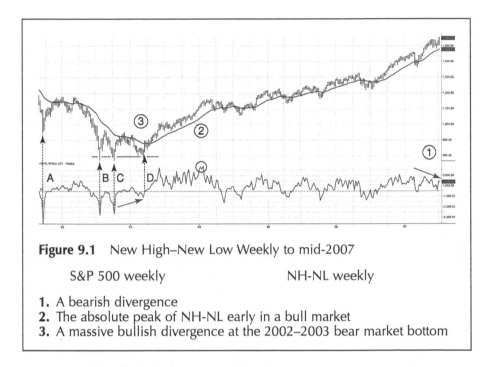

Figure 9.1   New High–New Low Weekly to mid-2007

S&P 500 weekly   NH-NL weekly

1. A bearish divergence
2. The absolute peak of NH-NL early in a bull market
3. A massive bullish divergence at the 2002–2003 bear market bottom

At the right edge of the chart (Figure 9.1) in zone 1, we can see that while the S&P 500 was charging higher, the weekly NH-NL was tracing lower peaks. The regiment kept attacking, but its officers were dropping out. A poorly led attack was likely to fail. That's when I began working on the first edition of *Sell and Sell Short*.

Looking further back, to zone 2, we can see that the weekly NH-NL reached its all-time high in early 2004. It is normal for NH-NL to reach its peak at an early stage of a bull market. Compare this to human development—we grow fastest early in life; later this rate slows down and even reverses. An early peak of NH-NL is normal; what is troublesome on this chart is that by 2007 so much time had passed since that peak—this bull market was getting old.

Finally, looking even further back, to zone 1, we can see how NH-NL helps identify bear market bottoms—intermediate as well as the major ones. Let's review these buy signals because we will be looking for them in the future.

- A downspike of the weekly NH-NL to a minus 4,000 level identifies an area of mass panic where crowds of traders dump their shares, creating great buying opportunities. When the weekly NH-NL spikes down to minus 4,000, it ensures several weeks, if not months, of strong rallying action—even in a bear market. Three such downspikes leap at you from this chart (Figure 9.1), marked with vertical dashed arrows.[1] We will soon see how such downspikes performed during the 2007–2009 bear market.

- A bullish divergence between the weekly NH-NL and the S&P offers an exceptionally strong buy signal. It occurs when the broad market falls, then rallies, then falls again to an equal or lower low; at the same time the weekly NH-NL spikes down, then rallies above its zero line, then falls again to a much more shallow low. This sequence of actions shows that while the soldiers are retreating, the officers have regrouped and are no longer running towards the rear; an attack is about to begin.

Returning to the right edge of the chart, we can see a bearish divergence (marked by a red diagonal arrow). It shows that the bull market was not nearly as powerful as it appeared. That action added to my conviction it was time to write a book about selling.

THE SENTIMENT INDICATORS ARE EARLY

Sentiment indicators tap directly into the mentality of market crowds. Their list includes bullish consensus, percentage of bearish advisory services, and the put/call ratio. These and many other tools track the patterns of crowd psychology and help identify trends, bottoms, and tops.[2]

One of the simplest sentiment indicators is the media. When the mass media exhibits an unusual extreme in mass sentiment, savvy traders start looking for a trend reversal.

In summer 2007 I flew to Asia to speak for a major international firm. On my flight from Tokyo to Singapore, I opened the *Financial Times* and sat bolt upright. The paper's Shanghai correspondent was reporting on labor shortages in local service industries, as hotel maids and dishwashers were leaving their jobs en masse to become daytraders.

---

[1] The Spike group was named after such spikes.

[2] My favorite window into such indicators is the website www.sentimentrader.com.

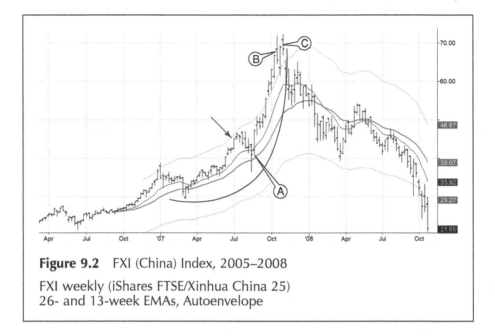

Figure 9.2   FXI (China) Index, 2005–2008

FXI weekly (iShares FTSE/Xinhua China 25)
26- and 13-week EMAs, Autoenvelope

I thought I could hear the bell ring. With all due respect for the folks who make beds and wash dishes for a living, the stock market has not been designed for them to win as a group. The article reminded me of the story of Bernard Baruch, one of the most prominent stock market operators of the early twentieth century. Baruch managed to sidestep the 1929 crash by selling all of his stocks after the man who shined his shoes gave him a stock tip. When the people least likely to speculate start piling into the stock market, you know the numbers of new gamblers are becoming exhausted, and the bullish game is nearing its end.

I brought the newspaper to the conference in Singapore and borrowed a bell from the hotel to ring it for my audience of money managers. A red arrow on this chart shows the date of my talk (Figure 9.2). A better use for that bell would have been to whack myself over the head.

In the weeks following my speech, the Chinese market declined—but then reversed and tacked on another 60% before collapsing. A human soul can grow much darker—or brighter—than anyone expects, which is why sentiment indicators give good general alerts but are not suitable for precision timing.

The dark curve on Figure 9.2 shows that towards the end of the bull market, the Chinese stock index went parabolic. This pattern marks a psychological extreme. If you find yourself holding a long position in a parabolic move, buckle your seatbelt, toss out your indicators, and simply keep moving your stops to below each previous week's bar.

The Impulse system mentioned earlier in this book delivered a series of useful signals on this weekly chart of FXI. The system works by measuring the inertia. and the power of market moves. The slope of fast EMA tracks inertia, and the slope of MACD-Histogram tracks power. When both rise during a single bar, the Impulse system colors that bar green, and when they fall, it colors it red. When the two indicators contradict one another, the bar color turns blue.

At bar A, the Impulse turned green, signaling the resumption of the upmove. The rally continued for 9 weeks without a single lower low on the weekly chart (Figure 9.2). At bar B, the Impulse turned blue, showing that bulls were out of breath. Prices rallied for one more week, with the Impulse returning to green, but it turned blue again at bar C. Notice that bar C rose to a new record high before closing near its low. A false upside breakout is one of the most bearish signs in technical analysis. It was all downhill from there for FXI—it did not have a rally of any significance until it lost half of its value, and then it continued to move lower again. As the Chinese stock market collapsed, it is safe to assume that there was no longer any shortage of unskilled labor in Shanghai.

THE TOP OF THE BULL MARKET

The stock market does not try to deceive or trick you. Think of an ocean rolling its waves onto the shore. You have to read the waves to understand when it is time to swim, surf, or sail and when it is time to drop everything and run for high ground. Learning the language of the ocean requires patience and experience. The market speaks to us in its own language of signs and signals. Interpreting its language is the task of technical analysis.

What were the messages of the stock market near its 2007 historic top? Let's look at two weekly charts—one with NH-NL and the other with my favorite four indicators (remember Five Bullets to a Clip, which we touched upon in Part One).

Why begin with a weekly chart? This is a very important rule. The market is moving simultaneously in different timeframes. It may be

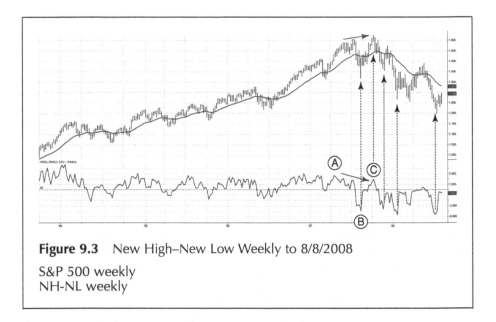

Figure 9.3   New High–New Low Weekly to 8/8/2008

S&P 500 weekly
NH-NL weekly

trending up on the monthly chart, down on the weekly, up on the daily, and down on an intraday chart—all at the same time. Most people focus on a single timeframe, usually daily, and miss the depth of market's messages.

I use the Triple Screen trading system, which requires me to begin by selecting my favorite timeframe. Since my favorite is the daily, Triple Screen prohibits me from looking at it—until I have examined the trend on a chart one order of magnitude longer. Rather than dive into the daily, I first explore the weekly chart and make my strategic decision there. Having decided whether to go long or short, I switch to the daily chart for tactical purposes—to find where to buy or sell.

The weekly chart of NH-NL exhibited a classic bearish divergence at the 2007 top (Figure 9.3). At point A the S&P rallied, confirmed by a rally of NH-NL. At point B the market fell—that was after the "maid shortage in Shanghai" article. Break B provided a major warning because NH-NL fell below zero, which I call "breaking the back of the bull." Afterwards, the U.S. stock market recovered and rallied to a new high, albeit less extreme than the Chinese market. At the same time, the NH-NL rose to a much lower peak.

Higher prices accompanied by a lower peak of NH-NL call for trouble ahead. When the weekly NH-NL ticked down from top C, it gave a signal to sell and sell short, marked with a red dashed vertical arrow on this chart. Precision does not get much better than that!

As an aside, notice that when weekly NH-NL spikes down to the minus 4,000 level, it provides timely buy signals. Even as a bear market gets going, such downspikes, marked with green dashed vertical arrows, tell us that at least a few weeks of rallying action are ahead.

BEARISH DIVERGENCES AT THE 2007 TOP

Let's explore the messages of my favorite indicators at the 2007 stock market top. In July 2007 the market rallied to a peak (marked A on Figure 9.4). It then dropped sharply, sliced through the value zone and stabbed the lower channel line, entering the undervalued area. This was the deepest drop in more than a year, showing that bears were growing stronger. Notice how these indicators behaved as they traced out the bottom B.

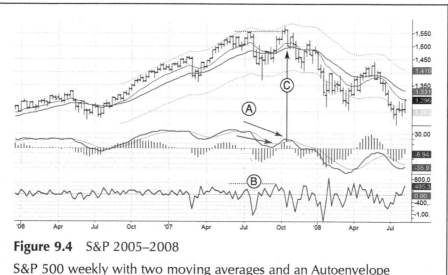

Figure 9.4   S&P 2005–2008

S&P 500 weekly with two moving averages and an Autoenvelope
MACD-Histogram and MACD Lines
Force Index—13-week EMA

In August, MACD-Histogram fell lower than it did at the March 2007 low or any other low for the preceding year. The Force Index also fell lower in August 2007 than it did it March. These bearish signals confirmed one another—providing evidence that the bears were becoming stronger.

The stock market rallied again in October 2007 and reached a new historic high, but the key indicators topped out at much lower levels than in July, creating glaring bearish divergences. These occurred in MACD-Histogram as well as MACD Lines. The divergences of MACD Lines occur much more rarely than those of MACD-Histogram, but they provide even more powerful trading signals.

The only indicator that did not diverge at the October top was the Force Index. Two indicators were flashing major sell signals, while one was basically neutral. That was good enough for the bears—you cannot be obsessive in the markets and wait for every single duck to get in line.

In October 2007, the weekly S&P touched its upper channel line. This is where the market becomes overvalued, and the crowd turns happily bullish. Amateurs love upside breakouts and expect them to continue. Professionals know that most breakouts fail and like to fade them—trade against them.

I like to draw a horizontal line across the previous top. When prices break out above this line and key indicators show potential bearish divergences, I attach an electronic alert to that recently violated line. As soon as prices close below that line, I consider it a false breakout and begin shorting—with a protective stop near the level of the latest peak.

THE BUBBLE POPS: MGM

As I flew back to New York from Asia in October 2007, I learned that the man in the seat next to me was a fundamental hedge fund analyst. He told me that he specialized in gaming stocks, and I asked him which gaming company had the best fundamentals. He stated that without a shadow of doubt it was MGM.

Both of us were returning from Macau, where MGM had recently unveiled the Venetian, the largest casino in the world. My seatmate said that the huge public hall I saw on the ground floor was no more than 40% of the casino—higher up were the VIP levels, culminating in something he called VIP-VIP. One had to deposit a million Hong Kong dollars—about $130,000—to gain admission. He was hugely bullish and said that some of his clients held millions of shares of MGM.

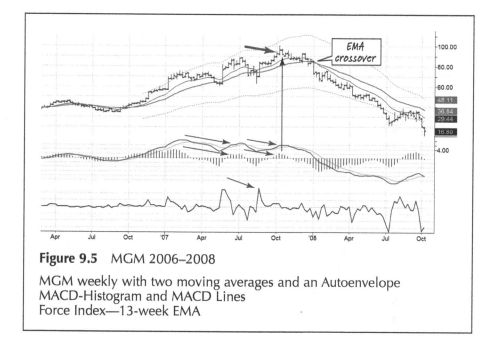

Figure 9.5   MGM 2006–2008

MGM weekly with two moving averages and an Autoenvelope
MACD-Histogram and MACD Lines
Force Index—13-week EMA

I pulled out my laptop and opened an MGM chart—our conversation
took place at a point marked with a diagonal blue arrow (Figure 9.5).
I told my seatmate that with MGM near $100 the uptrend looked won-
derful, but I would not buy it above value—above both moving averages. I'd wait for a pullback below value and get long there.

As I look at this chart today, I wonder where my eyes were. Mass bullishness has a way of infecting even sober analysts. As MGM began to
decline, I actually bought a bit below $70 but was soon stopped out.
Today I see massive bearish divergences leaping from this chart and
screaming "sell short!" There are bearish divergences of MACD-Histogram
and MACD Lines (an especially powerful sign), which in October 2007
were joined by a bearish divergence of the Force Index—a trifecta! In
January 2009 the fast 13-week EMA crossed below the slow 26-week
EMA—a classic sign of a bear trend. It was all downhill from there. My
only consolation about missing this short is in the sentence with
which I ended my first book: "Like all serious traders, I continue to learn
and I reserve the right to be smarter tomorrow than I am today."

I never saw my seatmate again, but thought of him and his clients.
When you lose a few dollars on a thousand shares as I did, it is unpleasant;

but to hold a million shares of a stock that slides from near $100 down into single digits is a disaster. When you think of the fortunes that have been wiped out, you know that the people who lost them are unlikely to return to the stock market. A bubble like we had in 2007–2008 will repeat—but not until a new generation of traders comes into the market.

SHORTING A HIGH-FLYER

Whenever I document a trade, I include its source. I want to keep in mind how I found it—during a market scan, an email from a friend, and so on. One of my main sources for trading ideas is the SpikeTrade group. The idea to short ISRG came from Dave F., one of our most successful Spikers.

In planning a trade, I make my strategic decision on a long-term chart (usually weekly) and the tactical decision on a short-term chart (usually daily). This weekly chart of ISRG shows one great signal and two middling ones (Figure 9.6). The great signal is a false upside breakout, marked with a blue arrow.

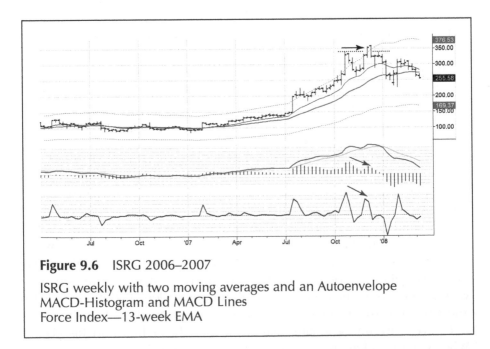

Figure 9.6   ISRG 2006–2007

ISRG weekly with two moving averages and an Autoenvelope
MACD-Histogram and MACD Lines
Force Index—13-week EMA

When a stock breaks out to a new high, but cannot hold that level and sinks below the breakout line, it shows that the mass of traders has rejected the recent high—and prices are likely to swing in the opposite direction. This principle works in reverse at market bottoms—a false downside breakout tends to precede a rally.

Beginners love to trade in the direction of a breakout. The pros know that most breakouts fail. They are much more likely to fade them—trade against them.

While the false breakout was great, the two middling signals came from the weekly MACD-Histogram and the Force Index. Both trended lower, although neither showed a bearish divergence. A true bearish divergence consists of two peaks—the second lower than the first, separated by a dip below the zero line. If an indicator does not cross into negative territory between the two peaks, it is not a true divergence.

The daily chart of ISRG shows a gorgeous triple bearish divergence (Figure 9.7). The third top of MACD-Histogram was so weak that

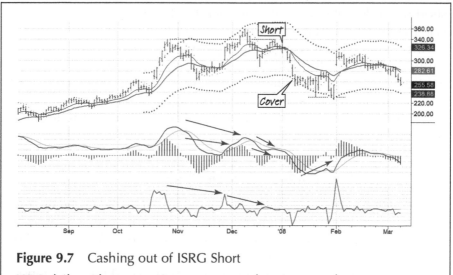

Figure 9.7 Cashing out of ISRG Short

ISRG daily with two moving averages and an Autoenvelope
MACD-Histogram and MACD Lines
Force Index—2-day EMA

it could not even rise above the zero line. We call this type of a divergence "a missing right shoulder". A bearish divergence of MACD Lines,
MACD-Histogram, and the Force Index delivered a perfect trifecta.

The fact that the weekly chart suggested shorting and the daily
screamed to short created a very tradeable combination. When the weekly
and daily charts contradict one another, I do not put on a trade. When one
is mildly conducive to a trade and the other very powerful, I go along
with that combo.

During a bull market, prices typically rally, pull back to the moving
average, then rally again. The opposite occurs in a bear market, where
value is being destroyed (just think of MGM). A pullback to value in a
bear market creates an opportunity to sell short and profit from the next
round of destruction.

As you can see on this chart, I sold short in the vicinity of the value
zone and covered as ISRG fell towards the oversold zone, near its lower
channel line. This pick came from SpikeTrade, whose typical trade lasts
a week or less. I generally try to be out of my Spike pick by the end of
the week, although occasionally I carry a Spike trade for a longer time.
Here I shorted value and covered below value, following my system for
shorting in downtrends. Catching such brief swings is much more realistic than riding a major trend from start to finish.

After I covered, ISRG stabilized, then twice stabbed even lower before
gapping up in a rally. This behavior provides a good example of the
frequent symmetry of trading signals. At the December top we had a
false upside breakout with a bearish divergence, which led to a downtrend. In February, a false downside breakout with a bullish divergence
preceded a sharp rally.

A BEAR MARKET IS A DESTROYER OF VALUE

In the wake of the economic crisis, the media has been brimming with
reports about the damage inflicted on the public by recession. While un-
employment and bankrupt businesses make the news, Figure 9.8 shows
what a bear market does to capitalists.

The vast majority of shares in SHLD—Sears Holding Corporation—
are held by institutional investors. The 2007–2009 bear market took
SHLD down from nearly $200 to below $40, wiping out over 80% of
its value—not quite as disastrous as the 95% decline of MGM, but still
plenty of blood, sweat, and tears.

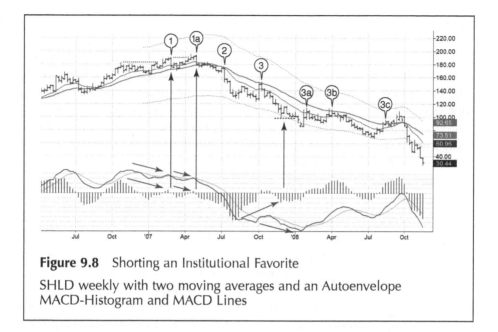

Figure 9.8 Shorting an Institutional Favorite

SHLD weekly with two moving averages and an Autoenvelope MACD-Histogram and MACD Lines

As we review the massive downtrend of this institutional darling, let us see how a private trader can profit at the expense of large institutions.

1 and 1a. As the bull market rises to its final peak, two bearish divergences, both coupled with false upside breakouts, signal the end of the bull market. These loud signals tell savvy traders to sell and begin shorting.

2. The fast 13-week exponential moving average crosses below the slow 26-week exponential moving average, confirming the bear market.

3, 3a, 3b, and 3c. Pullbacks to value. A bear market does not move in a straight line. The downtrend is periodically interrupted by rallies, some of them quite sharp. Look at the rally 3c—the stock gained nearly 50% from its intermediate low before collapsing again. Just imagine trying to sit through this rally, while holding a short position. This is an example of why shorter-term trading is less stressful and generally more rewarding.

In the area following 3b, the massive downtrend triggers "The Hound of the Baskervilles" signal. This signal (described in *Trading for a Living*) occurs when a normally reliable pattern fails to deliver its usual result.

A bullish divergence of MACD-Histogram is one of the best signals in technical analysis. Following such a divergence, we expect prices to rally from the second bottom. If they fail to rally and instead break through the latest low, it means that something is fundamentally changing below the surface of the market. At that point, one should not only sell but also reverse and go short, when the latest bottom is taken out. Notice that the MACD Lines did not diverge but rather fell to a new low while MACD-Histogram was diverging; when these two indicators go against one another, it is best to skip entering a trade.

Before we zoom in on several segments of this chart, let me make two "big picture" statements:

- As major bear markets destroy value, they tend to overshoot any reasonable downside projection. This is a mirror image of a bull market, which tends to overshoot any reasonable upside projection. Major bull and bear markets reflect major trends in the economy as well as huge tides in mass psychology. The power of the market crowd is greater than that of any individual. The strength of a major trend is so vast that its extent often defies our imagination, making the ultimate target very difficult to forecast.

- When we glance at a long-term chart, it may seem easy to ride a position in a major trend. Buy-and-hold (or in this case short-and-hold) seems like a pretty straight road to riches. In fact, the opposite is true. It is extremely hard to ride a major trend from start to finish. You need to have almost super-human patience and be prepared to sit through huge drawdowns while your trend corrects.

A much more practical approach is to use weekly charts to define a trend and then switch to the daily charts for shorter-term trading in the direction of the weekly chart. Let's see how a nimble trader can profit from catching shorter waves rather than entire tides.

As a private trader, you have one major advantage over institutional investors—you are allowed to sell short.

The charters of many institutional funds prohibit shorting. In the summer of 2007, I had a working breakfast with one of the largest fund managers in Asia. I showed him my charts, which indicated that the bull market was nearing its peak and a bear market was approaching. The man turned to his staff members and half-joked: "Our bonuses are in danger. We need to assume a more defensive position." He was in charge of tens of billions of dollars, but his hands were tied—he was not allowed to short.

A private trader has no such limitations. We can profit from a bear market by selling short. While institutional investors are holding their long positions and hoping for a reversal or desperately looking for "defensive stocks," you can swing into short trades when prices rally and cover when they fall again. Let's now apply this concept to SHLD during the 2007–2009 bear market.

SWINGING IN AND OUT OF A MAJOR DOWNTREND

Remember that the bearish divergences on the weekly chart gave signals to sell and sell short. Those powerful signals were confirmed by the downward crossover of two moving averages. Once the long-term chart gives you a strategic command to sell and sell short, turn to the daily charts to make tactical decisions about entries and exits—this is the essence of the Triple Screen trading system.

This chart (Figure 9.9) represents the first six months of the bear market, as SHLD slid from just under $180 per share to below $100. Let's use a very simple tactic—monitor the daily MACD-Histogram and go short whenever it ticks down from above its zero line. This reversal of a bullish upswing is a sign that a major downtrend is about to reassert itself. Let's take profits on short positions when prices fall into the vicinity of the lower channel line on the daily chart, marking an oversold level.

You can see four such shorting signals on this chart, each marked with a vertical dashed arrow. Each signal occurred within a day of the actual top—a very high level of precision. The first two signals to cover shorts were timely, while the third and fourth came very early, leaving big chunks of profit on the table.

This is not a perfect system, not by a long shot. It is, on the other hand, a well-functioning system. If you select a small number of stocks whose weekly charts give you strategic shorting signals and then switch to their daily charts and use this system, you should do well.

It is important to realize that perfection is the enemy of the good. Forget about perfection, even though it is great for the ego when it works. You are not in this game for your ego, you're in to make money. Accept the fact that you will not catch the absolute top, nor the absolute bottom. Keep grabbing nice chunks from the middle of a trend and be happy with the outcome.

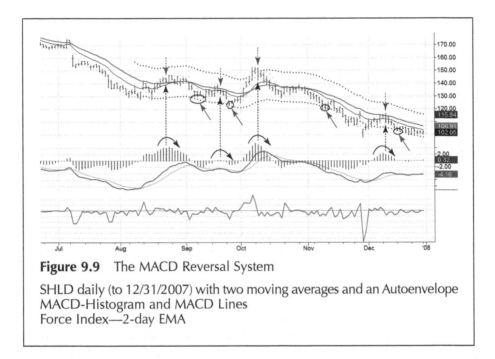

Figure 9.9   The MACD Reversal System

SHLD daily (to 12/31/2007) with two moving averages and an Autoenvelope
MACD-Histogram and MACD Lines
Force Index—2-day EMA

Now, let's follow up with the next daily chart of SHLD to see how the
system held up in 2008.

TRADING IN A DOWNCHANNEL

Sometimes you can catch a stock in a major uptrend or a downtrend
soon after it gets into its groove. This does not happen with all stocks, but
when you recognize this pattern, trading it becomes like going to a cash
machine. I feel reluctant saying this because I do not want to create a
false impression that trading is easy. Just keep in mind that sooner or
later your stock will jump its groove, this pattern will disappear, and your
last trade will be a loss. This is one of many good reasons to keep the
size of your trades stable and to avoid increasing them in the middle
of a trading campaign. If you keep increasing the size of your bet, the
inevitable loss at the end of a trend will hit when you are maximally
exposed, wiping out multiple profits. If perfect is the enemy of the good,
then greed is the enemy of success.

An absolutely essential point to keep in mind is that all of these daily
charts—the current one, the previous one, and the one that will follow—

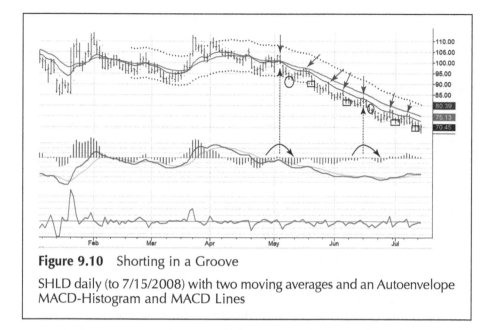

Figure 9.10 Shorting in a Groove

SHLD daily (to 7/15/2008) with two moving averages and an Autoenvelope MACD-Histogram and MACD Lines

must be examined against the background of the major downtrend on the weekly chart. I simply refuse to look at a daily chart until I have examined the weekly and made my strategic decision there.[3] Every trader needs an edge. An important part of my edge is that I use stereo vision, looking at every stock in at least two timeframes, while most of the world looks at the markets with one eye shut.

Two short-term trading systems pop up from this chart (Figure 9.10). One is the MACD reversal system, described above. Its shorting signals are marked by vertical red arrows; its signals to cover are marked with green circles at the lower channel line.

The other system—Shorting in a Groove—calls for sharper timing and requires more experience and closer attention.

When a daily downtrend becomes well established, it starts running in a groove. Prices keep pulling up into the value zone between the two EMAs, only to reverse and collapse to the oversold level near the lower channel line. These shorting opportunities are marked with diagonal red

---

[3]Clients sometimes send me e-mails with a chart attached, asking for my opinion about a stock. If they send me a daily chart only, I send back my standard reply—I refuse to look at a daily chart without first analyzing the weekly.

arrows, and the areas where one should cover are marked with green rectangles.

Even experienced traders miss the first one or two such signals, but afterwards the pattern becomes very visible: short in the value zone, put a stop just above the high of the next bar and a take-profit order to cover at the lower channel line.

At some point, the downtrend will bottom out, a strong rally will begin, and your stop will get hit. When a stock jumps out of its groove, it tells you to look for a different game. No system delivers consistent profits year in and year out, but while a trend is in a groove, milk it for what it's worth. Do not discard a system that has stopped working. Put it on the shelf and wait for the market environment to change—you may very well use this system again in the future.

Notice how the daily channel of SHLD becomes narrower with time. Its height was over $20 in 2007, but less than $10 by the middle of 2008, due to the lower price of the stock.

A channel, also called an envelope, provides a useful tool for setting profit targets. The height of a channel reflects the spread between optimism and pessimism, mania and depression. I consider any trade that captures 30% of a daily channel an A trade. Of course, there is nothing wrong with trying to be a star student and aiming for an A+ or even an A++. Occasionally this works. Just keep in mind that to earn a higher grade you have to spend a longer time in a trade. That's where the risk lies—in holding an open position.

Think of yourself as a merchant and your trading positions as your merchandise. Most retail merchants will tell you that fast turnover is a sign of a healthy business. Keep turning over your merchandise, buying low and selling high, or shorting high and covering low. Grabbing an A trade will teach you more about successful trading than holding out for an A++ trade with its greater risk.

PREPARED FOR A SURPRISE

Trees do not grow to the sky, and bear markets do not go down to zero. As investors and traders become distressed, disgusted, and desperate, they keep selling out. Much stronger, better capitalized, and farther-looking investors buy up their shares. Gradually the supply of shares for sale begins to shrink. This reduces the downward pressure on prices,

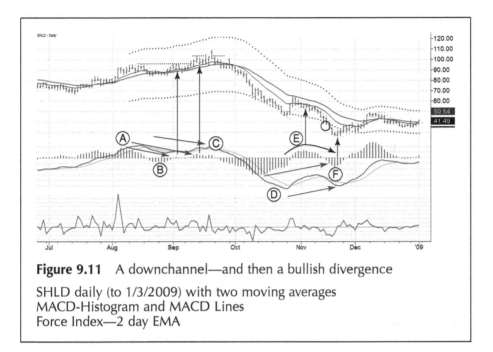

Figure 9.11 A downchannel—and then a bullish divergence

SHLD daily (to 1/3/2009) with two moving averages
MACD-Histogram and MACD Lines
Force Index—2 day EMA

and the decline stalls. Meanwhile, savvy bargain-hunters start coming out of the woodwork. The pervasive feeling of gloom and doom among distressed sellers creates the foundation of the next bull market.

On this 2008 daily chart of SHLD, we see how a bear market rally in September 2008 ended in a bearish divergence A-B-C (Figure 9.11). There was a high peak A of MACD-Histogram, followed by a crossover B below zero, then a feeble rally C, while the stock rallied to a new recovery high. Notice that this bearish divergence was pretty sloppy, in terms of a complex top C.

There were two sell signals at that top, both from MACD-Histogram downticks. The first one aborted, and even the second signal was followed by a quick rally before prices slid lower. That final rally kicked out traders who used tight stops. One of the key differences between the beginners and the pros is that newbies leave after getting stopped out. Professionals expect to encounter some market chop. They feel comfortable attempting several reentries and accept small losses while working on their entry.

The bear reasserted himself with a vengeance in November, and there was another "MACD reversal short" signal, but by then a much more important pattern was starting to emerge.

Look at bottom D of MACD-Histogram in October: its record depth showed that bears were very strong. A rally after such a record bottom tends to be a short-lived affair. Still, it lifted MACD-Histogram above the zero line in November. This meant that the back of the bear had been broken!

Whenever an index or stock traces a record deep bottom of MACD-Histogram and then rallies above zero, I put that ticker on my watch list. I begin waiting for the next bottom—and if the indicator turns up again from a more shallow level, I am eager to buy. This is a bullish divergence of MACD-Histogram—one of the strongest signals in technical analysis.

Prices slid to a new low later in November, but MACD-Histogram declined only to level F. Its uptick from there completed a bullish divergence—the latecomers to the bear camp were trapped. Notice how clean that divergence was: both MACD-Histogram and MACD Lines diverged in a totally orderly manner, without any whipsaws or other noise. An MACD divergence on the daily charts is the only signal that will prompt me to disregard the status of the weekly chart. Even if the weekly Impulse is still red, but a daily chart traces a bullish divergence, I will go long. Of course I'll protect that position with a stop in the vicinity of the recent low.

"BULL MARKETS HAVE NO RESISTANCE AND BEAR MARKETS HAVE NO SUPPORT"

In the long-gone days of easy credit, banks were giving out loans right, left, and center. Their misdeeds are amply documented in current literature, including the fabulously engaging *The Greatest Trade Ever* by Gregory Zuckerman and *The Big Short* by Michael Lewis. In 2007, the chickens headed home to roost. In 2008, some of them were processed into chicken nuggets and others tossed into the trash. Bank of America (BAC) was one of those hapless birds.

Figure 9.12 delivers several important messages:

- Notice several bearish divergences, marked by diagonal red arrows, as BAC huffed and puffed towards its final peak near $55.

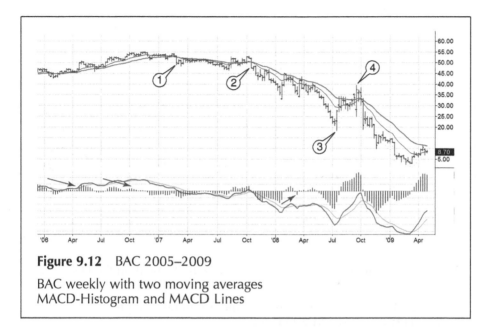

Figure 9.12 BAC 2005–2009

BAC weekly with two moving averages
MACD-Histogram and MACD Lines

- In the area marked "1," the fast 13-week EMA swung below the slow 26-week EMA, confirming the bear market. BAC never again rallied above that point—not in 2007, not later, not to the day of this writing in 2010.

- Bullet "2" marks a whipsaw—the one and only week when the fast EMA rallied above the slow one before sinking again. This illustrates that no pattern is perfect, and an occasional whipsaw is a normal risk in trading.

- The downtrend was temporarily interrupted by several sharp rallies. The strongest of them took BAC from point "3" to point "4"— from $19 to a whopping $39 in less than two months. The stock had briefly more than doubled in the midst of a bear market, which was to sink it into the low single digits! Do you still want to hold a short position for the entire duration of a bear market?

These bear market rallies are so sharp because hapless shorts whose fingers had been caught in the door first procrastinate and then panic to cover at any price. Once these desperate shorts have been burned out of the game, the decline resumes.

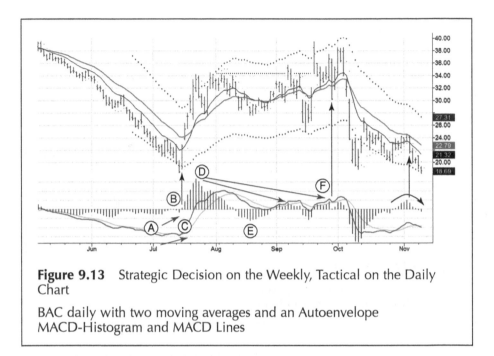

Figure 9.13   Strategic Decision on the Weekly, Tactical on the Daily Chart

BAC daily with two moving averages and an Autoenvelope MACD-Histogram and MACD Lines

The ongoing bear market ground BAC down from its intermediate peak near $39 to below $3 per share. If you ever need a reminder that it is better to make strategic decisions on the weekly chart and execute on the daily, take another look at this weekly chart of BAC. It gives you the strategic direction—and now you can turn to a shorter-term daily chart and use it to make tactical decisions about entries and exits.

Let's see what light our daily charts can shed on a period that seemed so wildly frustrating on the weeklies. We need to examine the interruption of a bearish slide by a sharp rally that took BAC from under $20 to near $40. That rise shook out many bears just before the stock took a bullet and continued its slide into the single digits.

First of all, the daily chart of BAC (Figure 9.13) gave ample warning that a bear market rally was around the corner. Take a look at the bullish divergence A-B-C, one of the strongest signals in technical analysis. Its clear message was that you could either buy or stand aside—but there was absolutely no reason to keep shorts in the teeth of a bullish MACD-Histogram divergence. When you see a steam-roller headed in your direction, get out of its way!

Most shorts were killed during the first five days of the rally that followed. The rest were mostly huffing and puffing, with false upside breakouts. Meanwhile, MACD-Histogram was building a bearish divergence D-E-F. Once it was completed, a swift drop followed. At the right edge of the screen, the MACD reversal system kicked in again, giving a shorting signal.

While the weekly charts give you a strategic direction for a trade, the daily charts are much more specific on when to get in, when to get out, and when to stand aside. This is the advantage of examining every market in two timeframes when you plan your trades.

Begin by examining the weekly chart to make your strategic decision. If you begin with a daily chart, it will prejudice you and interfere with your planning. Approach the long-term chart with a fresh and unpolluted eye. Make your strategic decision, write it down—and only then proceed to the shorter-term chart where you will plan your entries and exits.

FOR WHOM THE BELL TOLLS OR THE HOUND BARKS TWICE

A mortgage from Freddie Mac (FRE) used to be an American icon, right up there with apple pie. These days poor Freddie sits disgraced, its former executives canned, its share a despised penny stock. If the implosion of the credit bubble was at the core of the 2007–2009 bear market, then FRE was at the epicenter of that disaster.

Figure 9.14 reflects its slow-motion crash, as the stock rolled down from above $70 in 2006 to a measly 76 cents at the right edge. Let's review its technical signals to see what we can learn from this wreck.

At the point marked "A," the fast EMA crossed below the slow EMA, confirming the bear market. FRE still traded above $60 at the time. This signal remained in effect for the duration of the slide. This is one of the key lessons of this chart—do not hold long positions in a bear market! Whenever you see this EMA crossover on a weekly chart, get out of your long position. Any trader who followed this essential rule would have sidestepped the great majority of disasters so lustily profiled in mass media over the past decade—not just FRE but also Enron, Global Crossing, and the rest of the pernicious bunch.

In 2007, weekly MACD-Histogram twice attempted to rally above its zero line. Each time it ticked down from its top above that line, it

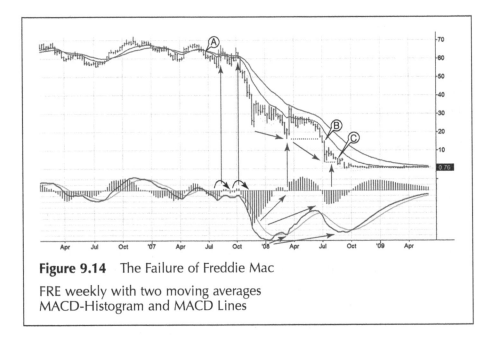

Figure 9.14   The Failure of Freddie Mac

FRE weekly with two moving averages
MACD-Histogram and MACD Lines

reinforced the bearish message—this is a bear market, get short and stay short. These MACD downturns are marked by vertical red lines.

A bullish divergence of MACD is a very rare signal—you can expect to see it on a stock's weekly chart no more than once every few years. A Hound of the Baskervilles signal,[4] which is essentially a failed bullish divergence, is even rarer. For two hounds to appear, one after another, on the same chart is virtually unheard of. Yet this is exactly what happened with FRE.

The vertical green lines mark bullish divergences. The first one was completed in March 2008, but the rally fizzled out within two weeks. By July, at point "B", FRE took out the March low, canceling the divergence and triggering the Hound of the Baskervilles shorting signal by declining below the latest bottom. Prices fell from the teens to under $4.

The second bullish divergence immediately followed—both of MACD-Histogram and MACD Lines. Still, FRE failed to ignite, and at point "C,"

---

[4]This signal, described in *Trading for a Living*, occurs when a normally reliable pattern fails. If you see a bullish divergence and then the market declines instead of rallying, it shows that something is fundamentally changing below the surface of the market and suggests reversing and going short.

prices slid below the July bottom of $3.89 to the unimaginable level of 46 cents—and into the arms of the Federal government, which stepped in to rescue the firm.

It is extremely unusual to have two Hound of the Baskervilles signals back to back—I cannot recall when I last saw this. This is a good lesson never to say "never." Statisticians inform us that stock market probabilities have "long tails." This is a fancy way of saying that if you look for seemingly improbable events, the market is the place to look.

Another lesson of this chart is never to say that the price is "too low." FRE, a $70 stock, looked "too low" when it tried to bottom out at $20. It looked "too low" at $5 and again at $3, but anyone who bought it at $3 still had an 85% decline ahead of them. There is no such thing as "too low." If you decide to buy above support after seeing bullish indicator signals, you may do so only if you get insurance—protect your position with strict stops.

I continue to get questions about FRE to this day—is it too low, is it a buy? My answer is that I refuse to look at this stock as long as it is being controlled by the federal government. Technical analysis is a study of mass psychology. The behavior of a small committee deciding the fate of a company cannot be fathomed using technical tools. Once the government took over, technical analysis was no longer useful. If you have a lobbyist friend with a good feel for inside information, he might be able to give you better advice on FRE than your charts. Just keep in mind that one of you may end up testifying against the other!

MR. BUFFETT BUYS TOO SOON

Warren Buffett is widely recognized as a genius of finance. As a child, he built his initial stake by delivering newspapers and selling used golf balls. He traded that stake in the stock market to become one of the richest men in the world. The story of how Warren Buffet grew up from a gifted but miserable child into his present position of great success and popularity is engagingly told by Alice Schroeder in *The Snowball.*

I greatly respect Mr. Buffett, but respect does not mean mindless worship. Buffett has been hugely successful in the long run, but he does make mistakes. Not all his picks pan out well, and people always learn more from losses than from successes.

The U.S. stock market was nearing a meltdown by the end of 2008. Bear Stearns had been sold for a song, essentially wiping out its investors; Lehman Brothers was told to go jump in a lake. There was a

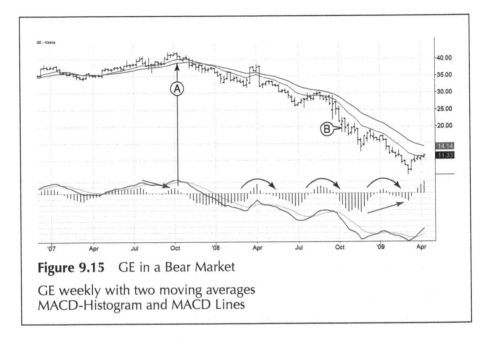

Figure 9.15 GE in a Bear Market
GE weekly with two moving averages
MACD-Histogram and MACD Lines

pervasive sense of doubt and fear—no company was safe. Everybody won-
dered which giant would implode next. You saw the chart of Freddie Mac.

Amidst this gloom and doom came a cheery announcement—Buffett
was investing 3 billion dollars in General Electric (GE). To attract him,
the company was paying 10% annual interest on his investment, almost
double the then current 5.5% rate on its debt. In addition, Buffett received
warrants for $3 billion worth of shares at $22.25. I immediately turned to
my screen to check out the stock (Figure 9.15).

The announcement came out at the point marked B on this chart. GE
had been in a steady downtrend for almost a year. At the point marked
A on the weekly chart, it gave a fantastic sell signal by tracing out a bearish divergence coupled with a false upside breakout. A bearish crossover of the weekly moving averages came two months later, and it was
all downhill from there. GE's slide was repeatedly punctuated by rallies,
producing MACD reversal system signals, marked with curved arrows on
this chart.

The first feature that leaped out at me from this chart on the day of
Mr. Buffett's announcement was the red color of the weekly Impulse
system. I apply this system to all my trades. Every market move in any

timeframe can be defined by two parameters. One is inertia—the slope of the fast moving average. The other is power, defined by the slope of MACD-Histogram. When the current bar of MACD is rising relative to the previous one, bulls are gaining power, and when it sinks, bears are gaining the upper hand. When both the inertia and the power are pointing up, my software colors the price bar green; it tells me that I am only allowed to go long or stand aside; shorting is not permitted. When both the inertia and power are pointing down, that price bar gets colored red, allowing me to go short or stand aside; buying is out of the question. The Impulse system does not tell me what to do, but it tells me what I am prohibited from doing; it serves as a censor, creating a useful level of control that most people in the financial markets lack.

The week Mr. Buffett bought into GE, its Impulse system was red. Had the great man asked for my opinion, I would have suggested waiting. Three weeks later, the weekly chart of GE turned from red to blue, but by then MACD-Histogram hit a record new low. A record low is a signal of great bearish power, and such bottoms are usually retested. Prices may have a brief rally but then tend to decline to the same or lower level. If MACD-Histogram traces a shallower bottom on the second attempt, we'll get a bullish divergence—one of the strongest buy signs in technical analysis. This is exactly what happened in March 2009 when I bought the stock, thanking Mr. Buffett, who first drew my attention to it. I had not been paying much attention to GE until Mr. Buffett's purchase hit the news.

These comments are not intended as a criticism of Mr. Buffett. He may have had his corporate or political reasons for investing in GE when he did. Also, the sweet deal that the company offered him might not have been available at a later date. Still, since Buffett bought GE until the time of this writing more than a year later, GE has remained well below the level of his purchase.

This discussion shows that even when you have great fundamental reasons for investing, it pays to look at the charts and apply some of the basic tenets of technical analysis. The best insight lies at the intersection of fundamental knowledge and modern technical analysis.

MAY I POUR SOME GASOLINE ON YOUR FIRE?

While working on this chapter, I received an email from Grant Cook, a Spiker (an elite-level member of SpikeTrade):

What I found truly remarkable was that this bear market coincided with the introduction of the 2× and 3× ETFs. The volatility and newness of these trading instruments created incredible swings. Probably the most notorious moves were in UYG/SKF and URE/SRS. SKF reached a high of 300 during the collapse with every hedge fund manager piling in, and now it is trading under 20. SRS reached a high also around 300 and now it is trading around 6. Clearly these moves were exaggerated by the leverage and the unusual time decay in these trading tools—but OMG! what moves! The emerging markets—also wild swings, as they responded to the threat of total deflation.

On the upside, what was remarkable was how much support the U.S. Fed gave the market. Despite the animosity and even hatred that much of the media and general public had for Wall Street and the financial markets, the Fed was unwavering in its support—low interest rates, buy-backs, etc. The recovery bounce was much stronger than anyone (including me) anticipated. Some, including me, would describe it as unapologetic manipulation. I think the Fed refers to it as "saving the international financial system," which it appears they did.

This chart (Figure 9.16) offers a view of the vertiginous decline in the financial sector. UYG—ProShares Ultra Financials—slid from above $70 when it was introduced in 2007 down to $1.37 in March 2009 for a 98% decline. It illustrates several key principles we have discussed:

- The relative position of the fast and the slow weekly EMAs (13-week and 26-week) defines bull and bear markets. When the fast EMA crosses below the slow EMA, it confirms a bear market. This is a lagging indicator, which nevertheless defines major trends. It remained in a sell mode throughout the bear market until finally turning up in September 2009, near the $6 level.

- In a bear market, when MACD-Histogram rallies above its center-line and then turns down, it gives a signal to short. You can see four such signals within a year on this chart. If you monitor a group of stocks from different industry groups using this method, you will see quite a few of these signals. It will be like having a stable of horses, one of which might be ready to run at any given time—sometimes on its own and sometimes in a group.

- Trading intermediate swings is easier than holding a position for the duration of a bear (or a bull) market. Take a look at the March–

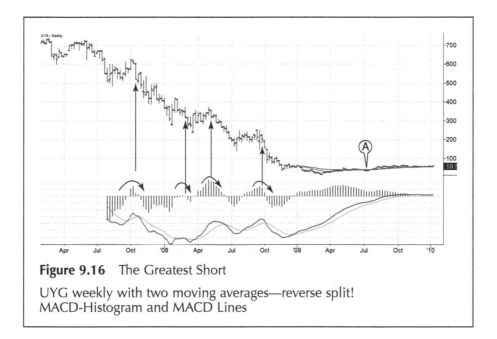

Figure 9.16 The Greatest Short

UYG weekly with two moving averages—reverse split!
MACD-Histogram and MACD Lines

May 2008 bear market rally, which lifted UYG from $240 to $372—a
rise of over 50% in only six weeks. Would you want to hold a short
position during that explosion?

- Be ready to take profits on short positions when your trading
  vehicle reaches the vicinity of its lower channel line.

This chart illustrates the depth of panic and despair in the financial
markets. Amateurs were being wiped out and professionals were losing
their jobs. But just as spring begins with water running under the snow,
the markets were getting ready to turn up.

KEEP SHORTING ON THE WAY DOWN

You do not need to sell the very top in order to profit from a bear
market. Many shorting opportunities emerge during a lengthy decline.
Some falling stocks remind me of drowning people—they keep coming up for air before sinking below the surface again.

This example comes from my trading diary. O'Reilly Automotive (ORLY)
belonged to the multitude of stocks that cracked to a new low in

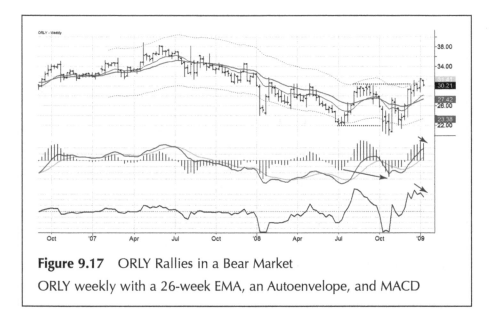

Figure 9.17   ORLY Rallies in a Bear Market
ORLY weekly with a 26-week EMA, an Autoenvelope, and MACD

October 2008. Its weekly MACD-Histogram also fell to a new low, reflecting the bears' great power and flashing a message that the October bottom was likely to be retested or exceeded.

During the recovery from the October 2008 bottom, ORLY rallied above the high it had reached in summer of that year. The rally looked nice on the surface, but it did not cancel October's bearish signals, which called for trouble ahead.

At the right edge of the weekly chart, a number of bearish signals emerged in rapid succession (Figure 9.17). Their message was that ORLY was tracing a top and nearing a downside reversal. First, prices refused to follow through on their breakout and basically stalled in the vicinity of the resistance level. The weekly Force Index began deteriorating and then weekly MACD-Histogram ticked down. That turned the weekly Impulse system from green to blue, allowing me to short.

The daily chart (Figure 9.18) presented a set of beautiful signals: a false upside breakout with three bearish divergences—MACD-Histogram, MACD Lines, and the Force Index. I sold ORLY short at $30.35 on Tuesday, January 6.

I covered my short position on Friday, January 9, at $28.49. The daily Impulse system was red, allowing me to continue to hold, but this was

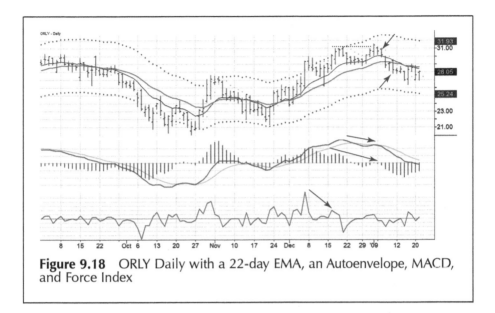

Figure 9.18   ORLY Daily with a 22-day EMA, an Autoenvelope, MACD, and Force Index

a Spike pick, and I prefer not to carry those over a weekend. Also, my favorite type of trading is swing-trading. This is a faster timeframe than position trading but much slower than day-trading. I enjoy catching a good swing, then closing the book on that trade before the weekend, and looking for a fresh idea on Saturdays and Sundays.

It is important to select a method that fits your personality. My approach may feel too short-term to some, too long-term to others, but it feels right to me. Select the time horizon that works for you and stick with it.

CHAPTER 10

GROPING FOR A BOTTOM

As the stock market kept relentlessly grinding down in the fall of 2008, the mood of most market participants became darker and darker. Even the short-covering rallies that normally punctuate down-moves were becoming more brief and feeble.

THIS STOCK MARKET IS NOT GOING DOWN TO ZERO

When we looked at a weekly chart of S&P earlier (p. 260–261), we saw that when the weekly NH-NL fell below minus 4,000, it provided strong buy signals. Here (Fig. 10.1), those signals are marked with vertical green lines on this chart. You may notice that while the first of these lines preceded quite a substantial rally, the last two led to brief and fairly weak advances. This indicated that the bears were growing stronger and the bulls weaker.

Occasionally, a decline would carry the weekly NH-NL below minus 4,000, but in the entire history of the U.S. stock market, this indicator has never fallen below minus 6,000. Then, in October 2008, the unprecedented happened—the weekly NH-NL crashed to minus 18,000.

This downspike reflected an absolutely wild level of panic. Bear Stearns ceased to exist, sold for a price below the value of its downtown headquarters. As Lehman Brothers was forced into liquidation, the most often heard words on Wall Street became "counterparty risk." Institutions were afraid to trade with each other for fear that the other party would not be able to deliver on its obligations.

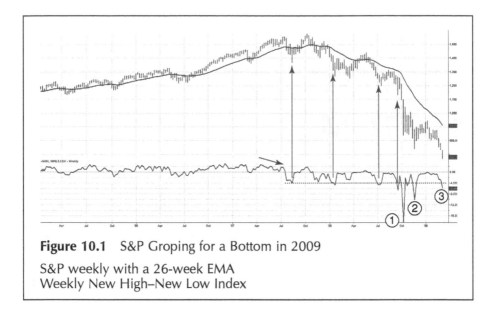

Figure 10.1   S&P Groping for a Bottom in 2009

S&P weekly with a 26-week EMA
Weekly New High–New Low Index

In this atmosphere, the federal government stepped in. It saved the day by reliquefying the system—pouring a major amount of money into the markets and issuing guarantees. To this day, critics are pointing to the government's missteps and to the vast sums misdirected and misused, but many of us believe that had the government not stepped in, the market could have seized up and stopped functioning.

The unprecedented spike of the NH-NL at point 1 showed that the market had reached its "do-or-die" point. As this indicator recoiled from that severely oversold level back towards zero, it showed that it chose "do" over "die." The fate of the market became clear, and the key question became: when will it bottom?

In November 2008, the market fell to a new low, but the weekly NH-NL bottomed at a more shallow level of "only" minus 10,000. It rallied back up to zero in January 2009, but then the stock market weakened again.

In March 2009, stocks slid below their October and November lows on low volume. And what about the weekly NH-NL? This index declined to minus 5,854—a zone that had been reached before at bear market bottoms. This reading alone does not tell us whether this is the absolute bear market bottom or just an intermediate low prior to a bear market rally. Of course, the massive bullish divergence between the bottoms 1, 2, and 3 indicated that the first option was more likely.

A "DOUBLE HELIX" GIVES A BUY SIGNAL

The message of this chart was unmistakable (Figure 10.2). It told traders not to panic. It signaled to cover shorts and get busy drawing our shopping lists.

Whenever you look at a market using different timeframes, technical trading signals seldom emerge at the same time. Professionals have rules for dealing with this challenge, while beginners do not even recognize it and obsessional traders keep waiting for perfection until the train leaves the station.

A case in point: the behavior of the New High–New Low Index at the market lows in March 2009. While the signs of a bottom leapt out at you from the weekly chart, the daily chart remained silent on the matter. While the market kept falling to new lows, daily NH-NL kept falling in tandem with prices, with no sign of a divergence.

During that final decline, the red line in the lower pane of this chart showed an expanding number of New Lows, while the flat green line reflected a small number of New Highs (Figure 10.2). While the weekly NH-NL was screaming "bullish divergence!", the daily NH-NL showed none in March. What should we do?

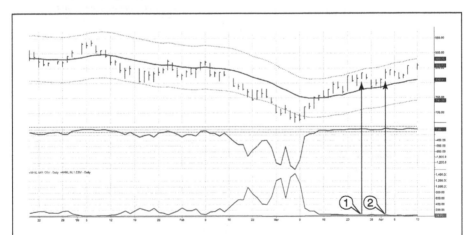

Figure 10.2 The Daily NH-NL Confirms Upside Reverse

S&P daily with a 22-day EMA and an Autoenvelope
Daily New Highs, New Lows, and New High–New Low Index
1–the first crossover of New Highs above New Lows;
2–the second crossover.

The signals from the longer-term chart are more important than those from the shorter-term, meaning a weekly chart trumps a daily. In a perfect world, both would sing the same tune, but in the messy world we live in, you have to make choices. The Triple Screen tells us to always begin our analysis on the longer-term charts. That's where we make strategic decisions, before turning to the dailies for shorter-term tactical timing.

The daily chart of NH-NL finally caught the weekly's tune in April, when the number of New Highs (the green line) rose above that of New Lows (the red line). Because the daily NH-NL is very sensitive, I tend to wait until its second bullish crossover before accepting it as a confirmed buy signal. Stephen Morris, a Spiker in Idaho, jokingly called this "Double helix" or "double Alex."

JUST IN TIME FOR THE PARTY

These three charts of Deckers Outdoors (DECK) (Figures 10.3–10.5), along with several intraday charts omitted for the reasons of space, came

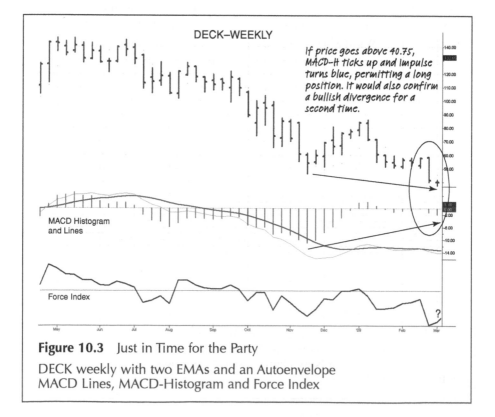

Figure 10.3　Just in Time for the Party

DECK weekly with two EMAs and an Autoenvelope
MACD Lines, MACD-Histogram and Force Index

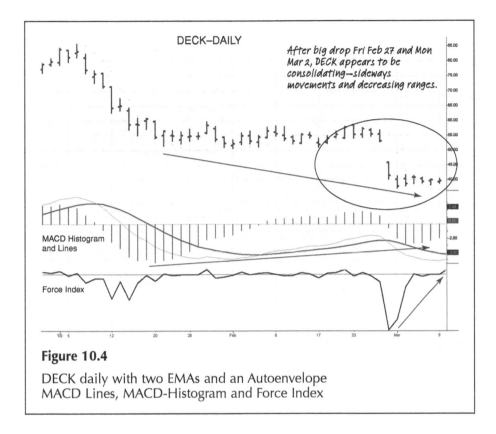

Figure 10.4

DECK daily with two EMAs and an Autoenvelope
MACD Lines, MACD-Histogram and Force Index

recently from Steve Alcorn, a member of SpikeTrade, who wrote: "I've attached my diary from my very first trade, which was on March 10, 2009, the first day of the big upmove. I went long DECK, which headed upward for six weeks. I traded the stock awkwardly, but made a profit. A lesson, as I look back on those halcyon days, is that there were many, many opportunities all of a sudden, and one could make money without a lot of experience and skill, so very different from the current environment."

Steve is a modest man—he is a strong performer in SpikeTrade. The comments on these charts belong to him. I've often said to my students: it is hard to teach a good skill—but even harder to learn it. It looks like Steve has heard my lessons—and had the courage to apply them at a time when many people were fearfully hugging the sidelines.

There is not much to add to Steve's comments or to his chart mark-ups. Notice how he uses his charts both as a planning tool and a diary. When I was a beginning trader, I used to write quite a bit on my charts

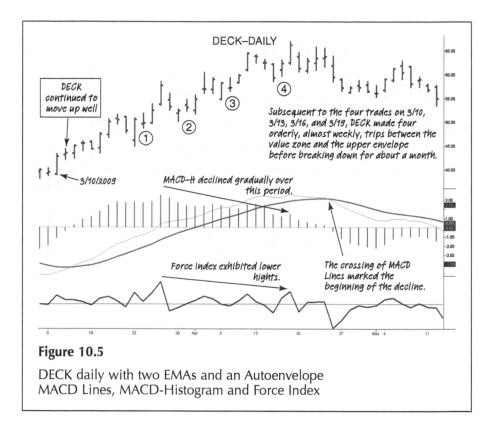

Figure 10.5

DECK daily with two EMAs and an Autoenvelope
MACD Lines, MACD-Histogram and Force Index

about technical indicator signals. These days, just a few arrows or circles
will remind me of every factor I consider important.

In a very professional manner, Steve traded the same stock repeatedly. Most beginners hit a stock, win or lose, and move on to the next
one. They remind me of an insecure man in a bar, trying to chat up
different women, but never taking the time to listen or develop a
relationship. They also take rejection very poorly—if someone ignores
them, they never speak to that person again. Professional traders, on the
other hand, tend to trade the same stock repeatedly. When they get
stopped out, they have no problem approaching that stock again and
again, until they finally get a good entry in the direction they want.
Steve, despite his inexperience at the time of these trades, took several swings at this stock until the crossing of MACD Lines told him that
the pattern of DECK's movement was changing.

In my early days, I used to include extensive psychological comments in my diaries. I used to write down how I felt entering and exit-

ing trades. Your mind is a trading instrument, and paying attention to how it operates helps you become a successful trader. After you gain experience, one's psychology tends to fall in place, and we shift our focus to risk control and money management.

MY FAVORITE MAJOR BOTTOM SIGNAL

One of the most important patterns for identifying market bottoms is a false downside breakout accompanied by a bullish divergence. This pattern tends to deliver results in all timeframes, but of course the longer the timeframe the more important the signal. Here we will look for this pattern on a weekly chart—a timeframe which helps identify major tops and bottoms.

Research in Motion (RIMM) is a technology company whose Blackberry product is half-jokingly called "crackberry" for its addictiveness (Figure 10.6). The stock held up better than most in the early stages of

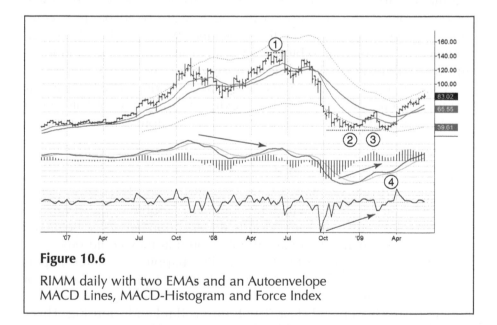

Figure 10.6

RIMM daily with two EMAs and an Autoenvelope
MACD Lines, MACD-Histogram and Force Index

the bear market, rising to a new high in 2008. That summer it popped above its resistance level but could not hold and closed below the resistance line in the area marked "1" on the chart. A bearish divergence of weekly MACD added to the gravity of that sell signal from a false upside breakout. It was all downhill from there for RIMM. Within a year, it slid from near $150 to below $40, losing three-fourths of its value.

In October 2008, RIMM found support below $40 (area 2). It rallied in January 2009, with its MACD-Histogram crossing above the zero line, "breaking the back of the bear" (area 3). In area 4, RIMM fell back to support again, and then broke down to a new low. The lowest point RIMM reached in 2008 was $35.09, but in March 2009, it declined to $35.05, four cents lower. That penetration must have been enough to chuck out traders who like to put their stops "one tick below the latest low."

One of the advantages of looking for such breakouts is that they are easy to find. Set an alarm below an important low, and when it goes off, be ready to buy when the market crosses back above its recently violated support line. Scanning for such breakouts provides a rich selection of potential buy candidates.

The bullish divergence that occurred in area 4 is of the "missing right shoulder" variety. Bottom 2 was below zero, top 3 showed the break of bear power, and at bottom 4 the bears were so feeble they could not push this indicator below the centerline. When the Impulse system changed color from red to blue, it gave a permission to buy—and it was up, up, and away for the crackberry stock.

A similar approach, only in the opposite direction, works well at market tops. There you need to make an extra allowance for volatility, which tends to be higher near the tops than at the bottoms.

SELLING A BULL

Past tops and bottoms are easy to recognize; good buying opportunities are crystal clear in the middle of a chart. Trouble is, the closer you get to the right edge, the more cloudy the situation becomes. Beginners looking at old charts often have the illusion that they could buy at the bottom of a trend, sell at the top, and live happily ever after. Experienced traders know that this dream is about as practical as betting on last month's lottery numbers.

The past is frozen and clear. The future is fluid and suprising. This is why the pros are more humble than amateurs. We are perfectly happy with catching an occasional swing. We wait for an orderly pattern to emerge from the chaos of the markets, jump on it and ride it to a nearby target, and then hop off.

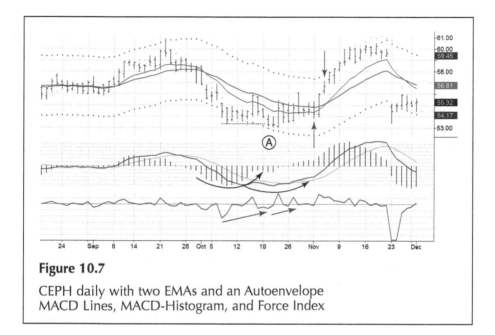

Figure 10.7

CEPH daily with two EMAs and an Autoenvelope
MACD Lines, MACD-Histogram, and Force Index

Repeat this process hundreds of times while using good money management, and your equity curve will trend up at a very satisfying angle. Let me share with you some recent trades from my trading diary to illustrate this principle.

My attention was drawn to Cephalon Inc. (CEPH) on the first weekend of November 2009 when one of the leading Spike group members selected it as his pick for the following week (Figure 10.7).

CEPH had been in a bear market, but on Monday the Impulse system on its weekly chart (not shown) turned from red to blue, meaning that buying was no longer forbidden. On this daily chart, you can see a false downside breakout A. At that time, the Force Index traced out a bullish divergence. It showed that bears were running out of steam. This was followed by a bullish pattern of MACD—not quite as strong as a divergence, but positive enough, with rounding bottoms of MACD-Histogram as well as MACD Lines.

On Monday, CEPH briefly dipped below its value zone, where I went long at $54.62 on the day marked by a vertical green arrow. On Tuesday there was a very satisfying upside reversal, putting the trade firmly in the black. On Wednesday the rally continued but its thrust shortened, while prices almost reached the upper channel line—the oversold zone. I took profits at $57.06, on the day marked by a vertical red line.

My trade grade was 53%—I captured a bit more than half of the total channel height. I consider any trade that captures over 30% of a channel height an A trade.

Did I sell too soon? I sure did. It would have made sense to continue to hold until the daily chart had lost its green color and turned blue, showing that bulls were becoming exhausted. Still, this is the kind of mistake I can live with. I bought value and sold near the overbought zone, clearing the deck for the next short-term swing trade.

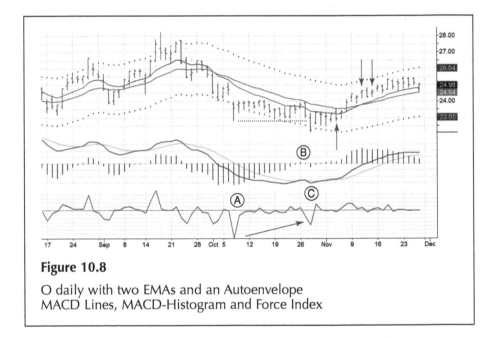

Figure 10.8

O daily with two EMAs and an Autoenvelope
MACD Lines, MACD-Histogram and Force Index

In another trade, a false downside breakout, coupled with a bullish divergence A-B-C shouted "buy!" (Figure 10.8) The weekly chart of Realty Income (O, not shown) was blue, permitting buying. I went long just below the value zone during the bar, which is marked with a solid vertical green arrow. I exited this position in two steps, marked with vertical red arrows. I sold the first half on a green bar, as prices approached the overbought level near the upper channel line. This was followed by a blue bar the next day, prompting me to sell the balance of my position a day later.

Commissions are so low these days that doing multiple trades instead of a single one is no longer an issue. My trade grades were 39% and 44%.

This trade did not catch the absolute bottom, nor the absolute top of the upswing. Still, it took a very satisfying chunk out of the middle. The first signal to sell came when prices approached the overbought zone near the upper channel line; the second signal flashed when the color of the Impulse system on the daily chart switched from green to blue, indicating a loss of bullish power.

So many traders torture themselves for having "left money on the table." A calm and realistic attitude to profits is much more productive in the long run.

EVERY BULL STUMBLES

The spectacular upside reversal of the stock market in March 2009 was followed by a broadly based rise. By the end of 2009, there was hardly any doubt that we were in a bull market.

A bull market tends to last four or more years, but this does not go in a straight line. The classics of technical analysis, starting with Charles Dow and Robert Rhea, wrote that a typical bull market has three stages:

- Stage One is the recovery from the ridiculously low prices at the end of the preceding bear market
- Stage Two is the rise that reflects the growth in the real economy
- Stage Three is the speculative blow-off after the previous two stages building a stand from which to jump into the next bear market

The transitions between these stages are not smooth. Quite the contrary, these typical stages of a bull market are punctuated by severe corrections.

At what stage were we by the end of 2009? It was certainly not the happy third stage, nor the second stage, since the economy was still very much in the doldrums. We were in Stage One, in recovery from the lows of the preceding bear market. With Stage One already nine months old and the signs of weakness appearing in the New High–New Low Index, it was reasonable to expect a temporary drop in the market.

Google (GOOG) has been one of the leaders of this bull market. Notice its relative strength during the preceding bear market—in March 2009, while the market averages sank to a new low, GOOG stayed well

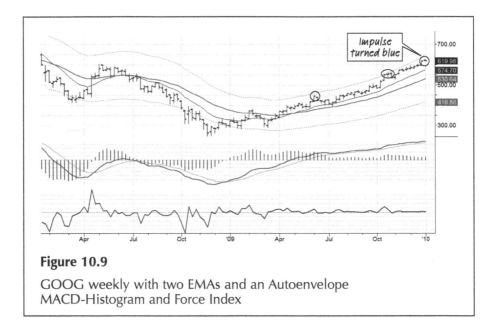

Figure 10.9

GOOG weekly with two EMAs and an Autoenvelope
MACD-Histogram and Force Index

above its 2008 bottom. This indicated that the stock was likely to become a leader of the new uptrend. Still, even leaders need a rest. This
weekly chart (Figure 10.9) shows that whenever GOOG approached
its upper channel line, it became overbought and required a pause of
several weeks before resuming its rally.

At the right edge of the chart, the overbought signal reemerged, and
at the same time the weekly Impulse system turned blue. Its loss of green
meant that traders were no longer prohibited from shorting.

The courage to act springs from several sources, and one of them is
confidence in your analytic tools. In December 2009, GOOG appeared
super-strong, rising to a new high for the year. Still, with the weekly
Impulse turning from green to blue and the daily chart showing massive bearish divergences in many indicators, this stock presented a relatively low-risk shorting opportunity (Figure 10.10).

The vertical red arrow on December 31 marks the day of my entry
into a short position. After the daily Impulse stopped being green
and changed to blue, I shorted well above value, with a protective
stop in the vicinity of the previous day's high. GOOG fell towards its
lower channel line, where I covered, capturing 64% of the channel
height.

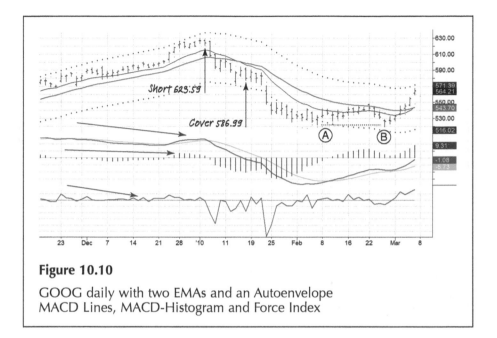

Figure 10.10

GOOG daily with two EMAs and an Autoenvelope
MACD Lines, MACD-Histogram and Force Index

The stock paused, then continued to slide, but that was fine by me. I had already grabbed my profit, and once GOOG hit its lower channel line, my system would no longer allow me to sell short. It is important to trust your system if you are going to live with it.

Notice the upside reversal in February 2010. At point A, GOOG declined to $522.46, then, at point B it broke down to a new low of $520, but closed at $526.43. That was a false downside breakout—one of the best signals of a bottom! Looking at this chart, do you recognize the messages of MACD and the Force Index during that time?

Before closing this chapter, let us review one more trade from my diary. I made it while finalizing this revision of the book.

A SCREAMING SHORT

I first saw this chart (Figure 10.11) on Sunday, April 11, 2010 while teaching a class in New York. There were two Australians in the room, and I pulled up a chart of iShares MSCI Australia Index (EWA)—the Australian ETF, which I had never traded before. The weekly chart flashed exciting signals—a year-long rally off the March 2009 bottom appeared to be ending. EWA was forming a double top, just a few cents above

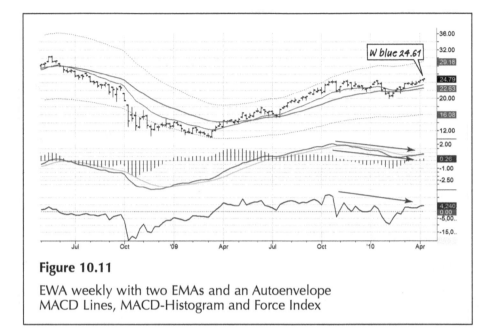

Figure 10.11

EWA weekly with two EMAs and an Autoenvelope
MACD Lines, MACD-Histogram and Force Index

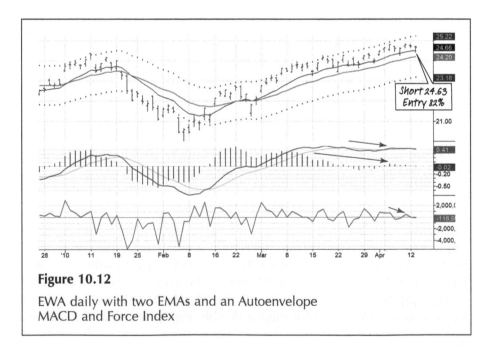

Figure 10.12

EWA daily with two EMAs and an Autoenvelope
MACD and Force Index

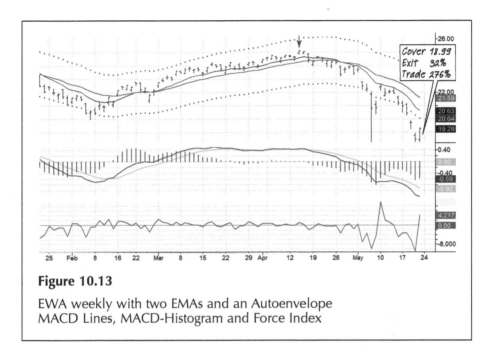

Figure 10.13

EWA weekly with two EMAs and an Autoenvelope
MACD Lines, MACD-Histogram and Force Index

the point where the weekly Impulse system would turn blue. If that came to pass, we would have a trifecta of weekly bearish divergences—MACD-Histogram, MACD Lines, and the Force Index. I turned to the daily chart shown in Figure 10.12.

The daily signals looked very similar to the weekly, and on Tuesday, after the Impulse system turned blue, I went short. With a stop above the recent peak, my risk per share was just pennies, allowing me to short thousands of shares with a very low dollar risk.

As the decline accelerated, I continued to hold (Figure 10.13). Even after EWA fell near its lower channel line on the daily chart, I continued to hold because the Impulse system was still red. When the mini-crash took place, I was traveling in Asia. Away from the screen when it took place, I missed a fantastic opportunity to take profits. I did not despair—in my experience, crashes are usually followed by a reflex rally and then a slow grind down towards the crash low—a retest of the lows on low volume. That's exactly what happened to EWA, and I covered shorts when the daily Impulse turned blue, at a level not far away from the crash low.

Lessons of this trade: it pays to have a simple trading system, risk relatively little, have a scenario in mind, and implement one's plan in a peaceful and relaxed manner.

CONCLUSION

Successful trading demands clarity and discipline. The vague and indecisive meanderings of so many traders and investors tend to reflect the way they live their lives. The folks keep postponing hard decisions, as if they had all the time in the world. They keep dreaming that, in the words of a Broadway song, "the sun'll come out tomorrow." In fact, their time is limited, and with their kind of decision-making, tomorrow is likely to be worse than today.

While structuring your life is outside the scope of this book, we can certainly begin by structuring your trading. What are your specific entry and exit plans for the next trade? How will you manage risk and keep records? When will you sell the stock you own? Are you ready to sell short and profit from a decline? You should be able to answer these questions much better now, after you have worked through this book.

I have shared with you the discovery which had a hugely positive impact on my own trading and that of my students. The single most important factor in your success or failure is the quality of your records. Beginners keep toying with the parameters of various indicators. Those issues are chicken feed in comparison to the importance of good trading records. I have shown you what records to keep and how to use them. Will you follow these instructions? Will you try to improve on them?

We've taken a quick look at buying but have spent the bulk of our time in this book on selling and shorting. You saw how to establish profit targets as well as stop-loss levels for every stock you buy. We have discussed several methods for setting both. You need to choose the techniques that fit your personality and apply them to your trading.

If, like most traders, you have never sold short, I encourage you to find a stock that you hate and sell short a few shares. Do it several times, practice shorting a small size. You are not obligated to become an active short-seller, but if you decide to specialize in buying, I want you to make that choice as a free person, and not out of ignorance and fear.

One topic we have not addressed is the tax aspect of trading. I am not an expert in this area and can only suggest that you read up on it and seek competent advice.

HANDLING PROFITS—
THE PERSONAL DIVIDEND

As Oscar Wilde said over 100 years ago, "Every true idealist is after money—because money means freedom, and freedom, in final analysis, means life." Money can be a powerful motivator—I remember being driven hard by my desire to be able to spend more time with my children instead of being on call at the hospital; to live in a nicer house; to go to the Caribbean to escape the northern winter, and so on.

When you begin making money, it is important to know what is enough, when it is the time to jump off the carousel. There is always a bigger carrot to chase—a bigger house, a nicer villa, a shinier toy. If you do not shift gears when you are good and ready, you can spend the rest of your life chasing the almighty buck—and that would be a sad life. Remember, the goal is freedom and not a shinier toy.

Your solution to this challenge is going to be as unique as you are. When you begin to implement your own solutions I would like to hear from you.

One thing I continue to do, unrelated to the pursuit of money, is write books. Their royalties cannot begin to cover the profits that I give up by taking thousands of hours and a lot of energy away from trading. I like the work of writing and the reward of dealing with readers who are attracted by it.

My other pursuit is teaching. A couple of years ago I volunteered to teach a class called "Money and Trading" at a local high school. To make the experience more real for the kids, I opened up a $40,000 account and told the kids that if our account showed a loss at the end of the school year, I would eat it, but if it showed a profit, I would donate one-half to the school and distribute the other half among members of the class.

The Personal Dividend

As long as I achieve 100% or better of the goal I set for myself each quarter, I create a pot of 5% of quarterly profits as the dividend. That is then divided equally among the recipients who can do what they want with the money.

No one was told about the dividend program at first. The first dividend for Q4-2002 was issued in person, by surprise. My presentation approach was to staple a bunch of hundred dollar bills into a card. The impact sure had its desired effect!

The recipients now include 6 key constituents, plus a local charity where they do an amazing job focusing on specialist palliative care. The 5% dividend does not change the world, but it is appreciated by the recipients!

Some quarters I don't meet my goal, and that keeps each quarter fresh, with everyone keen on knowing how well I am doing! I let people know during the 3rd month each quarter if the dividend is "likely or not." It has certainly helped me be more focused, and helping my family in a methodical way adds a very rewarding dimension to the work. I like having my "shareholders."

From *The Unconventional Trader* by Robert Bleczinski

As the year went on, I was surprised to discover that I often focused more on this small account than on my own. We ended up having a good year. The kids loved the experience, and the school keeps inviting me back. Teaching a class and making decisions in front of a group reminded me of those athletes that get an extra edge from playing a game in front of their fans.

THE ROAD INTO THE FUTURE

Think about the fact that year after year we trade the same stocks. Once in a while a new company comes out with an IPO—Tesla Motors Inc. (TSLA) went public the week I wrote this—but mostly we buy and sell the same shares year in and year out. How come the pros keep winning and the outsiders usually lose?

There is an old Russian saying: prepare your horse-cart in winter and your sleigh in summer. Professionals buy low, hold while the stocks rise, then sell and go short at a higher level, when they see a decline is in the cards. This is like buying winter clothes in March, after they go on sale or summer sports gear on sale in the fall.

Of course, with stocks there is an added complexity of having to sell them. Imagine selling your winter jacket during a cold snap in March because you know the cold days are numbered and it is time to take profits on those positions. Researching the markets, uncovering their patterns, and anticipating changes allows us to enter and exit positions opposite to the market crowd.

If the size of your trades is too big for comfort, it will make you tense. Feeling anxious, you invariably fall in with the crowd. How can you remain relaxed and independent? Especially in the beginning, you must reduce the size of your trades.

You already know about the 2% Rule, but it is a good idea to risk even less. The lower your risk, the more relaxed you'll feel. You will be more flexible while making decisions on taking profits, cutting losses, or giving a trade a bit more time.

Greed and fear are two deadly twins. If you control greed by trading a relatively small size, especially in the beginning, you will automatically reduce the fear factor, and your mind will become clear. On the other hand, if you greedily pump up the size of your trades, then fear will come in and play games with you.

Low fear equals good decisions and profits. High fear equals bad decisions and large losses.

One of the great attractions of trading is its promise of freedom. Another great attraction is that trading is a lifelong pursuit in which you can grow better as you grow older. Memory, patience, and experience—the virtues of age—are the essential assets for trading. But first, in order to benefit from your experience, you need to survive and stay in the game long enough to master it. You need to set up your money management so that no big loss or a string of losses can kick you out of the game. You need to organize your record-keeping system to learn and profit from your experiences.

If you take the message of this book seriously and use its rules and lessons, you'll have a fascinating road ahead of you. I want you to make the correct choices at many crucial forks in the road ahead.

I wish you success.

References

Alcorn, Stephen. Personal communication, 2010.

Angell, George. *Winning in the Futures Markets*. New York, NY: McGraw Hill, 1990.

Appel, Gerald. *Technical Analysis: Power Tools for Active Investors*. Ramon, CA, Financial Times, 2005.

Bade, Margret. Personal communication, 2003.

Benyamini, Zvi. Personal communication, 2007.

Bleczinski, Robert S. *The Unconventional Trader*. An unpublished paper, 2007.

Bruin, Gerard de, Personal communication, 2007.

Buffalin, Dr. Diane. Personal communication, 2007.

Cooke, Grant. Personal communication, 2010.

Elder, Alexander. *Come into My Trading Room*. New York, NY: John Wiley & Sons, 2002.

Elder, Alexander. *Entries & Exits: Visits to 16 Trading Rooms*. Hoboken, NJ: John Wiley & Sons, 2006.

Elder, Alexander. *Trading for a Living: Psychology, Trading Tactics, Money Management*. New York, NY: John Wiley & Sons, 1993.

Faith, Curtis. *The Way of the Turtle*. New York, NY: McGraw Hill, 2007.

Friedentag, Harvey Conrad. *Options—Investing Without Fear*. Chicago, IL: International Publishing Corporation, 1995.

Gawande, Atul, *The Checklist Manifesto*. Metropolitan Books, 2009.

Grove, Nicholas. Personal communication, 2004.

Hieronymus, Thomas A. *Economics of Futures Trading*. New York, NY: Commodity Research Bureau, Inc., 1971.

Kreiz, Shai. Personal communication, 2007.

Lewis, Michael. *The Big Short: Inside the Doomsday Machine.* New York, NY: W.W. Norton & Company, 2010.

Lovvorn, Kerry. Personal communication, 2007.

MacPherson, Malcolm. *The Black Box: All-New Cockpit Voice Recorder Accounts of In-flight Accidents.* New York, NY: Harper, 1998.

Mamis, Justin. *When to Sell: Inside Strategies for Stock-Market Profits.* New York, NY: Simon & Schuster, 1977.

McMillan, Lawrence G. *Options as a Strategic Investment,* 4th ed., Upper Saddle River, NJ: Prentice Hall, 2001.

Morris, Stephen. Personal communication, 2010.

Natenberg, Sheldon. *Option Volatility and Pricing.* New York, NY: McGraw Hill, 1994.

Parker, Jeff. Personal communication, 2007.

Patterson, Jacqueline. Personal communication, 2006.

Rauschkolb, James. Personal communication, 2007.

Rhea, Robert. *The Dow Theory.* New York, NY: Barron's, 1932.

Schroeder, Alice. *The Snowball: Warren Buffett and the Business of Life.* New York, NY: Bantam, 2009.

Smith, Adam. *The Wealth of Nations.* New York, NY: Bantam Classics, 2003.

Steidlmeier, J. Peter. Presentation at a CompuTrac conference, 1986.

Teweles, Richard J., and Frank J. Jones. *The Futures Game,* 3rd ed. New York, NY: McGraw Hill, 1998.

Weis, David. *Catching Trend Reversals: a video.* New York, NY: elder.com, 2007.

Weissman, Richard L. *Mechanical Trading Systems: Pairing Trader Psychology with Technical Analysis.* Hoboken, NJ: John Wiley & Sons, 2005.

Wilder, J. Welles, Jr. *New Concepts in Technical Trading Systems.* Greensboro, SC: Trend Research, 1976.

Winters, Deborah. Personal communication, 2007.

Zuckerman, Gregory. *The Greatest Trade Ever: The Behind-the-Scenes Story of How John Paulson Defeated Wall Street and Made Financial History.* New York, NY: Broadway Business, 2009.

ACKNOWLEDGMENTS

I am grateful to my editor, Kevin Commins, for being "present at the creation"—encouraging me to write this book. Many thanks to the good folks at John Wiley & Sons, with whom it has been my good fortune to work on a number of books. Outside of Wiley working with Joanna V. Pomeranz, Gabriella Kádár, and Nancy W. Dimitry felt like repeating a journey with a group of old friends. Ted Bonanno, my agent, helped ensure the smoothness of this as well as many other projects.

Both my daughters helped edit this book. Miriam is a journalist in Moscow and Nika is working on her doctorate at Princeton, but both found the time in their busy schedules to review the manuscript and make constructive suggestions. Carol Keegan Kayne, the reliable guard against sloth and imprecision, performed the final check of the book, weeding out mistakes that had eluded everyone else's eyes.

Kerry Lovvorn, a trader in Alabama and my co-director of the Spike Group, generously helped produce many charts for this book. Jeff Parker, a trader and a member of the Spike group in North Carolina, has read the manuscript and asked tough questions that helped improve the book. Patricia Liu was an invaluable sounding board, as I read the manuscript out loud to her, making sure it flowed just right. All the while, Inna Feldman, my manager at elder.com, ran the company alone for weeks, making sure I had enough time to write and edit.

I am grateful to all of you. Without your help this book would probably not see the light of day. Thank you very much.

Dr. Alexander Elder
New York City, 2011

ABOUT THE AUTHOR

Alexander Elder, M.D., is a professional trader and a teacher of traders. He is the author of 10 books, including *Trading for a Living* and the *Study Guide for Trading for a Living*, considered modern classics among traders.

Dr. Elder was born in Leningrad and grew up in Estonia, where he entered medical school at the age of 16. At 23, while working as a ship's doctor, he jumped a Soviet ship in Africa and received political asylum in the United States. He worked as a psychiatrist in New York City and taught at Columbia University. His experience as a psychiatrist provided him with unique insight into the psychology of trading. Dr. Elder's books, articles, and reviews have established him as one of today's leading experts on trading. Many of his own trades are featured in this book.

Dr. Elder is the originator of Traders' Camps—week-long classes for traders. He is also the founder of the Spike group, whose members are professional and semi-professional traders. They share their best stock picks each week in competition for prizes among themselves. Dr. Elder continues to trade, conducts webinars for traders, and is a sought-after speaker at conferences. Readers of this book are welcome to request a free subscription to his electronic newsletter by contacting his office:

elder.com
PO Box 20555, Columbus Circle Station
New York, NY 10023, USA
Tel. 718.507.1033
e-mail: info@elder.com
websites: www.elder.com
www.spiketrade.com